MW00615710

you
are not
alone

for Parents and Caregivers

The NAMI Guide to Navigating Your
Child's Mental Health—With Advice from
Experts and Wisdom from Real Families

you are not alone

for Parents and Caregivers

CHRISTINE M. CRAWFORD, MD, MPH

zando

NEW YORK

Zando
zandoprojects.com

First Edition: September 2024

Text design by Aubrey Khan
Cover design by Evan Gaffney
Cover art by June Glasson

The publisher does not have control over and is not responsible for author or other third-party websites (or their content).

Library of Congress Control Number: 2024934554

978-1-63893-080-8 (Hardcover)
978-1-63893-081-5 (ebook)

10 9 8 7 6 5 4 3 2 1
Manufactured in the United States of America

CONTENTS

PART I
How to Think About Your Kid's
Mental Health

PART II
Exploring Mental Health Conditions
in Children and Adolescents

PART III
Lessons from Lived Experience

FOREWORD

During the book tour for *You Are Not Alone*—the first book from the National Alliance on Mental Illness (NAMI)—author Dr. Ken Duckworth had some wonderful moments meeting people who had been helped by the book. He was also asked many questions that he did not address in that book: What did you learn about the mental health of younger kids in your interviews? What can help parents with the challenges of childhood diagnoses changing?

One of NAMI's main goals is to ensure people get help early. Our robust programs and resources are intended to help young people get the mental health support they need. NAMI's second book, *You Are Not Alone for Parents and Caregivers*, is designed to advance these conversations, address these questions, and provide guidance and support for mental health concerns.

This book will be a vital resource for anyone with a young person in their life, helping them discern if their child is struggling with their mental health, how to understand different diagnoses, and the best path forward for supporting the child and getting them the care they need. The author, Dr. Christine M. Crawford, is both a mother of young kids and physician to teens and parents in her child and adolescent psychiatry practice. Combining Dr. Crawford's own experience and interviews with real parents and kids, and integrating practical experts, this book is unique in its approach. These multiple perspectives give readers a holistic view of youth mental health while also offering real-life stories that offer guidance and support.

Dr. Crawford is thoughtful, approachable, and makes complex ideas easy to understand. She is the perfect person to take on this important task to help parents and caregivers. We at NAMI are fortunate to have her as the associate medical director and are proud to add this important book to our portfolio of resources.

If you are looking for answers and multiple perspectives on mental health and development to become a more informed parent or caregiver, this is the book for you. Whether your child has a history of mental health difficulties, or you are approaching this subject for the first time, I hope this resource will help you on your journey. The NAMI community will always be here to provide guidance, encouragement, and support, and to remind you that you are not alone.

Ken Duckworth, MD,
Chief Medical Officer, National Alliance on Mental Illness
Assistant Professor of Psychiatry, Harvard Medical School

and

Daniel H. Gillison Jr.,
CEO, National Alliance on Mental Illness

INTRODUCTION

When your child, or a child you care for, is struggling, and you don't know what to say or do to ease their pain, it is hard to focus on anything else. You may know intellectually that every child is likely to experience feelings of sadness, frustration, anger, confusion, loneliness, and even grief during their journey to adulthood, but it can be difficult to bear witness to the intensity with which your child experiences those feelings when they haven't yet acquired the skills to deal with or regulate them. You may feel uncertain whether the emotional difficulty your child is experiencing is typical for children of their age or evidence of a serious developmental issue or mental health condition.

The search for answers and solutions can provoke a whole host of other uncomfortable feelings: Why is this happening? Is it my fault, or my spouse's/partner's/ex's fault? Am I overreacting? Is my child in the wrong school, or the wrong class, or being influenced by the wrong friends? Am I a bad parent? *What should I do for my child?* Whether the child you are concerned about is a tantrum-throwing toddler or a teenager with depression and anxiety, these are the questions that keep you up at night and make daily life difficult. They create a sea of confusion and an unsettling uncertainty about the future—not only your child's future, but yours.

One of the ways we try to better tolerate the uncertainty we feel when we're worried about a child is to quickly enter into problem-solving mode. Our minds become engaged in a perpetual process of assessing the situation, thinking about the problem, trying to figure out why the problem exists and what needs to be done to solve it. We may feel that if we don't immediately intervene, the problem is going to persist or worsen. Paradoxically, though, this problem-solving mode of think-ing can lead to a heightened sense of worry, fear, dread, sadness, or even anger. Everyone always says that parenting is hard. You likely already know that to be true, and sometimes it's not all that validating or help-ful to hear.

Very often, people with troubled kids feel alone in a world full of "normal happy" families, isolated with the unbearable weight of their child's pain. That's why the National Alliance on Mental Illness (NAMI) asked me to write this book. As NAMI's associate medical director, and as a child psychiatrist who has treated several families with children who are living with mental health conditions, and as a mother, there is at least one thing I'm sure of: While your situation may be unique, and your child certainly is unique, you are not alone.

The challenges that come along with being a parent of a child who is experiencing a mental health issue, and the desire to form a sense of community to support caregivers who are going through this same ex-perience, is at the heart of NAMI's origin story. We're an organization that was formed in 1979 after two mothers who both had children liv-ing with schizophrenia decided to meet to share their experiences navi-gating their role as caregivers while supporting their children with severe mental illness. The power of those meetings and the exchange of ideas and support ultimately drew a community of other caregivers of children with mental illness, which expanded again to include people living with mental health conditions themselves, who found empower-ment and comfort in support from others who had shared similar experiences.

Over the years, NAMI has grown from a lunch meeting of two mothers to an organization that now has more than six hundred local affiliates and forty-nine state organizations across the United States—the nation's largest grassroots organization focused on improving the lives of individuals living with mental illness. NAMI aims to be a bea-con of hope and recovery, and its mission is centered on the lived expe-riences of families and individuals who are impacted by mental illness.

People turn to NAMI—our support group sessions, our educational workshops, and our social media platforms—to get the tools and resources necessary to navigate their mental health journey and to feel less alone.

NAMI's programming has also evolved over the years. We seek to provide concrete tools and resources for caregivers to support their children through support groups and educational workshops such as NAMI Basics and NAMI Family-to-Family. Additionally, through NAMI's Youth and Young Adult Initiatives, educators can access resources to support the mental health needs of the children in their classrooms. Among these resources is NAMI Ending the Silence, a program delivered in middle and high schools that provides an opportunity for students and teachers to learn about the signs and symptoms of various mental health conditions as well as to hear young adults share their personal journeys to recovery.

NAMI's growth in part reflects the advancement in the public's understanding of mental illness and how it can touch the lives of countless families regardless of where they are from or what they look like. On the other hand, NAMI's growth has simultaneously paralleled a disturbing rise in childhood mental health concerns. To many adults, it seems as though there is something about the world we live in that is making more children vulnerable to mental health conditions such as depression, anxiety, substance use disorders, and psychotic disorders. Others may still wonder: Do children actually "get" mental health conditions, the way adults do?

The statistics that have been shared throughout the media and in clinical literature certainly demonstrate that kids are struggling emotionally. Fifty percent of all mental health conditions start to appear before the age of fourteen, and 20 percent of children between the ages of three and seven have a diagnosable mental health condition. As a result of the Covid-19 pandemic, we have seen a dramatic increase in the rates of depression and anxiety experienced by all kids: One out of every six adolescents is diagnosed with a major depressive episode, and rates of anxiety have *tripled* in the last two years. The gravest indication yet that our children are struggling is reflected in the data that demonstrates that suicide is the second most common cause of death among people ages ten to thirty-four and, astonishingly, the eighth leading cause of death among children ages five to eleven.

The data speaks for itself: Mental illness does present during childhood. At NAMI, we know the struggles of individuals and families behind this data. We learn every day about the experiences of ordinary families who have shared their stories with countless NAMI volunteers and members across the United States, through calls and texts to the NAMI HelpLine and discussions in support groups, classes, and workshops. All these individuals reaching out to NAMI about their children are eager to learn how they can better understand their child's emotional state and find strategies for navigating the mental health system. Their experiences remind us that, while the number of children who are impacted by mental illness is already staggering, each of those children also affects the lives of family members, friends, teachers, and other members of their community.

Despite our growing recognition of mental illness in children, many do not receive the care that is so critically needed. Only *half* of those diagnosed with a mental health condition get the help and treatment that they need. Notably, the average delay between symptom onset and treatment is eleven years, which unfortunately encompasses many critical years during a child's development. Opportunities for intervention are missed. This treatment gap is in part a consequence of barriers like discrimination and limited access to mental health services. Delays also sometimes occur because people in the child's life find it difficult to accept that the child's emotional and behavioral issues are more than "just a phase," or because it is hard to discern behavior typical for a child at a given stage in their development from behavior consistent with a mental illness. And even when it's clear there is a mental health concern, it may not be clear what exactly to do next. Even families with social and financial resources can find it difficult to access effective help.

If you picked up this book because you are concerned about your child, you are right on time. What you are concerned about may resolve itself, but you don't know that it will. Being concerned at all is a sufficient reason to seek help. If you are already engaged in helping a child struggling with mental health issues, I hope you will find more help, hope, wisdom, and empathy in these pages.

You Are Not Alone for Parents and Caregivers is intended to serve as a practical guide, compendium of ideas, and supportive companion to anyone concerned about a child's mental health. In it, I will share what I've learned about childhood and adolescent mental health from my own practice and experience, as well as perspectives and advice from leading experts from a wide variety of professions. The book also channels the collective wisdom of parents and other caregivers of children with mental health concerns, particularly those who are part of the NAMI community, and provides a forum for them to tell their personal stories and share their hard-earned wisdom. These "lived experience experts" spoke so candidly with me about their own journeys because they wanted to support you on yours. They keenly understand the healing power of community and want to welcome you into it.

If a child in your life is struggling, this book is for you.

· · ·

The best feature of my office in the clinic at Boston Medical Center is a very large window. Broad beams of light shine through to illuminate paintings of colorful animals on my walls and bookshelves stacked with coloring books and board game boxes. Right in front of the window is a box overstuffed with a variety of toys: Jenga, dolls, Slinkies, cars, trains, and trucks, just to name a few. A wooden dollhouse is perched right on top of my heating vent, which some overzealous children have spontaneously marked up with crayons and markers. On the surface, my office is cozy and inviting, bursting with color and joy, reflective of the spirit and energy of the children I see in this clinic. I often reflect on how the children interact with all the items in this room: Do they run straight to the dollhouse? Or are they more interested in my swivel chair and want to take a quick spin? Or perhaps they're the type of kid who walks straight into my office, takes a seat in one of my fabric-lined chairs, stuffs their earphones into their ears, and fixes their gaze on the screen of their cell phone.

I can't help but be fascinated by how these children navigate this unfamiliar environment and my unfamiliar presence when, most of the time, they have no idea who I am or why they are here. The children and adolescents I treat in this clinic rarely show up to my office alone, so I'm never viewing the child in isolation. In the rare cases when a child does come alone, that fact in and of itself gives me a helpful glimpse into some of the challenges they are already contending with. But most of the time there is a caregiver with them, an adult who is invested in their emotional well-being, whether that adult is a parent, grandparent, adoptive parent, foster parent, caseworker, or other relative. These adults are often the ones who are full of questions, confusion, frustration, bewilderment, anxiety, fear, or even excitement to see me. They are coming to me to get an answer; to find a solution to something that they feel is, or that someone has labeled as, a "problem" in their child. They want my guidance on how to understand what is happening to the young person in their lives, and what, if anything, they can do to help.

Unfortunately, getting to see someone like me, a child and adolescent psychiatrist, is not an easy feat. According to the American Academy for Child and Adolescent Psychiatrists, there are roughly ten thousand child psychiatrists in the United States—a number that pales in comparison to the sixty-thousand-plus pediatricians available in this country. In the state of Massachusetts, there are thirty-six child psychiatrists for every one hundred thousand children. However, in a state such as Wyoming, there are only four child psychiatrists per one hundred thousand kids. In addition to the challenges of finding a child psychiatrist, there are often tremendous financial barriers to overcome to access mental health care for your child. Overall, less than half of child psychiatrists accept insurance, which means that the majority of caregivers are paying out of pocket for their child's mental health care. Additionally, psychiatrists accept Medicaid, which provides insurance coverage for millions of American low-income families, at much lower rates compared to other physicians. Even for those with private insurance, there are still tremendous challenges in identifying and successfully securing an appointment with an "in-network" psychiatrist. One study was conducted in which the researchers posed as parents of a twelve-year-old with depression and called the offices of child psychiatrists who were listed as "in-network" for Blue Cross Blue Shield, one of the nation's largest private insurers. Only 17 percent of the researchers who called this list of child psychiatrists were able to schedule an initial appointment. Many child psychiatrists are motivated to see children with various forms of insurance, but insurance companies pay very little to reimburse providers. Given the countless hours child psychiatrists devote to each patient—talking to other health providers, calling collateral sources to better understand the child, advocating for school services, and providing ongoing guidance to parents on how to best support their child—the hurdles involved in getting even minimal reimbursement, and the costs of running a practice, many child psychiatrists are pushed into establishing "cash only" policies.

Given the limited accessibility to child psychiatrists, chances are high that the people I meet in my office waited several months or more to see me. And when you wait several months or more to see a child psychiatrist, you might well expect that, when you finally reach the head of the line, you'll gain the clarity that you need to better understand your child. The reality is, though, that by the end of that first visit with me, you likely would not have definitive answers to your questions. Understandably, this can be incredibly disheartening—you've waited this long just to be told that a child psychiatrist will only be one piece of the recovery puzzle. What most caregivers don't know when they come to see me is that seeing me is just the first stop on their child's recovery journey, not their destination. And, most importantly, that I am not the only expert in the room.

Just like the people who come into my office, you probably picked up this book because you're looking for answers, to better understand why your child is feeling or behaving a certain way and what resources you need to "fix it." What drives and fuels your desire to obtain answers is an inherent need to better connect with your child, to ensure that they are safe and healthy. Something may be interfering with your ability to support your child, and there may be vulnerabilities on the child's end that make it difficult for them to connect with you and with others. The child's behaviors, and the feelings that the behaviors may bring up for you, can be overwhelming and can alter the dynamics in the relationship that you have with that child.

All caregivers at some point in time have pondered these questions: Is my child okay? Should I be worried? Why are they acting this way? For some, the questions are rooted in a desire to determine whether they are alone in dealing with particular issues in their child; whether the behavior and emotional challenges they are facing are common to other caregivers dealing with children of the same age; and if not, what they need to do about it. I hate using the word *normal* when it comes to discussing how children express their emotional states, but in truth, that is often what caregivers want to know most: Is my child normal or not?

As human beings, it is natural to be curious about and want to understand whether our child's behavior is "normal" or "abnormal." Especially as parents, we can't help but get caught up in comparing our child to other children of the same age to gauge whether our kid is "like the other kids." When we start playing that game of comparisons, however, it isn't good for anybody involved. The fear, anger, or anxiety that are generated through these comparisons can emanate through the ways we engage with our children. Simultaneously, we may feel bad or guilty that we haven't parented in such a way that our kid is just like everyone else. It's important to try to shift perspective to focus on the child's unique path, and to understand a child's challenging moods and behaviors as signals of their need for more support at this stage in their socioemotional development. Doing so will often help take the pressure off both caregiver and child.

As you can imagine, neurodevelopment is complicated. It's important to understand that children's and adolescents' brains are still developing. Reliable and efficient connections between the various regions of the brain that govern planning, decision-making, and insight, as well as parts that are responsible for our memories, our emotional reactivity, and our body's responses to emotional content, are still being formed and strengthened. Knowing how to react and respond to social and emotional interactions appropriately doesn't just happen because someone tells us or shows us how. It also involves an enormous number of complex interactions between various parts of the brain that are responsible for our behavioral responses to stress and highly emotional content. Given this fact, and the fact that development happens differently in different brains, it is impossible to determine with 100 percent certainty when in a child's development they should act and behave in a certain way. The timeline for socioemotional development is governed by multiple sources: genes, the environment, responsive caregiving, trauma—all factors that can influence the architecture of the brain and the trajectory and speed at which these essential brain connections are solidified.

One of the reasons why I can't provide definitive answers to a caregiver's questions in a sixty-minute initial visit is that it is hard to assess all the factors that may be influencing a child's behavior. Besides the neurodevelopmental piece of the puzzle, relationships also play a role, specifically, how the child interacts with the people in their life. Children's relationships with the adults in their lives provide essential opportunities for them to acquire the skills necessary for socioemotional development. Relationships are all about connection and it is through these social connections that children can learn, grow, and thrive. Yet emotional pain and distress in children tend to manifest in the form of disruptive, impulsive, and defiant behavior that can be challenging for a caregiver to navigate, and take a tremendous toll on the quality of their relationship with the child. Throughout this book, you will learn how to uncover the underlying issues interfering with your child's ability to be fully present and engaged in their relationships, and how to help them learn the skills they need to regulate their own emotional and behavioral states.

Supporting the mental health of a child is a journey on which many people will be involved in helping your child acquire the skills necessary to live well with, or without, a mental health condition. I am just one of the many supports that can be brought in at a particular stage in a child's journey to help strengthen some of those skills. This is key, and will be a theme echoed throughout this book: Ultimately, it's the caregiver and child who should lead the way on this journey, and the goal is not the discovery of definitive answers or solutions but to build a village of support around the child devoted to their socioemotional development. There is no way that any one person, any one expert, will have all the answers. It is also critical to understand that there is no single treatment protocol that will alleviate the symptoms of a given mental health condition the way there often is for physical health conditions.

Just as you may experience a wide range of emotions when you have a child with a mental health concern, you may experience something similar as you seek answers about how best to support your child from experts in the field. First comes the humbling dismay, anxiety, or defensiveness in response to hearing a "professional" express a concern about your child. You may wonder, *how could this be? There has never been a problem with me at home managing my child's behavior. The pediatrician never mentioned any concerns. So, what is this person talking about?* Then, very often, comes the confusing and frustrating experience of having different professionals from different disciplines give you conflicting feedback about your child, and about what you should or shouldn't do. Just as I rarely can provide such answers to the families I see in my office; it's important to know that bringing your child to see another professional—a psychologist, pediatrician, social worker, or any other mental health provider—may not provide that clarity either.

It's good to keep in mind that when different people see things differently, that doesn't mean that one is right, and the others are wrong. They are looking at your child through different lenses. None of these professionals is likely to explain how their specific training inclines them to conceptualize issues with a child's mood and behaviors in a certain way, and they are even less likely to explain that other professionals in other disciplines are trained to evaluate things differently, but they all have information and ideas to offer. This understanding is key, especially when a teacher or a pediatrician advises you to have your child seen by a "professional," or suggests that they need to be "evaluated." What exactly does that mean, and who should you see? I will explain more about the disciplines that may be involved in supporting the mental health of your child, and how their perspectives differ, throughout the book.

For now, it's useful to view the process of supporting your child's mental health as a journey to create a *team* of people who will help your child develop and strengthen skills. All the individuals you will meet along this journey will illuminate opportunities for your child to develop their socioemotional capacities—and for you to evolve in your understanding of how best to guide your child. Johanna, one of the interviewees for this book, is a fifty-year-old white cisgender lesbian Jewish woman from Ann Arbor, Michigan. Johanna, an art therapist, and clinical social worker specializing in early childhood and creative arts therapies, uses the analogy of hiring specialized coaches to help improve your soccer playing skills: There may be one individual who is good at footwork or another who is good at increasing your stamina on the field; all these different components and having skill in these areas will all make one a much better soccer player.

One of my roles in this book is to introduce you to a village full of experts who are devoted to loving and caring for children, whether as mental health or health care professionals, educators, child development specialists, social workers, athletic coaches, guidance counselors, family members, parents, or caregivers. Many of the experts who are featured have lived this journey firsthand, and know exactly what it is like to be in your shoes. A single person in a brightly colored office in a hospital, like me, does not have all the solutions, but I hope that as you read you will find the people whose voices and perspectives are most resonant for you, whose experiences best reflect your personal experience, or whose values and core beliefs are most in sync with yours. You may be surprised to find that the voice that gives you that "aha" moment may not be that of a psychiatrist, psychologist, or therapist. It may come from Nina Richtman, a mother in Iowa who adopted two children with significant trauma histories on her own and has been on a journey to identify the best therapeutic supports that meet her children's emotional needs; or from Jodi Bullinger, a former high school teacher and now school administrator from Ann Arbor, Michigan, who was juggling the role as educator while at the same time trying to meet the emotional needs of her students in the classroom.

Another of my roles in this book is to use my skills, training, and years of experience seeing children and families as a child and adolescent psychiatrist to provide a roadmap for understanding how to best support your child's mental health. Resilience is a word used often in recent years to describe one of the qualities children need to acquire to persevere and navigate all the challenges they may encounter throughout their childhood and beyond. As adults in the lives of children, we possess the skills and capacity to foster resilience in our children, and we need to do so given the multitude of emotional challenges our children face every day.

My perspective throughout this book is also heavily influenced by my most important role—a mother to two daughters. I understand the sense of urgency you feel, the pressure to find answers and solutions to address what is happening with your child, because I've been there. I know that having someone else tell you that your child has an emotional challenge is one of the most humbling experiences in life, no matter who you are or how much clinical knowledge you may have.

I also know from experience that while the challenges of this journey to help your child can be demanding, they can also bring about transformational self-discovery: deepening wisdom, development of skills, meaningful new relationships, and a wider worldview. Sometimes it may feel like your life has been subsumed by your kid's issues, but in the long run, you'll find that your efforts to help your child heal and grow will not only further deepen your connection to that child, but help you heal and grow too.

• • •

This book is divided into three parts. The first part aims to provide you with a framework for better understanding your child's mental health. I will provide you with a "conceptual toolbox" that will allow you to better approach your child from a place of curiosity, rather than to problem-solve and find immediate solutions. You will learn that recovery from a mental health condition is not as simple as finding a mental health provider, receiving a diagnosis, and starting medication or therapy—though those can be important interventions—but is rather a journey to better understand the "why" behind the behavior and mood changes, and the supports your child needs to grow, develop, and experience recovery during those many hours when they are not receiving formal therapeutic care.

You will learn about a concept that I call the "Distress Radius," and how to use it to assess whether your child's mood and behavior are reflective of a need for help. I'll define the distress signals that indicate reason for concern, and the factors that may make it challenging for some caregivers to recognize these signals. You'll learn that it is important to be mindful of factors such as fear, stigma, and your own childhood experiences dealing with mental health issues and how they shape the lens through which you view your child.

We will then talk about the process of getting your child help, which will involve assembling a support team ranging from medical professionals to community members with whom you or your child have a strong bond. We will talk about empowering yourself with the knowledge that you and your child are in full control of your child's therapeutic supports and treatment plan, and provide you with an understanding of the variety of perspectives mental health professionals, educators, and others bring to the table. You'll learn how to filter their recommendations and opinions to best meet the specific needs of your child.

Communication is key both in connecting with your child and in working with the support team you assemble for your child. You will learn about strategies to effectively communicate with team members—whether they be teachers, other family members, or mental health professionals. Caregivers will share their stories about how they advocated for their child's needs within their own family and in schools, health facilities, and other settings.

The second part of the book will explore the various challenges related to supporting a child and adolescent with specific emotional and social difficulties. I'll provide a general overview of underlying factors that may contribute to various types of emotional distress experienced by kids including trauma, depression, anxiety, anger, psychotic symptoms, and addiction and address how to understand and deal with self-harm and suicidal ideation. We'll explore how best to communicate with a child who may be experiencing behavioral and emotional problems and the tools and resources that are available to children and caregivers to navigate these emotional challenges.

In part III, we'll look at the challenges and opportunities of your child's transition to adulthood, and hear from kids and their parents about their mental health journeys: how they grew, what they learned about themselves, and the ways people have made their experiences meaningful, and to leverage their experiences as mentors, advocates, and activists.

Given the sense of urgency that might have led you to pick up this book, you may be tempted to quickly jump to the section of the book that pertains to your child right now. But I highly recommend that you start at the beginning to equip yourself with the conceptual and practical tools you'll need throughout your mental health journey with your child. Understanding how your child is influenced by the environments that they spend the majority of their time in, through multiple relationships and interactions with others, can help you better understand the "why" beneath your child's moods and behaviors.

I hope that the guidance in this book, and the words of wisdom you'll hear from experienced family members, educators, children, and professionals, will illuminate the path forward on your journey to understand your child and to effectively support your child's mental health.

AUTHOR'S NOTE

The individuals and families you will meet throughout this book have each provided me with a brief description of who they are and how they would like to be identified. While many included their race, ethnicity, sexual orientation, or other cultural identity in their description, some did not.

I intentionally did not offer my opinion on, interfere with, edit, or consider outside opinions on how people chose to identify themselves. The inconsistencies are therefore a reflection of the unique personalities and individual choices of the people who have so generously shared their experiences and perspectives.

Because this book features the critical first-person voices of many young people as well as caregivers who shared details about the children in their lives, contributors were given the option to identify by their first name only or remain anonymous.

Methods

People in the NAMI community and beyond volunteered to be interviewed for this first-person-as-expert book. Before the actual interview, I spoke to each person about the idea of the book and addressed their questions. After they gave permission, my colleagues Jordan Miller, Alexa Zielinski, and I conducted the interviews in the form of online Zoom conversations. The conversations were recorded and then transcribed. When people elected to share their understanding of their diagnoses, I took them at their word, as no doctor-patient relationship was entered.

Given the informality of spontaneous conversational speech, I have taken some liberties in polishing quotes from verbatim transcripts so that they read well and convey meaning clearly as written text. For example, we eliminated some "ums," "likes," and repetitions, and occasionally reordered sentences to clarify the sequence of events in someone's story. Interviewees were given the opportunity to review the edited quotes to ensure that the text accurately reflected both how they spoke and what they meant to say.

Demographics

In this book, you will meet each person individually as they describe themselves in their own words. Note that not every person answered every demographic question, and there were no predefined checkboxes.

That said, our community of lived experience experts were from

- thirty states,
- of twenty-four races and ethnicities, and
- across the spectrums of both gender and sexuality.

Interviewees represented

- eleven different faith orientations,
- thirty-five occupations, and
- reported ages from ten to seventy-one.

I am grateful to each of them.

Scope and Substance

Finally, this book addresses the experience of recognizing, getting help and treatment for, and living with and recovering from a mental health condition, regardless of the diagnosis. While it does contain some information on treatments, research developments, and best practices for some specific conditions, it is not comprehensive.

For example, eating disorders (which can also co-occur with other mental health conditions) and dissociative identity disorder (which can be rooted in trauma) are only touched on in these pages. There are many other helpful and enlightening books and resources available that focus on treatments for and recovery from specific diagnoses and conditions. We guide you to some of the ones NAMI members have found most helpful in the Resources section (page 387).

While in the mental health field the term *youth* applies to young adults into their midtwenties, kids legally become adults at the age of eighteen. At that point, the role of a caregiver or parent changes in certain ways and becomes more circumscribed, whether we like it or not, and whether our child is ready or not. I have not talked about the issues involved in that transition in this book. I recommend that you, and your child, consult NAMI's book for adult peers and their family members, *You Are Not Alone: The NAMI Guide to Navigating Mental Health* by Dr. Ken Duckworth, for useful information.

A Note About Medications and Treatment Options

This book will describe various evidence-based treatment options that are used to address mental health symptoms experienced by children and adolescents. Most treatment options for kids include a combination of different therapeutic interventions such as parent management training and psychotherapy. However, some of the treatment options described in this book will include the use of medications. Please note that the medication and treatment options that are discussed should provide you with a general overview of available approaches that can be used to address certain mental health symptoms. The book's discussion on medication is provided to equip you with information that can be helpful as you navigate conversations with your child's mental health provider about treatment options.

Your child's psychiatric prescriber may recommend medications that are considered "off-label" for use in children and adolescents. *Off-label* is the term that describes the process when a licensed prescriber uses a medication that has not been approved by the FDA to treat a specific condition, or has not been approved for use within a certain age group. This is often because the clinical research on the effects of psychiatric medication among children and adolescents is limited, and impacts the speed at which certain medications are approved by the FDA.

Many licensed psychiatric prescribers often recommend medicines that are off-label. However, this is a common practice in child and adolescent psychiatry. I recommend talking with your child's prescriber about their reasoning for recommending a particular medication and exploring the potential risks and benefits associated with it. I hope that the information on medication provided in this book will aid in the collaborative decision-making process around a treatment plan that I hope that you have with your child's prescriber so that you can be the best advocate for your child.

PART I

How to Think About Your Kid's Mental Health

ONE

Does My Child Need Help?

When a child points to their stomach to communicate a belly-ache or their knee to show you a new scrape, they are using a commonly understood distress signal to let an adult know they need help. From a very young age, we learn how to signal to caretakers when physical needs arise—and almost as early, we learn to respond to certain universal distress signals from others. If someone holds both hands to their neck, we know they are choking. If someone becomes unresponsive to calls of their name or physical touch, we know to immediately seek help. The impulse to respond to someone in a state of urgent distress immediately and without question has been socialized into our beings since we were children. And we are especially and exquisitely attuned to signals of physical distress in our children.

Now, think about the signals of distress that indicate someone is experiencing a mental health challenge. How do children and adolescents express that something is wrong; that something hurts? How about adults, for that matter? The answer is certainly not so straightforward.

We aren't socialized to understand signals of mental distress in the way that we understand signals of physical distress. But there are signals, nevertheless. Children and youth have several ways of communicating to us adults that they are suffering emotionally, and there are a multitude of factors that influence how their emotional distress signal is sent. For parents and caregivers, developing an ability to recognize and respond to those signals is key to swiftly getting them the help they need.

What Is a Distress Signal?

If a child is struggling with a mental or emotional health issue, our ability to recognize distress signals and intervene early is critically important. Sometimes a child's distress signals are easy to detect, but because kids express distress in different ways at different ages, there may be signals you don't recognize as such. When we talk about distress signals, and how to better notice when our children are communicating their struggles, it's important to take a step back and reevaluate how we interpret a child's behaviors.

Distress may manifest in ways that confuse us, test our patience, or seem counterintuitive. The signals may be more evident in some settings than others and vary from person to person. But they very commonly manifest in the realms of social interaction, behavior, and mood.

Social Interactions
One of the first social indicators of distress that we often notice is when children disengage from social and extracurricular activities that they previously enjoyed. You might notice that your child has less interest than they once did in hanging out with friends, or is significantly less talkative. Any physical fights or outbursts of verbal aggression, especially with peers and/or family members, are another indicator that a child is experiencing distress. You might notice that the child is having increasing difficulty separating from you or other caregivers, or that they're being more clingy than usual.

Behaviors
Behavioral indicators can vary significantly, but there are several primary red flags that health care providers look out for when assessing a child's distress levels. Changes in eating habits—eating significantly

more or significantly less—or the emergence of routines or rituals associated with food might be an indicator that a child is attempting to
manage distress by managing their relationship with food. Difficulty
falling asleep and staying asleep, or sleeping an excessive amount, might
be another indicator. Appearing restless and having difficulty staying
still, or being noticeably tired or lethargic throughout the day are all
things to take note of. A child might run or wander away from their
caregiver without permission—this is referred to as eloping. Refusing
to attend school or sudden changes in academic performance are indicators to pay attention to. You might notice a decline in attention to
personal hygiene, such as bathing, grooming, and overall physical
appearance.

More intense or alarming behaviors, however upsetting they are for
caregivers, are also indicators that a child is experiencing inner turmoil.
Many families we spoke to for this book shared stories of significant
disruption to their child's life resulting from the child's behaviors.
Ongoing meltdowns or tantrums, actions such as lying, stealing, property destruction, or impulsivity and a lack of acknowledgment of potential negative consequences of the impulsive behavior are all behaviors
that should be approached with compassion and curiosity. (We'll talk
more about how to think about especially disruptive behaviors in chapter 12.)

Mood

Mood changes can also be indicators of distress in children. Most
commonly, children will display symptoms of irritability. You might
feel as though you're walking on eggshells whenever you're around the
child, out of concern that they might lash out. Or the child might
begin expressing constant worries, which may seem to you overblown,
excessive, and impervious to soothing, or tell you that they are having
difficulty controlling these worried thoughts. They might become oppositional or argumentative, tearful, sad, or despondent. On the other
side of the spectrum, they might display a "flat affect": a lack of

emotion or emotional responsiveness. All these shifting emotions can be indicators that a child is experiencing distress.

Distress Signals and Acute Safety Concerns

When it comes to matters of safety, we certainly do not want to delay in getting a child access to help. What are some of the safety concerns that would warrant immediate intervention? In the mental health field, there is no more immediate safety concern than that of suicidal thoughts. Devastatingly, suicide is the eighth leading cause of death among children aged five to eleven years old. Studies have found that those within that early age group who complete suicide are more likely to be Black males and that suicide rates among those younger than thirteen years old were two times higher for Black children when compared with white children. Additionally, according to the CDC, nearly 19 percent of high school students aged fourteen to eighteen seriously considered attempting suicide in the past twelve months. Suicidal behavior in children and adolescents is a significant public health concern; however our ability to predict whether children who contemplate suicide, also known as suicidal ideation, actually go on to attempt suicide is quite poor. Given that fact, we must take immediate action whenever a child's distress signals include suicidal thoughts. We will provide further discussion about the immediate steps to take when there are concerns of suicide in chapter 10.

But I do want to note some other distress signals that may be communicating severe distress that cannot be overlooked. In terms of safety, we need to be mindful of the moods and behaviors that may inflict harm on the physical body. Our bodies must engage in basic functions such as eating, sleeping, and having enough energy to get up and complete the necessary tasks of a given day. These are functions that we can take for granted, but when a child is experiencing depression, anxiety, trauma-related symptoms, psychosis, or even problems with their ability to plan, focus, and remember details, the symptoms related to these conditions can make it such that the very basic tasks that are essential to living cannot be done.

Observing changes in sleep, energy, and appetite is not reserved for older kids who may have more established routines in these domains, it can be observed in children of any age. If you notice that your child is having persistent problems with being able to fall asleep and stay asleep or even if your child is sleeping more than usual, take note of that change and try to identify any patterns that may be contributing to those changes. Are they taking more naps during the day, whether that be in school or at home? Studies have found that poor sleep in children is associated with impulsivity, behavioral dysregulation, cognitive problems, and inattention so you can imagine that consistent sleep can be one of the greatest indicators of overall well-being. Or do they appear more agitated or restless or have difficulty settling into their routines? Energy level changes can be quite interfering and distressing for the child to potentially overcome, while at the same time these are signals that can be misinterpreted as laziness or impatience by those around them.

Lastly, consistent food intake is paramount to ensuring that the body is functioning properly. Yes, we all know preschool and elementary school kids who are very picky eaters and would have no problem walking away from a full plate of food. However, if this is a persistent pattern over two weeks or you are noticing changes in their weight, that is an immediate sign that seeking out help, mainly from a pediatrician, is warranted. You can also imagine the link between adequate nutrition, energy, and sleep. The manifestations of emotional distress experienced by the child can easily be transferred to their overall physical well-being and can exacerbate their underlying mood symptoms.

I mention some of the safety concerns having to do with the physical body first since disturbances in areas around sleep, energy, and appetite can be overlooked and minimized; however if these areas are impaired it can certainly increase the potential for impulsive and risky behaviors.

The Distress Radius

It is important to take note of all the ways a child's moods, behaviors, and/or their internal distress are affecting them in all areas of their life. Throughout the book, I will be referring to this concept as the *distress radius*. It is a concept that will help you set the gauge on your internal barometer that determines whether there is cause to be concerned about your child.

Children behave in different ways in different settings. They also may experience mental and emotional distress, and manifest it differently, in particular situations or scenarios. Each domain of a child's life—including home, school, extracurricular activities, social interactions with peers, and social interactions with adults—serves a critical function in their overall development. Distress that affects a child's moods and behavior in a particular setting may interfere with their ability to acquire important life skills in that area.

Considering the impact that the child's mood or behavior has on their functioning in the worlds around them is a clarifying approach. What is the degree of the collateral damage, and in what domains?

It can be difficult to determine when a child's behavior should concern us. As caregivers, we love our children for who they are. We accommodate their behavior and automatically adapt our home and lifestyle to best suit our children's needs. Often, these adjustments are nurturing, and allow our children to feel secure as they develop at their own rate. However, caregivers may not fully realize that they are adjusting their behavior and homes to mitigate the potential for a child's problematic behavior, to such an extent that conditions and behavioral expectations at home depart significantly from those the child will encounter in the outside world. And if the adaptations that are put in place result in the family limiting its activities outside the home, or if despite the adaptations the child's behavior is having a mental and physical impact on everyone else in the home, then it may be time to seek out additional supports.

Children develop in different ways and on different timescales, in both brain and body. What should concern us is not whether a kid is "normal" or not, since there is a lot of variation in normal development, but to understand whether a child's behavior is disruptive in such a way that, if it continues, it could potentially further jeopardize their development.

Take a step back and think about your child's experiences in the world beyond your relationship. If you are experiencing some distress yourself because of interpersonal struggles you are having with your child at home or are concerned because your child's intense emotions, problematic behaviors, or difficulties adapting to the little challenges and frustrations of daily life are affecting your family's home life, take note of how your child's struggles are affecting them outside the home, in other domains. Has their behavior led to strained relationships with their peers? Does their mood impact their ability to engage in their schoolwork? Are there other people in your child's life expressing a fair amount of discomfort or concern in response to this child?

Parents and primary caregivers may feel that they already have a strong sense as to how their child functions and behaves out in public, around other family members, and with friends because they've spent so much time with their kid in all these settings and circumstances. But the reality is that during all those interactions, your child's demeanor and behavior may be influenced by the dynamic that exists while you are there. Caregivers are often surprised to hear that their child shows up differently in your absence. When caregivers are informed about mental health concerns by others, their first response is often disbelief or denial. But the truth of the matter is that kids do behave differently when they are no longer influenced by your proximity. Children are often better behaved when they are out in the world without the parent because whatever is going on with them is most commonly due to challenges within the parent-child relationship.

Sometimes when parents are absent, children behave perfectly because they are afraid that the parents will be angry if they hear that they have been impolite. Sometimes when parents are present children are more likely to be clingy and needy—particularly if they are afraid of novel situations or overwhelmed by sensory stimulation. On the other hand, sometimes when kids are without their parents they miss them and cry for them, and are unable to accept comfort from other adults. It can be hard to see your child as an independent person who navigates the complexities of our emotionally charged world, whatever age they may be. However, it is important to understand and accept the fact that other people may experience your child differently than you do.

The Risks of Underestimating a Child's Distress

In thinking about whether your child's behavior, moods, or interactions indicate that the child is signaling a need for help beyond what you know how to provide on your own, you also need to make an honest assessment of your abilities and liabilities as the receiver of those signals. As adults, we cannot ignore the fact that we may underestimate or overestimate the distress a child experiences. For some of the adults in a child's life, the distress signals a child is "sending" may be apparent. Some of us may be so anxious about our child's well-being and so determined that they be happy and well-adjusted that we overreact to passing phases, mistaking noise for signal. Others may be blind to the severity of distress experienced by the child.

For parents and caregivers most intimately connected to the child, it may be especially difficult to see or acknowledge your child's distress. Our lens on our child can be clouded by the intensity and intertwining of our relationship with them. We are like lobsters in a pot, the temperature of the water rising so slowly that we don't detect it. We also may not want to acknowledge that our child is struggling even though we have cared for them so devotedly and love them so deeply. It can also be quite easy to chalk their moods or behaviors up to other factors: *This is how teenagers are, they're moody,* or *She's only six, she'll grow out of it.* Some of these sentiments about the mood and behaviors of children and adolescents can of course be true. But we could also be minimizing the signals of distress for reasons we aren't yet conscious of.

As caregivers, we often use a different set of lenses to view own children than when we view the children of others. How we perceive our child's mental health has a significant impact on the timing of the child's entry into mental health care, and that can influence the trajectory of the child's illness and recovery. Our previous experience with mental illness, stigma, and existing dynamics with our child has a direct impact on how we may view any changes in our child's mood and behavior.

Caregivers essentially serve as gatekeepers to mental health supports. They play a vital role in the recognition of symptoms, particularly when it comes to children who may not perceive their moods and behaviors as problematic and may not seek out help on their own. Yet nearly two-thirds of parents who have children experiencing mental health symptoms do not perceive these symptoms as part of an underlying mental health condition. Let's examine some of the factors that can result in a caregiver potentially underestimating their child's distress.

Stigma

One of the significant factors that influence the caregiver's ability to perceive their child's behavior as being concerning for a mental health condition is stigma. *Stigma* is a word that comes up often in conversations about mental health, but to better understand why it creates such a tremendous barrier to recognizing mental illness and getting help we need to better understand what stigma is. According to researchers Link and Phelan, who have done extensive research to understand the concept, stigma involves the convergence of several factors, which include stereotype, discrimination, labeling, separation, and status loss. This concept of labeling and the fear of having your child be assigned a particular label if you bring them to a primary care provider or a mental health professional can be particularly daunting for people who have had previous experience navigating mental illness. Some people from marginalized communities who experience daily forms of discrimination, stereotype threat, and "othering" may feel significantly less inclined to have their child assume a label that will bring yet another set of challenges.

It is not sufficient to just say that stigma gets in the way of recognizing mental health symptoms, and of seeking help. For some caregivers, stigma may influence their ability to accept or deny the presence of mental health symptoms. They may even reframe their perceptions of mental illness to deny the possibility that their child may have one.

The impact of stigma related to mental illness impacts not only the youth who is manifesting symptoms but the entire family. Some researchers talk about the concept of separation and a desire to have their children be socially distant from individuals with mental illness. This separation factor can lead to the development of bias on the part of the caregiver as to what constitutes a mental illness. When a concern regarding the mental health of a child is brought up to the caregiver, stigma may make it such that parents may rationalize their symptoms as normal to protect their child and/or family from being labeled with a mental illness. Given that the caregivers are the ones responsible for making mental health care decisions, the potential burden due to stigma may weigh heavily on their decisions, which in turn could bias the caregiver to not think much of the child's symptoms.

Anticipation of the negative consequences of stigma can alter your perception of what is going on, and the denial that a mental illness may be present starts to seep in. I hope that, as you continue to read this book and hear from the families and young people who have personally been touched by mental illness, you will see how crucial it is not to let fear of judgment and discrimination delay opportunities for you and your child to get the help that is needed.

Prior Exposure to Mental Illness

Whenever I meet with a family and a child, I always inquire about their family history of mental illness and their overall thoughts and impressions of the field of psychiatry. I recognize that it can be uncomfortable for family members to tell me honestly how they view medication and therapy, given that I'm a mental health professional. However, I need to have a basic understanding of their previous experience with mental illness since it will shape how they talk about their child's mood and behaviors. There are certainly benefits to having an understanding of the impact of mental illness based on previous firsthand experience. Caregivers with lived experience are better able to recognize mental health problems and symptoms, know where to seek help and information and understand that mental health problems can and should be treated. Researchers have found that parents who have a personal experience with mental illness, either with their own mental illness or that of other family members, are better able to recognize signs and symptoms of mental illness, particularly the signs of moderate to severe psychological distress. For some, that increases the likelihood that they will seek out care for their child.

How parents understand the origin of mental health problems also influences how they perceive mental health symptoms. Studies show that parents who believed that mental health problems are due to "biopsychosocial" beliefs—meaning they think that mental illness is caused by physical, personality, relational, familial, or traumatic issues—were more likely to seek out mental health supports. Parents who believed that mental health problems were due to "sociological" factors such as negative peer relationships, American culture, discrimination/prejudice, or economic problems were less likely to seek out help for their child.

Jose Julio Murillo is a Hispanic first-generation male in his early thirties from California who told me he has been diagnosed with borderline personality disorder. He currently is a board member for NAMI Coachella Valley and state trainer for NAMI California. The son of immigrants from Mexico who had to give up on their educational aspirations in order to enter into the workforce to provide for their family, Jose told me that he had a difficult time having his family appreciate his symptoms of depression and anxiety. Rather than understanding that his mood and behavior were reflective of a more serious mental health concern, they believed that he was just lazy because he was playing too many video games and sleeping too much. "Take it seriously. I'm not making this up . . . Just because we have the basic necessities doesn't mean that I'm making excuses. It's mental illness," Jose said, expressing to me what he could not effectively convey to his parents at the time.

We know that the way the caregiver conceptualizes their child's mental health is influenced by several factors. But some caregivers may have a biased perception of their child's mental health, which can lead to minimizing the child's overall distress. In the clinic where I work, I have met several caregivers who had their own experience with mental illness during their childhood, either because they experienced mental health symptoms themselves or witnessed the development of mental illness in close family members. Some experienced stigma related to their own childhood mental illness or felt traumatized by interventions such as involuntary hospitalization (even if they were meant to be lifesaving and supportive)—and want to protect their child from having a similar experience. It is important for us to discuss these experiences early on during our work together not only because they will influence how they perceive and interpret their child's mood and behaviors while the child is in treatment, but also to ensure that treatment with me does not repeat some of the traumas they may have experienced. The whole process of helping a child struggling with mental or emotional health challenges can be triggering for caregivers who have had their own negative experiences interacting with the mental health system, and I want to make certain that the caregiver feels comfortable discussing support and treatment options for their child, not pressured or coerced.

If you had a negative experience dealing with mental illness in your childhood, it may be reassuring to hear how much the approach to providing psychiatric care to children has evolved over the years. There are now many more evidence-based therapeutic interventions available, such as cognitive behavioral therapy, dialectical behavior therapy, parent-child interaction therapy, and specific programs such as psychologist Dr. Ross Greene's Collaborative and Proactive Solutions, which will be discussed in detail later on in the book. There are new and more effective medications, and we have a better understanding of how to employ them and mitigate side effects. We have recognized the importance of having a team-based approach toward supporting children's mental health through collaboration with schools, and schools are more mindful about creating environments that support a culture of mental health and emotional wellness. We have also become much more aware of how important it is to work with the whole family to ensure that the adults who play an active role in supporting the socio-emotional well-being of a child have their own needs met. For example, support for caregivers is an essential feature of psychiatrist Dr. Bruce Perry's Neurosequential Model for supporting children who have experienced trauma and who are highly emotionally reactive. A lot has changed in the mental health field over the years, and the experience you may have had as a child will inevitably differ from that of a child born in the twenty-first century.

None of this is meant to invalidate the lasting impact of your own negative experiences. Tragic and traumatic things have happened to people who sought or required care for mental illness in the past. You may have had a bad reaction to psychiatric medications and do not want your child to experience the same side effects. You may have been ostracized or discriminated against and don't want to put your child through the pain that you experienced. As caregivers, we naturally want to protect our children from ongoing emotional distress. But it is important to reflect on how our own experiences with mental illness may instead hinder our ability to recognize emotional distress and to seek out help for our child.

The Risk of Overestimating Distress

Some parents have a heightened sensitivity to signals of distress from their child and are eager to seek out help. In the same way that a caregiver's personal experience of mental illness can cloud their view or make them reluctant to acknowledge or seek help for their child's emotional distress, personal experience can sometimes make caregivers oversensitive, hypervigilant, or overeager to intervene when they believe their child is struggling. Of course, mental health literacy can be a positive asset. I have met caregivers who are living with a variety of mental health symptoms who benefited from mental health treatment and don't want to deny that intervention for their child who needs support, or who struggled for too long without support and don't want their child to suffer unnecessarily. However, I've noticed a trend in my clinical practice in which the caregiver's anxiety alters their perception of their child's behavior such that they become worried while their child and other adults in their child's life lack the same level of concern.

A key element of anxiety is difficulty tolerating uncertainty, and caregivers and parents face so much uncertainty, day to day, about how our children are doing and what their future will be. If our child has been in an irritable mood, we may experience uncertainty about whether that mood is transient or indicative of an underlying mood disorder. And because we cannot control our child's emotional or behavioral responses or "fix" their mood, but do have direct control over how we respond to our child, some of us respond by reaching out to someone else—our primary care provider, or the child's school, or mental health professionals—who we hope may be able to identify what's going on with our kid and thus how to stop or control how the child is feeling or behaving. This process of engaging in problem-solving behavior is one way in which caregivers deal with the distress and anxiety that they may be experiencing in response to their child's mood and behaviors.

It can be incredibly challenging as a parent to see your child experience distress. But it is essential, developmentally, for children to experience sadness, anxiety, anger, and frustration to learn tools and strategies for coping with intense emotions. If parents quickly intervene at the slightest hint that their child may be distressed, they may be depriving their child of opportunities to learn how to recognize their own distress signals and how to effectively communicate their distress to others.

Mismatch of Expectations

It's also important to remember that kids develop differently. Just as some kids learn to soothe themselves and fall asleep more easily than others, so do some struggle more than others to understand and manage their own emotions.

Our ideas about how children should behave and display emotions are often influenced by the expectations that our own parents placed on us when we were children. They are also influenced by what we see or read about in the media, or expectations set forth by our child's school. They can also be shaped by prior experiences parenting or caring for other children. The challenging part about having a set of expectations for a child when it comes to their mood and behaviors is that we often fail to take into account that child's unique temperament and developmental trajectory. Our child's ability to modulate their behaviors and their emotional responses is a developmental process that must occur through trial and error, and according to psychologist Dr. Mona Delahooke, caregivers can overestimate children's ability to manage big emotions. The best thing we can do is gently guide a child toward distinguishing how to appropriately respond to given situations.

This scenario is not uncommon: In describing ongoing challenges they have managing a child's behavior at home, parents make comments like, "None of my other children behaved like this. I don't know what's wrong with them!" It can be perplexing to caregivers to see how differently their children respond to their home and school environment and interact with those around them. Caregivers may feel as though the approach that they are using in their parenting or teaching can be universally applied to every child, but there is a well-established body of research to suggest that factors such as genetics, environment, temperament, cultural factors, and biological vulnerabilities have an impact on how each child experiences and displays emotion.

Is It Time to Intervene?

Ongoing delays in providing support to a child who is experiencing prolonged distress can have a significant impact on the child's overall development. Whether their distress manifests in a dysregulated state in which they are throwing a tantrum, yelling, becoming physically aggressive, or engaging in risk-taking behavior, or in a preoccupied and uncommunicative state in which they are struggling with intense internal feelings and distancing themselves from others, it will compromise their ability to learn in a classroom setting and their academic advancement. But perhaps the most worrying negative consequence is relational: Children learn a tremendous amount through their relationships with others, so when their behavior interferes with their ability to positively connect and form sustainable relationships, it ultimately compromises their ability to function in the world.

Children rely heavily on adults to provide the supports and tools necessary for them to understand how to effectively cope with their own distress. If, having applied the distress radius framework, you believe your child is struggling mentally and/or emotionally and needs more support than you can provide, it's time to act.

How to Apply the Distress Radius Framework

To understand the collateral impact of a child's behavior and emotional state in domains beyond the home, you first need to be receptive to feedback from others about how your child is doing. You can make a proactive effort to reach out to people who regularly interact with your child outside of your home, including your child's teachers, coaches, guidance counselors, and other adults who may support your child in various extracurricular activities. These adults have ongoing opportunities to observe how your child acts and behaves in your absence. They are able to notice how your child may be interacting with their peers or how it is that they are responding to stress and disappointment. If you have more specific concerns related to their interaction with peers and you're curious about how they behave in other people's homes, consider reaching out to parents of the children who socialize with your child to gather some more information on how your child behaves in a different home environment. You want to function as a detective, collecting clues to paint a broader picture of how your child functions in the world. In chapter 2, "Look, Listen, and Lock In," I'll talk in more depth about the kind of information you're looking for, and how to communicate both with your child and with others as you assemble it and assess its meaning.

It can be hard to receive this information about your child from other people in your child's life. On the one hand, you may be surprised to hear feedback that reflects only glowing, positive views about how your child is behaving at school, or at other children's homes. It may be painful to realize that your child's emotional and behavioral challenges are limited to your home. But if that's the feedback you get, be reassured by the fact that when your child is out in the world, they possess the tools and skills to adapt and modify their behavior in such a way that it doesn't interfere with their ability to function in other domains of their life. Think about some of the factors within your home that may make it a challenge for your child to regulate their emotional state. This exercise is not about pointing fingers at anyone or assigning blame, but involves facing the reality of a situation that can be difficult to face. If the problems are limited to the home, it could be beneficial to seek out more family-specific interventions. You can begin by having a conversation with your child to better understand some of the challenges that they experience in the home. You can ask them directly why they think it is different for them outside of the home when it comes to managing their moods and behaviors. I'll also discuss how to have these conversations in chapter 2, "Look, Listen, and Lock In."

On the other hand, you may learn during this process of gathering information from others that your child is exhibiting this sort of behavior in most areas of their life outside of the home. This is a clear indication that it is hard for your child to modulate their emotional state in different settings, which can lead to negative consequences both socially and academically and create collateral damage in other areas of their lives. Either the triggers and stressors that may elicit certain behaviors from your child are widespread, or there are no specific triggers to this behavior, reflecting that your child lacks certain skills, or that significant emotional distress makes it difficult for the child to engage in rational thinking and problem-solving in the heat of the moment.

It can be hard to accept that your child may be struggling, but learning that your child is experiencing emotional distress in more than two different settings is very important information to have. It indicates that you need to get help—both for your child and for the sake of you and your family. Intervening sooner rather than later is critical for several reasons.

First, it's a matter of safety. Witnessing your child experience emotional and behavioral distress at home can be hard, but when it happens you have some sense of control over the environment. You have some authority over who gets involved and how to respond to the situation. When your child exhibits similar behaviors out in the world in other settings, you have no control over how another individual may respond, especially if they are a stranger. As caregivers, we need to keep our kids safe first and foremost. We need to make sure that their behaviors do not put them at risk for being in unsafe situations resulting in potential harm to themselves or others.

We also want to provide our children with safe spaces in which they can be free to exhibit a wide range of emotional and behavioral responses and to be met with the care and support that they need to navigate that moment. You can keep your child safe by sharing tools and strategies with them on how to manage themselves in the moment, and with other people in their life. But you first have to know what they are. Getting the help that your child needs is also the path to learning what supports are needed, both inside and outside of the home.

Delaying help for your child can have lasting consequences on their ability to learn and to grow during their most formative years. If a child is distracted by feelings of anxiety, depression, and anger, it's going to be hard for them to be fully present and engaged while in the classroom or while interacting with peers, disrupting both educational learning and acquiring critical social skills. They won't be able to absorb all the valuable life lessons that come along with experiencing the world every day. When kids who lack social and academic skills notice that they are not keeping up with their peers or fitting into their friend groups, it exacerbates their distress and can worsen their mood and behavior.

Children who are experiencing ongoing emotional distress need the help and support of others. But the reality is that some of the behaviors children exhibit during these periods of intense emotions can push other people away. If they are pushing people away, their social network starts to shrink, and they become more isolated. Kids thrive from connections and community. They need to form and maintain these relationships.

Children and adolescents are trying to acquire all the tools they need to navigate the emotional stressors that they encounter daily. If there is a delay in recognizing and appreciating how widespread and far-reaching their emotional and behavioral problems are, then kids may develop coping strategies that may not benefit them in the long run. We want children to use positive coping strategies early on. The more they resort to negative ones—such as controlling their eating habits, using drugs, getting into fights, or engaging in self-harm—the harder it becomes for them to stop. The negative coping strategy eventually becomes a problem in and of itself—another source of distress. To help kids learn healthy coping strategies, we need to recognize the radius of our child's distress as early as possible, and quickly intervene.

TWO

Look, Listen, and Lock In

I think it's about connection a lot of times. It's not about fixing. It's about being with them as they're experiencing the problem and walking with them on that journey. Often, they don't know what they're going to need. We don't know what they're going to need.

—**LAURA HORNE,**
chief program officer, Active Minds, a nonprofit
organization mobilizing young adults around
mental health advocacy and suicide prevention

• • •

The distress radius is a tool we can use, much like a thermometer, to assess the state of things as they are in our child's life. But how you go about the process of assessing the distress radius, determining whether and what help is needed, and engaging with your child along the way, is important. And this process is one you may engage in not just the first time you have a concern about your child's mental health, but many times as your child grows and develops. Later in the book, we'll look specifically at how to communicate effectively with your child directly about their mental health. But more broadly, making use of the distress radius concept involves three steps: (1) look for a pattern, (2) listen with curiosity, and (3) lock in and embrace.

Look for a Pattern

Are there times when you are left wondering why a child behaves one way in a certain context and differently in another? Or why certain situations, times of the day, or even people may elicit a certain reaction from your kid? If a school or another caregiver has brought up a concern about your child, have you ever questioned it because you never observed such issues within your own home? It's important to closely examine these scenarios to see if a pattern exists. We need to be mindful of the fact that we may not have a full understanding of how our child interacts with people and other environments in our absence. See if you observe a pattern in your child's shifts in mood or behavior, in their academic performance, peer relationships and social activities, or in family dynamics.

As a child psychiatrist, the thing that I am most curious to hear about is whether a child's mood and behavior is interfering with their ability to function. Why is that? Well, we all experience anxiety, sadness, anger, and fear, but these experiences do not always persist or get in the way of our ability to carry out the daily tasks of our lives. Sometimes when we're in the midst of one of these mood states, we may not fully be aware of the fact that it is getting in the way, but people close to us may be able to recognize subtle changes in our mood and behavior.

Given that children spend a large chunk of their time in a school, which can be quite challenging for some, we often observe signs of distress within that demanding environment. Look for any patterns that may indicate that mental health symptoms may be impacting your child's ability to fully access their education. Oftentimes the clearest distress signal that caregivers can recognize is declining grades, but there may be other indications that a child may be struggling in the school environment. Does the child seem to be taking longer than usual to get ready for school or refusing to go altogether? Are they frequently leaving class to go to the nurse's office, complaining of various physical ailments? Or is the child frequently calling you during the school day asking you to pick them up and take them home? At first glance, it may appear as though these moments are just attempts to avoid doing schoolwork, but if you notice that on a weekly basis there seems to be some kind of conversation about school that is fraught with conflict, then that should be recognized as a clear distress signal.

Challenges in academic performance may be subtle, and harder to perceive for kids who are already high achieving or who may not be engaging in disruptive behavior that the teacher can't ignore. When a child who used to be voluble now gazes out the window, or when a kid who got As is now getting B-pluses, it's hard to know whether they're struggling with mental health challenges or just not as interested in the subject matter. And as a caregiver, it is hard to know what exactly is going on in the school environment. But take notice of changes in the types of communication you're receiving. Are you receiving more phone calls or emails from the school about your child? In the clinic, I often ask caregivers if they have received any concerning reports from the school or if there has been an increase in communication from the school.

Mental health–related symptoms may interfere with your child's ability to interact with their peers in a positive way. You may not be privy to all the conversations that your child is having with their friends, but it is important to take note of the stories that your child shares with you. Have you noticed a pattern in the stories about how your child is being excluded or bullied by their peer group, or that they are constantly complaining about conflicts with different people? Are they talking about avoiding certain peers or turning down invitations for playdates or get-togethers? Other patterns to notice within social relationships:

- Is there a lack of interest in spending time with their friends?
- Has the child's behavior at school negatively affected peer relationships in enduring ways?

- Are they no longer interested in playing with a familiar
  playgroup in the neighborhood?
- Are friends stopping by the house less often?
- Did the child's meltdown or altercation with a schoolmate
  result in any physical injury to the child or others?
- Did the duration of the meltdown or altercation persist so
  long that all strategies to soothe, regulate, or restrain the child
  were exhausted?
- Are they no longer staying late at school to participate in
  extracurricular activities but instead coming straight home?

These are just examples of some behaviors to take note of that may suggest that something may be getting in the way of their peer relationships.

It's also important to take a step back to reflect on whether there has been a change in you and your family's relationship with your child. In the hustle and bustle of family life, when caregivers are busy juggling several responsibilities, it may be difficult to notice changes in the dynamics involving your child from within the home. Ask yourself:

- Does my child have tantrums so frequently that I avoid taking
  the child to stores or restaurants, turn down invitations to
  family social events, or feel unable to relax at the playground,
  pool, or even my church, mosque, or synagogue?
- Has my child become more irritable, oppositional, and
  argumentative toward me and other family members when
  they get home from school?
- Has my child been spending a lot of time in their room, with
  minimal interactions with the family? Do I feel as though I
  have to walk around on eggshells whenever other family
  members are around, worrying that the child is a ticking time
  bomb ready to go off?

Lastly, have you noticed a pattern change in your child's relationship with themselves? Think about how they are functioning day to day and accomplishing basic tasks. With kids of all ages, we're looking at things such as sleep, their appetite, and, for older kids and teens, their ability to attend to their personal hygiene. Yes, kids can be messy and may need to be reminded of when to brush their teeth, bathe, brush their hair, or wear clean clothes. But if you notice a pattern change such that the child is refusing to engage in these activities more often, then that would be cause for concern.

Listen with Curiosity

Once you've noticed the pattern, it is important to address the issue. The question that often arises is *how*. Yes, as caregivers we want to protect our children by stepping in and immediately solving problems, for example by pointing out concerning behavior patterns or offering up suggestions for changing them. We may make comments such as, "You need to stop doing x, y, or z behavior" or ask questions like "What is wrong with you?" It is important to understand that the child may not know exactly how to stop what they're doing or even understand why they are doing it. It will be more helpful to approach your child with the intention of listening to them and to listen from a place of curiosity.

Throughout the conversations that you may have with the child, keep in mind that the ideal balance would be for the child to do most of the talking and for you to do most of the listening. This approach is not only helpful when navigating conversations with the child but also in conversations with other adults in the child's life who are offering feedback about patterns that they're noticing in the child.

Lock In

Lastly, once you have heard from the child and others about changes in their patterns of thinking, feeling, or behaving, and what may be driving those changes, you want to lock in with support. You can effectively provide support to your child only after you connect to them by listening to what they have to say about their situation. The idea of "locking in" is to ensure that the distress radius, meaning the impact of the concerning mood or behavior pattern, will not continue to extend into other areas of that child's life and result in more adverse consequences over time.

Imagine that you are emotionally embracing your child not only with your love and understanding but with the resources that are needed. "Locking in" doesn't necessarily have to mean immediately connecting them with mental health support. It is rather about mitigating the distress your child is experiencing by letting them know that you have heard them, understand the distress they are experiencing, and will ensure that they do not have to navigate this journey alone. You are letting them know you are in it, with them.

Notice, Listen, Validate, and Engage

If you're not sure if your child is in fact in distress, a great place to start is by talking with your child. A conversation can begin at any age at which the child can verbally communicate. But how you conduct these conversations is key—not only to discern what's going on with your child but to provide them with the fundamental support necessary to manage their distress.

We communicate constantly with our children—consciously and unconsciously. In our hectic and busy lives, we generally do not think much about *how* we communicate, and opportunities to slow down and become intentional with how we do so can feel infrequent. But communication is a powerful tool, one we all possess the ability to utilize, that can have a profound impact on our relationships with our children and others. All the steps I describe previously—look, listen, and lock in—are all contingent upon one's ability to communicate effectively. We often take our ability to communicate for granted (*Of course I know how to talk to my kid!*), but it may be the tool that, if we use it skillfully, can have the greatest impact. How do we harness the power of communication to better support our children?

In this chapter, we will talk about a few different communication tools to use as you look, listen, and lock in to best support your child, and discuss how to sharpen the communication skills that you already possess. We will address all the different components of communication, considering not just the actual words that we say, but so much more.

Slow Down

To notice and be curious about a child's behavior without reacting to or focusing on the behavior itself requires you to slow down. Slowing things down allows you to take a step back and reflect on changes in your child, and on what may be causing or influencing these changes. It's important to try to reflect without rushing to judgment—of your child, yourself, or others—or into action. I encounter many families who live lives in which they are moving at a swift pace throughout the day. Rushing to get everyone dressed and fed and out the door, then coming back home late for the evening routines of preparing dinner and getting ready for bed. For some, there may not even be a nighttime routine, since they may be working jobs in which the schedule doesn't allow for them to be home during these moments in their child's lives— through no fault of their own. We can become so preoccupied with just getting through the day, running in survival mode while putting out the daily fires that may arise, that we lose sight of what is right in front of us. There is so much noise and movement throughout the day that it may be difficult to truly notice your child. We have to slow down whenever we can, to truly notice and acknowledge changes in their mood or behavior.

Acknowledge and Manage Your Own Distress

In trying to identify a pattern of change in your child, it's also important to ask yourself why you are noticing certain things about your child at this particular moment in time. Noticing changes in yourself in response to your child's behavior is equally as important as noticing changes in your child. It is natural for parents or caregivers to experience distress themselves when they notice their child is in distress or exhibiting concerning behaviors, but it is important to develop tolerance for this distress. Distress tolerance is a skill—one that can be learned and practiced. It means tolerating difficult feelings without either disconnecting from or numbing them or rushing instantly to problem-solve. You want to be able to sit with your child in the discomfort of distress and resist the urge to minimize it or offer platitudes about the importance of positive thinking. You want to give the child the space and time to figure out what they're going through, and to help them do so, and that will take time.

Look and Take Notice—Nonverbal Communication

We all have a deep desire to be fully seen by those around us. We also possess the power to truly see our children for who they are. For children, being seen by us as caregivers is incredibly important. By "seeing your child," I don't just mean knowing their whereabouts and acknowledging changes in their physical appearance, moods, or behavior; I mean going beneath the surface to understand what is driving their feelings and actions. This may seem self-evident to many caregivers, but when a child's behaviors become problematic or disruptive, our first instinct is often to reprimand them or lecture them. If the behaviors are a symptom of distress, though, these tactics are ineffective and even counterproductive. First, just notice what is going on. This step is imperative. Once we slow down, noticing your child is the first step in communicating with and being able to provide support to your child.

There are so many children who are not truly seen in their daily lives. They go through the world hoping that people are curious about them and interested in their internal experiences. Noticing a child gives them a sense that their existence has some impact on others—it lets them know that they matter. Noticing children, acknowledging their presence by checking in and letting them know that they've been on your mind, can open the door for a child to share with you how they are feeling. Your acknowledgment of them is an invitation for them to be their true selves and to share whatever is on their mind.

It can be hard to notice changes in a person when you see them every day. You're just too close. Your own internal biases toward your child influence what it is that you can see and tolerate. Noticing things in our surrounding environment is easy for us. You notice when someone new moves into your neighborhood, when construction is taking place at a neighbor's home, or when someone is blasting loud music out their window. But it can be hard to notice signals of change in our own homes or our own lives. If you feel that you are only now noticing things that you "should have" noticed before, don't blame yourself. There are many other factors influencing when we come to notice changes in our child's mood, behavior, or relationships, as well.

Noticing Beyond When Behaviors Impact Others

Unfortunately, when adults do take notice of a child's behavioral changes it can often be out of concern for how that behavior is impacting others, rather than concern about what is driving the behaviors in the first place.

Sierra Grandy, now a twenty-seven-year-old disabled bisexual public speaker and law student from Minnesota who has experienced mental health and chronic pain symptoms since childhood, describes her experience as a young person:

> Looking back, treatment followed when my symptoms were negatively affecting others even when the symptoms had been negatively affecting me for much longer. It often seemed that the main goal of the people who were trying to help was to make sure that I was not affecting others

with my internal dilemmas. So, there was limited empathy, compassion, and understanding that children are human and they're going through complex and intense emotions that are brand new for them.

Taking the time to fully notice the child, without getting caught up in how inconvenient or disruptive the child's behaviors are, is a skill. We need to ask ourselves why the child is behaving in this manner and why they are doing it right now, without placing the burden of explaining and intellectualizing the behavior on the child. The child likely does not know and cannot articulate why they are behaving as they are. When parents come into my office, they often provide an extensive recount of an episode involving a child who demonstrated "problematic" behavior. They will discuss the inappropriateness of the behavior, and mention how they reprimanded the child or how the school attempted to discipline the child. There is so much attention being paid to disruptive behaviors—and this makes sense! It's natural to want to stop certain behaviors in our children, especially ones we fear might elicit judgment from others, or have a detrimental impact on those in our families and communities. But the behaviors are very often a symptom of a problem that we need to understand. We need to play the role of detective to understand the things that are impacting our children's lives rather than blaming them for their behavior and rehashing all the details within an episode of dysregulation.

Dominique Freeman, a Black woman in her early thirties from Los Angeles, told me she has had diagnoses of depression and anxiety since childhood. Now a dedicated advocate for youth in foster care and working for NAMI, Dominique shared what it was like to have someone finally try to understand where her behavior was coming from as a child, instead of immediately trying to change it:

I think about how relieved I felt when I was finally asked, "What's going on at home?" I had never been asked that. It was always like, "What's wrong with you? You never act like this." It was always pointing at me. I think when someone asked me, "What's going on at home?" It just felt like I could talk about it . . . It wasn't me this time. It was what was happening around me.

Sometimes I think we question the behavior. What's going on presently in front of us? Rather than, "What's happening around you? What does your day-to-day look like? Something happened to you, and you showed up this way, and so let's get to that," rather than, "What are you doing?"

Active Listening: Explore, Don't Explain

Active listening requires making space for your kid and taking time to listen and understand them without offering input. Easier said than done for most of us. As adults, we have a wealth of knowledge that has accumulated over time through our life experiences. It goes without saying that "we know a thing or two about a thing or two" and we're eager to share those life lessons with the children that we care so deeply for. We hope to prevent them from making the same mistakes that we've made, or from experiencing any form of pain or disappointment. However, we do a disservice to our children when we listen to them speak with the objective or goal of offering them a solution or an explanation as to why they may be experiencing a particular challenge. It's almost as though we are half listening, because at the same time we're reviewing our personal library of lessons learned, trying to figure out what we could say, suggest, or offer to our child in that moment.

People we interviewed about their own childhood experiences dealing with emotional distress or mental health issues told us that caregivers were most helpful when they set their judgments and emotions aside and practiced active listening.

Brandon Smith is a Black man in his midtwenties from Ohio. He has experienced symptoms of depression, anxiety, and OCD since childhood. Brandon formerly worked for NAMI as a Next Gen young adult advisor, and currently works as a behavioral specialist at a local school.

"I think sometimes the solution is to stop trying to solve the problem and just listen," Brandon told me in our interview. He continued:

That would've gone such a long way. The people who I really connected with just listened. They asked open-ended questions. What do you mean by this? Or what are you really experiencing? What are you really feeling? They didn't judge, they didn't try to fix it, they just listened. Because very often, even if they did know what the solution was, they guided me to the solution that was already within my capability to obtain. And that helped me gain self-confidence and helped me to realize that the problems I'm facing aren't necessarily always a bad thing. They're an opportunity to grow.

Nora Flanagan is a white woman in her late forties from Chicago. She has worked to understand and support adolescent mental health as a teacher for twenty-five years, and as the mother of two teenage sons. She shares a similar sentiment from the perspective of an open and supportive adult:

I do think we as grown-ups look at young people and we can sometimes gravitate toward the simplest answer, which isn't necessarily the correct answer. "Well, they're doing this, so it must be this." We depend on our assumptions to guide our judgment.

Here's the difference: I ask and then I listen. I don't ask to say that I ask. I ask and then I listen on the assumption that they're going to tell me something I don't know, because I think also sometimes adults ask questions and this is our standardized testing mode of talking to young people. We ask a question that there is one answer for. Or at least in our minds, there's one answer, and we're just waiting to hear it. I try to approach both my own children and my students on the assumption that I have no idea what the answer to my question is, and so I'm going to shut up and listen.

Ziona, a CEO and outreach coordinator who is considered a peer in the Mental Health Recovery community and volunteers throughout the peer recovery movement in various organizations, shared a simple phrase with us to keep in mind while communicating with your child: "explore, don't explain."

Engaging in the process of exploration means creating a conversation less dominated by you talking at the child but rather full of opportunities for the child to truly convey how they are feeling and to appreciate that you notice and care about what they are experiencing. This kind of conversation will create the space that is truly needed to validate—not fix or change—their feelings. If we notice concerning changes in our children and the child is sending off signals inviting us to inquire further about what is going on, we need to initiate a conversation that is free of judgment and shame but full of empathy and validation.

Practicing Empathy and Validation

Conveying empathy is essential to truly noticing and understanding your child. Empathy is defined as the ability to understand and share the feelings of another. You might not be able to immediately understand why your child is displaying certain behaviors in response to a given situation, but you can undoubtedly relate to the emotions that the child is expressing through the behaviors.

Evelyn is an eighteen-year-old from Northern Virginia. She has struggled with anorexia, anxiety, and depression for many years. She shared with me the importance of coming alongside someone as they process their experience and trying to understand them as best you can:

> I can't fully understand what you're going through, but also I'm never going to be able to totally understand how you feel. I'm ready to be next to you through the whole time and learn from you if that's what you want to do, or else just support you.

Validation can be employed as a tool—a way to express empathy. It involves responding to a person's emotional state by making comments that convey that the person's feelings are being noticed and understood. To validate your child's emotional state, you do not have to understand exactly where they're coming from, agree with their view about a given situation, or apologize for things that you are truly not apologetic for. However, you do need to have patience enough to give space for your child to feel what they're feeling—and this can be frustrating! Validation of someone else's experience communicates that you acknowledge and respect their autonomous experience of the world around them, even if it's not the same as your own. In that moment, your child is feeling a certain way, and feeling that way is hard. Acknowledging that truth is a critical step in establishing healthy communication.

When a child is sharing their emotional experiences, caregivers can sometimes fall into the trap of minimizing the gravity of the situation or making suggestions about how to suppress the emotions themselves. Although such responses are well intended, they can make the child feel invalidated, as though their feelings don't matter, or that there is something wrong with having them. This creates a rift, a disconnect, when what they need most in that moment is to feel connected to you. Examples of invalidating comments include, "Everything will be all right, no need to worry," "Oh that's not a big deal, no need to get upset," "You'll get over it soon," "Tomorrow is another day," or anything that questions whether the child is overreacting to or wrong about the situation that has elicited their feelings. However well-intentioned, and regardless of whether they are true, these comments shut the door to further exploration with your child about their current emotional state.

We spoke to a Family-to-Family class graduate from Santa Barbara County who elected to stay anonymous. She is the mother of a child who experienced moments of intense mood swings and behavioral changes. She talked about how over time, through trial and error, she learned how to validate her child's experience:

> You tell them, "Don't worry, it'll be okay," try and encourage them, which now I realize is invalidating. And so what came across to her is, "There's something wrong with the way I'm feeling." Like, "Oh, I shouldn't be anxious, I shouldn't be afraid. It shouldn't bother me." All of these things that we thought were helpful were really being very unhelpful because we didn't know that validation was what she needed. It was like, "Well, what do you mean you don't have any friends? You're friends with all these people."
>
> And so I feel guilty, but we didn't know what we didn't know. I think I probably argued back and didn't really do the right thing. Had I known what validation would be, I could have handled it differently. And in our case, trying to offer solutions was harmful. Telling her what we think she should do or what she could have done better, that just makes her feel worse and ashamed, and it's very triggering and causes a lot of dysregulation on her part, which then causes dysregulation in me.

Engaging and Modeling

It's important not only to notice the cues given off by your child to signal a particular emotional state but also to give them space to identify their own emotions first. This step allows the child to learn to better recognize the thoughts and sensations in their body that signal a particular mood state and allows for them to receive feedback about how others perceive their mood states.

As a parent, one of the things you can do to help your children develop the ability to identify their own emotions is to point out what you notice in your child as they move through different emotional states. When you see that your child is experiencing anger, sadness, anxiety, fear—emotional states that you have certainly experienced before—you can make comments that reflect your awareness of how that emotion is manifesting in their body language and temperament.

This can help them develop an awareness themselves of what's happening in their bodies as they experience different emotions.

In preschool or the early grades of elementary school your child may recognize emotional responses when other people have them, but may still have some challenges identifying what they are feeling, articulating their emotional states, or expressing their needs in a way that is easily understood by parents. They may be able to tell you that they feel like something is wrong, but struggle to offer up an explanation for why they feel that way.

One great way to initiate a conversation with your child is to ask them to "translate" their distress signals to you: "Mommy was just thinking about ways that I can help you whenever you're not feeling happy but sometimes it's hard for me to tell when you're sad, mad, or scared. What are some ways that I can know when you're sad, mad, or scared? What sort of things do you say or do?" They may not know how to answer yet, but meanwhile you are enlisting them in coming to understand their own distress signals, so over time they'll more effectively communicate their emotional needs.

Another good strategy is to ask what they think they may need at this moment, that they are currently lacking. When I see a younger child who is experiencing some form of emotional distress, and I am trying to explore what they think they need in the moment, I ask the question: "If I had a magic wand, what would be the two things that you would want to magically change in your life to make you feel better?"

Demonstrating that you understand how hard it is to experience those particular feelings provides the child valuable information as to what they are feeling and how their emotions are being perceived by others. By doing that, you are reinforcing how to identify the emotional state, which allows them to learn the signals and cues that their body sends when they are experiencing it. Helping them to label their emotional states, conveying that you notice the change in their mood, and sharing how you relate to that emotional state will teach the child to understand what they are experiencing and reassure them that they are not alone in feeling that way. Once again, showing your child that you are truly listening and noticing them in the moment—and comfortable joining them as they process and move through their emotions—can go a long way.

Shared Goals and Ongoing Conversation

Communication is a two-way street. In the same way that the attitude and outlook your child brings to the conversation influences the tone and outcome, the way you as a parent are receiving and responding to your child will impact the interaction. Taking time to envision how we want a conversation to go ahead of time allows us to go in better prepared and reduces the likelihood of saying things that we may regret later. Another key to having conversations about mental health with your child is to initiate them when things are calm, when the child is not engaged in some activity that requires their full attention, and there is no evidence of an acute concern going on at the moment. This provides an even playing field for both you and your child, and a neutral place to start building a foundation. If you approach a child when s/he is in an emotionally aroused state or trying to play a video game, you will get nowhere. If you wait until your child is calm and engaged in an activity that allows for both playing and talking, you will have a better chance of capturing his/her interest in what might be a slightly uncomfortable or anxiety-provoking conversation.

Preparing for these difficult conversations by thinking about and establishing clear goals for you and your child can help make them easier too. For example, do you want to leave this conversation having reassured your child that you are a safe person to share their problems with? Do you want to establish boundaries for your child's behavior while offering positive ways for them to reach out to you when they experience distress?

There is always the possibility that when you ask the child about what they think would be helpful to reduce their distress, they just shrug their shoulders and run off. Don't feel dismayed by that response;

take it as a signal that they may not be ready, comfortable, or quite frankly interested in having that conversation with you, and that's okay. In fact, that goes for children regardless of age. The goal isn't to have one particular conversation; it's to continue to create spaces and opportunities that demonstrate that you're taking notice of your child's moods and behaviors and that you're interested in hearing their take on what's going on.

Considerations and Strategies for Kids at Different Developmental Stages

Ages Two to Five (Toddlers and Preschoolers)

Children this age have vivid imaginations and can engage in what is referred to as magical thinking. The question I mentioned that I typically ask them, "If I had a magic wand, what would be the two things that you would want to magically change in your life to make you feel better?" invites children to engage in a form of imaginative play with me, which makes it easier for them to connect and communicate. Engaging children this age in play and imaginative thinking can also reduce some anxiety they may be experiencing related to discussing their distress by allowing them to briefly escape the difficult, real world where they are struggling, and access a place in which they feel more competent and more comfortable.

One helpful recommendation from the American Academy of Pediatrics is that children this age have their own area in the house where they can manage difficult emotions. Create a cozy nook in their bedroom, or create a "fort" or tent to serve as a private retreat when they are overwhelmed.

Ages Six to Eleven (Middle Childhood or the School-Aged Child)

Children in middle childhood may ask you a lot of questions or even provide some pushback when you try to have a conversation about their mental health. The key is to keep them engaged in the conversation, and to keep them informed about thoughts you may have about how to support them. Here's a sample dialogue:

CAREGIVER: I've noticed you've been less interested in going to basketball practice and haven't wanted to play with your friends. Why do you think that is?

CHILD: It's too cold outside, and I hate the cold.

CAREGIVER: It seems like whenever it gets really cold outside, you tend to feel sadder. Is that something you've noticed?

CHILD: Why would I feel sad just because it's cold outside?

CAREGIVER: Well, I'm not sure, but I wonder if we should talk to someone about why you seem to become sadder and less interested in doing things during the colder months.

CHILD: How would talking to someone make me feel better when it's cold outside?

CAREGIVER: Well, there are professionals who talk to kids about how their mood and behaviors may change over time. For some kids, their moods get worse when it's cold out. Maybe this person can teach us ways to improve our mood so that things like cold weather don't bother us as much. What do you think would be helpful for you?

CHILD: I don't know.

CAREGIVER: Okay, we'll let's just see if a person like this can be helpful and start from there. Would that be okay with you?

CHILD: Sure, whatever.

In this example, both the child and caregiver have identified a pattern in which the child becomes less interested in their preferred activities during the colder, winter months. The child is able to make the connection between lack of interest in playing basketball and socializing and hating the cold but isn't able to connect how losing interest in preferred activities means that he is sad or that the cold weather may make him sad.

Some caregivers might walk away from this conversation thinking, "Well, my child doesn't really care or think it's important," and decide not to engage them in any further conversations. Keep in mind that it may be challenging for the child to make all the connections to understand why what you're talking about *is* important. That's why it's good to explicitly state why you're asking certain questions. And remember, the point of the conversation is to have the conversation, not necessarily to instantly solve what you consider a problem. Your child may think about the conversation later, and come to understand it—and their own feelings—better.

Ages Twelve and Over—Motivational Interviewing

Adolescents and kids who are twelve and older have developed the cognitive skills to think in more abstract and sophisticated ways. They are not as concrete and don't require a lot of extra support in making connections between certain concepts. Given this shift in the way that adolescents are able to process things, they are able to think more creatively and may have unique solutions to offer for how to support their own mental health. As caregivers, it is important to recognize their creative capacities and encourage their participation in conversations about their own well-being.

Dr. Emily Kline is a psychologist and author in Massachusetts. She works with young adults and their families at Boston Medical Center and is an assistant professor at Boston University. In her clinical practice, she has seen parents get into power struggles with their kids trying to get them to change certain behaviors or to solve problems in a manner that the parent approves of. Teenagers are at a developmental stage in which they want to assume more independence from their primary caregiver. They have the capacity to problem-solve, and to consider all the potential risks and consequences of their choices. It is easy to bump heads with a strong-minded teenager when you lose patience with the direction or pace of their "problem-solving," resulting in frustration, anger, and increased tension within the home. Dr. Kline has adapted elements from motivational interviewing—an evidence-based therapeutic approach developed for working with people who had substance use disorders—to help parents communicate with teens in a way less likely to provoke conflict. Dr. Kline describes motivational interviewing as "a set of conversational tactics to talk to people who are ambivalent or defensive about changing behavior." Caregivers have to learn to relinquish the idea that they ought to be in control, and instead use these techniques to encourage your child while also "backing off."

Key elements of motivational interviewing include asking open-ended questions, reflecting back how you understood your child's answers to those questions to ensure the child knows you've listened and understood them, providing affirmations, and working toward a solution with your child in mind. Dr. Kline continued:

> In order to get into a place where we're not feeling defensive, and we're willing to consider the pros and cons and practicalities of a change, we need to feel understood, confident, and in control. And in order to help kids feel that way, we have to approach them in a way that's nonjudgmental, curious about their perspective, and that assumes their strengths. I want parents to understand that they're much more likely to get there if they can slow down and react in a nonjudgmental and curious way, and help understand the teen's perspective. What's going on? What's getting in the way? How can we problem-solve this together?
>
> When I talk to parents, and they want to learn these skills, I always start with the question, "Who was an influence in your life when you

were your kids' age? Who were the adults that you actually would listen to, or that you liked to be around? What was it about [this person] that made them a safe person to talk to, whose advice you actually wanted?" And the answer is always the same. Parents from all over the world say, "They listened. They didn't judge me. They saw my strengths."

You can learn more about Dr. Kline's approach to using MI in her book *The School of Hard Talks: How to Have Real Conversations with Your (Almost Grown) Kids.*

. . .

Getting to a place in which you're effectively communicating with your child is not easy and requires you to notice all the ways (overt and covert) your child may be communicating their distress to you. Finding ways to manage your own distress when you are concerned about your child, and cultivating validation, empathy, and active listening skills can help you to build a foundation of trust so that your child feels safe sharing their feelings and knows that you are open to solving problems together. These communication skills can serve to keep that foundation sturdy as you and your child enlist support from others in the outside world.

THREE

Starting the Journey

To realize you have good reason to be concerned about your child, and that you can't just let them carry on functioning with the level of distress they have been experiencing, can usher in a wave of anxiety, fear, and for some, a sense of relief. Now you know: Your child needs more support than you can provide on your own. The next step is figuring out how, where, and from whom to obtain that support at this moment in time.

Acknowledging that your child is experiencing distress brings with it a palpable desire to know *why* your child is experiencing distress, so we can fix the problem as soon as possible. It is understandable for parents to want to figure it out on their own. After all, you know your child best and may have an intuition about what might be a suitable approach for supporting your kid. This approach can result in a feeling of triumph when you notice that changes your family makes seem to significantly improve your child's emotional well-being. But simply taking matters into your own hands without enlisting the help of others can also yield a fair amount of frustration, angst, and confusion. And in truth, most of us don't know what to do, exactly.

When we as caregivers do not have the answer as to how to help our kid, we want and *need* to believe that someone out there does. But finding answers is inevitably a process. No one else, regardless of their professional expertise, is going to have a magic solution. And the most important thing you can do first is to be present for your child. You may feel alone as you embark on this journey to get your child help; paradoxically, most people do! But in truth, while there are no instant answers or remedies, there are many, many people who are on the same journey, and many people you don't know yet are already in your corner.

In this chapter, I'll start with some guiding recommendations for starting your child's mental health journey. I'll also give a general overview of the professionals you might encounter as you navigate the mental health care system and their roles. I recognize that everyone's journey will look different but the general principles that we touch upon throughout this chapter apply to all, no matter how and when you decide to start your child's mental health journey.

Identifying the best point of entry for you and your child, given your particular circumstances, environment, and resources, can be a challenge, but as you are trying to figure it out, keep the following principles in mind:

- Trust is critical.
- Start in your own backyard.
- Rethink your assumptions about expertise.
- Remain vigilant and patient.

Trust Is Critical

The first person you reach out to should be someone you trust to hear your concerns about your child without judgment, and who can assist you in exploring different options for accessing help. Whether that's your spouse, partner, pastoral counselor, or a family friend who you know has experience dealing with mental health concerns, you and your child both need to trust the person you're consulting. Discussing a mental health concern can be a vulnerable experience. You first need support for yourself—an ally, not necessarily an expert.

You and your child will feel more comfortable being fully open and honest with someone you already have a relationship with. So, reach out first to leaders in your community with whom you have a strong relationship—and it doesn't have to be a single person. People you trust could include a leader in your faith community, a school counselor, a teacher, a medical provider, or a mental health clinician with whom you already have a relationship. That person's official title doesn't matter.

Your child's primary care provider, with whom you already have an established relationship, is a trusted resource for many families. Mental health–related concerns are also medical concerns, and therefore your primary care provider (PCP)—whether that be a pediatrician, a pediatric nurse practitioner, or a pediatric physician assistant—can serve as that initial point of contact at the beginning of your journey. As we've all experienced when a child is physically ill and we aren't sure what to do, the guidance and reassurance the PCP provides over the phone or in person during a visit gives you a sense of relief that you're talking to someone who not only has practical knowledge and training but has also accompanied many other families who are concerned about their child.

We spoke to Dr. Jeremy Daigle, a pediatrician based out of Oak Lawn, Illinois, about his role in supporting the mental health of the children who come through his practice. His perspective is informed by the relationships he's established with patients in their infancy. He reminded us that your pediatrician or pediatric primary care provider has been monitoring your child's mood and behaviors using various rating scales at every annual checkup. Remember those pesky, long questionnaires that you have to fill out in advance of the appointment, or on an iPad or clipboard in the waiting room if you didn't do so ahead of time? All those forms provide the pediatrician critical information about your child's development, mood, and behavior that they otherwise may not have the time to explicitly ask you about during the visit, so make sure to be as honest and as accurate as you can be when completing those questions. The answers that you provide on those questionnaires allow the pediatrician to focus on issues of concern to make more efficient use of the limited time that they have with you.

Dr. Daigle also mentioned that many states have programs that provide pediatricians direct access to a psychiatrist over the phone if a child patient has more complex mental health needs. In his state, Illinois, for example, they have a program called DocAssist that Dr. Daigle uses when he has specific questions on how best to support a patient. Dr. Daigle emphasized that primary care providers can also give you some direction on where you can find a therapist for your child. Several pediatric primary care clinics already have mental health clinicians serving on staff so you don't have to go too far from home or worry about whether or not the therapist will accept your insurance.

Finding someone you trust to share information with about your child's mental health and to guide you along this mental health journey is a great place to start. However, identifying a trusted individual who also has information about the next best steps to take is not necessarily easy. I spoke to many family members of children with mental health concerns who felt unable to approach faith leaders, teachers, counselors, mental health providers, or even a primary care provider since they came from small communities and had legitimate concerns about privacy. People we interviewed from Hawaii, Alaska, and parts of the Midwest where there are limited resources for addressing mental health concerns told us about how trusted individuals might also be trusted by multiple other family members, which can present a "conflict of interest" or create anxiety about even inadvertent breaches of privacy. Or the trusted individual or someone in their office was a friend, or there were other existing dynamics in their relationship with that person that made approaching them with concerns about their child problematic. We fully acknowledge and appreciate that these issues may present barriers to accessing support. But you may not have to branch out too far to figure out where else you can go.

Start in Your Own Backyard

When it comes to navigating the mental health system, there can be a tendency to feel as though you have to reinvent the wheel and develop a mental health team completely from scratch. I have worked with families who have spent hours doing internet searches for the "best" mental health clinicians that exist, and for some families, those practitioners were located in places far from where they lived or charged exorbitant fees that were not affordable for the majority of families in America. Finding help for your child can be an overwhelming and daunting process when you feel as though it is entirely your responsibility to materialize a treatment team from thin air. So, it is important to know that it doesn't have to be all on your shoulders alone.

I advise families not to look too far from home to figure out where to start and where to gain access to mental health care for their child. Teri Brister, who created NAMI Basics, a free educational program for caregivers of youth ages twenty-two and younger who are experiencing mental health symptoms, has always said that there are "no wrong doors" when it comes to gaining entry to mental health supports, and these doors don't have to be that far away. Initiating conversations within your local community can provide the opportunity for people to share resources that they have access to and use to help support their children. Most people feel as though they need to keep the information about the difficulties that they're facing behind closed doors. But as you get more comfortable with the idea that your child needs more support than you know how to provide, opening the doors and sharing with people what you're going through allows others to step through and offer up resources that otherwise we would have never known about. Community connections and tapping into supports that are right in your backyard can save you a lot of time and angst. Do yourself a favor: Talk to others in your community about what they've done to support their child. There's no need to keep it between you and Google as you figure out your point of entry to the mental health system.

Rethink Your Assumptions About Expertise

While, as Teri Brister said, there are "no wrong doors," certain doors may take longer to access. There are 60,000 pediatricians in the United States but, according to the American Academy of Child and Adolescent Psychiatrists (AACAP), there are only 8,300 practicing child and adolescent psychiatrists. That means that 70 percent of children live in counties that do not have a child psychiatrist on call at all. The situation is not much better when it comes to psychologists. Only 4,000 out of the 100,000 clinical psychologists (PhD, PsyD) are trained to see children and adolescents, according to the American Psychological Association, and it can take up to six months on a waiting list before a child can see a psychologist for therapy. Pediatric neuropsychologists, who are clinicians trained to evaluate and assess for different learning disorders (impairment in math, reading, and written expression) and neurodevelopmental disorders such as ADHD and autism spectrum disorders, and to develop appropriate interventions, typically have waitlists at least twelve months long in most major US cities. A lot of children and families do not have six to twelve months to wait to see a mental health specialist.

I share these statistics because it is important to understand that immediately reaching out to a psychiatrist or a psychologist will not always translate into gaining access to immediate support. As a caregiver, this delay in accessing help can seem unbearable. But you need not simply sit and wait for an appointment with a psychiatrist or a psychologist to become available. There are other specialists and available supports you can access in the meantime. We certainly want the best for our children, but that doesn't always mean that your child must wait to have their mental health needs addressed until the clinician with the most advanced degree has an opening in their schedule.

Remain Patient, Stay Vigilant

Knowing that your child needs help and that you're unable to obtain it from a psychiatrist or psychologist can be painful. I know that seeing your child experiencing any form of difficulty is something that you certainly want to be short-lived. But while many of the families I interviewed experienced this sense of urgency to find resources, many also often found that their expectation that there would be immediate results once they accessed these resources would prove to be unrealistic. For some, the process isn't as simple as finding a single mental health provider who then makes a definitive diagnosis and identifies one particular type of treatment that will resolve your child's distress in short order. Mental health–related concerns are complex, and your child is a moving target, learning, developing, and encountering new challenges and obstacles day by day. It's rarely as simple as, say, getting your child diagnosed with strep throat and starting them on an antibiotic and that's it. One must have patience while on this journey of finding the right mental health provider for your child—and an awareness that the kind of provider you need, or the kind of therapy or medication or help, is likely to change over time. The good news is that there are so many other ways, and so many other people, who can support our children, who can not only teach them the specific skills they need to learn to manage their distress, but also help them continue to develop socially, emotionally, and intellectually.

Who Are the Professionals?

There are several kinds of mental health professionals whom you may be referred to, who may have different perspectives, different kinds of expertise, and different tools and skills to offer. The list of professionals that you can call to address a mental health concern in your child can be daunting. Do you start with a psychiatrist or a therapist? Or a psychologist versus a social worker? A counselor versus a neuropsychologist? There's a whole cast of characters from a variety of different disciplines working as mental health professionals, and I know that most people start out unsure about their specific realms of expertise. Let's explore their roles in supporting your child—and you and your family—on your mental health journey.

Therapists

The first mental health professional most people engage with is a therapist. Therapists become credentialed in many different academic disciplines and have somewhat different, if overlapping, educational training. Most commonly, therapists have either doctoral degrees in psychology (PhD, PsyD, and sometimes EdD), master's level degrees in psychology, mental health counseling, educational psychology, or social work (MA, MS, MSW, MEd). There are also mental health clinicians with nursing degrees (CNS, PMHNP) and social workers (LISW, LICSW, LCSW). Don't be afraid to ask a mental health professional about their training and licensure.

Most caregivers may have a basic understanding of what a therapist does, but for some, their understanding of the role is based on what they might have seen on TV or read about on the internet or social media rather than through firsthand experience. We may have heard from others about their experiences with therapy, which could color the lenses through which we understand its role—whether good or bad. Or you may have preconceived notions about the utility of therapy—*Why would I pay someone to simply talk to my child? Couldn't they just talk to me or someone else that they know?* These are all valid thoughts and concerns. Whatever opinions, reservations, or feelings you have about therapy are important to acknowledge from the start and even to discuss with your child's therapist when you first meet them. Chances are it won't be the first time that the therapist has heard whatever it is you think or feel about therapy, nor the first time they've been asked the questions you have. Openly discussing your thoughts and concerns about therapy will create an opportunity to learn more about this effective form of treatment and support, and to understand its potential role in relieving your child of their distress.

Therapy, which can also be referred to as "talk therapy" or psychotherapy, is a form of support that will allow your child to discuss their innermost thoughts, feelings, and past experiences in a safe, confidential space with a trained therapist. Therapists meet with the child, typically weekly but sometimes more or less frequently, for individual therapy where they can further explore underlying factors that may be driving certain moods and behaviors. They also provide strategies and skills to help children better tolerate intense emotional states, cope with distress, and regulate their behavior. During therapy, your child will learn specific skills to mitigate the distress that they may be experiencing and will practice how to implement them. Attending regular therapy sessions allows your child to better understand their own emotions and recognize and respond to the distress signals they may experience in their body—or the pattern of their thoughts. Your child can become more in touch with their emotions rather than suppressing them or denying their existence. Learning how to recognize your feelings, label the emotion, and then access a skill in the moment of distress to better tolerate that moment are the primary goals for most types of therapy.

Therapists are also trained to evaluate underlying mental health conditions and can recommend strategies for improving some symptoms that may be causing your child distress. If your child is experiencing more severe symptoms that are interfering with their ability to function, the therapist can make recommendations for additional mental health supports. Therapists also may communicate with a child's school to better determine and assess how the child is functioning in the school environment and make recommendations for supports that should be put in place within the school to ensure that the child can progress academically.

Psychiatrists

A psychiatrist is a medical doctor who specializes in diagnosing and treating mental health conditions. Given that their training is in medicine, they can order blood tests and brain imaging and perform physical examinations in order to evaluate whether an underlying medical condition may be contributing to a child's behavior and mood changes. Psychiatrists prescribe medications to treat specific mental health conditions and monitor the child's symptoms while they are taking the medication. Many studies have indicated that a combination of medication management and therapy is the most effective form of treatment for a variety of mental health conditions. Your child's psychiatrist may provide psychotherapy in addition to medication management or refer your child to a therapist if they do not already have one.

The psychiatrist works in collaboration with therapists, primary care providers, schools, and families to ensure that appropriate supports are in place across multiple settings within the child's life. They can provide recommendations to schools for strategies that they could implement within the classroom to make the environment more tolerable for the child in light of their mental health symptoms.

Although therapy and medication management are helpful treatment plans for many patients who may be experiencing certain conditions, for those who are experiencing more significant symptoms of emotional distress including suicidality, disorganized and erratic behavior, detachment from reality, hallucinations, and extreme fluctuations of their mood into a state of mania, then a psychiatrist may be recommended before establishing care with a psychologist given that the child would benefit from medication first to provide more immediate stability in their mental health.

Neuropsychologists

In addition to supporting the emotional needs of children by providing treatment through therapy and/or medication management, it may be important to understand how the child's brain is developing and how that development impacts how they think, behave, and learn new information. A neuropsychologist is trained to use their expertise to assess for patterns in a child's brain development that may make learning more difficult for the child in certain ways, or that may manifest in how the child responds to certain situations behaviorally.

A referral to a neuropsychologist is often made if there are concerns about a child's academic performance. You or the school may notice that there are areas of weakness in the child's performance in different school subjects. An evaluation by a neuropsychologist can reveal important information about the root cause of difficulties in school. The neuropsychologist performs specific assessments and tests that can help determine if the child has a specific learning disorder. For some children, mood or behavior changes, particularly while in school, are often a by-product of their frustrations over not being able to keep up with their peers in class. The child may not say this in so many words, or even know the source of the feeling, but children are sensitive to where they stand relative to peers and can know at some level that something is difficult for them that is not hard for others.

A neuropsychologist can also detect areas of weakness and strength in how the child processes information—to determine if there are any challenges in their ability to process information that they have received in writing versus information that they've received by hearing it. Have you noticed a difference in how you understand and retain information that you read versus information that you hear? That difference reflects the fact that some people are more adept at learning through what they see (known as "visual learners") and some through what they hear ("auditory learners"). The neuropsychologist can make recommendations based on their understanding of how the child learns best, to help the child better tolerate being in a classroom setting learning academic material.

Neuropsychologists can also evaluate for any challenges related to a child's "executive functioning." Executive functioning refers to one's ability to remember information, focus, organize oneself to accomplish a task or a sequence of tasks, as well as the ability to do more than one task at a time. They can diagnose specific conditions that make it more difficult for a child to socialize or communicate with others, or sensitivities related to sensory processing—meaning their ability to tolerate different sounds, textures, smells, tastes, and visual stimuli. Neuropsychologists use their knowledge of brain development to determine whether a child demonstrates evidence of delays in achieving certain milestones in terms of their motor, language, social, and thinking skills as well as their ability to complete basic daily tasks such as getting dressed or toileting. If there are concerns about some of these skills, the child could be referred to an occupational therapist (OT) for help with sensory, fine motor, and coordination issues or a physical therapist (PT) to assist in the child's gross motor development.

There will come a point when you have found a provider for your child. You may experience a sense of relief, optimism, and hope that after all of your efforts, this person you've found will be able to fix things. You may want to hinge all of your worries and fears about the future of your child on this sole individual since in your mind they are now shouldering the burden of making whatever is distressing your child go away. But our child's mental health journey is not about identifying a problem and finding a person to fix it.

This problem-solving paradigm is something that we are quite accustomed to in other areas of life. We have an issue with our car, we bring it to the auto mechanic and expect quick results. But even after you bring your child to meet with a mental health professional, healing takes time. Your child is unlikely to immediately trust this provider with all the information about what is going on in their lives. Your child may not want to engage in therapy, may resist or dislike prescribed medication, or may not enthusiastically volunteer to change their behavior. Life may present new challenges. Their normal development certainly will. We as caregivers cannot force our child to forge that relationship with their provider nor push the child to learn, grow, or heal at a faster pace.

It is not uncommon for a child to express to a parent or caregiver their lack of interest in or connection with their provider. They may refuse to go back to the person, or when they do go it may be difficult for them to engage. Either they're sitting in silence, or you may have the impression that the conversation is too superficial for it to have any meaningful impact. You may start to question whether there is a good fit between your child and the provider after the first couple of visits. Give it some time. With any type of relationship that we form, things change. There may be an immediate connection that fades over time. Or there could be a lack of connection in the beginning before a relationship begins to blossom. We do not know what type of relationship will form, but we do need to provide some time and space to see how it grows.

That doesn't mean we should be passive in our approach and just sit back and wait for things to happen. Remain vigilant throughout this process since you, too, are forming a relationship with your child's provider and want to ensure that your child is in trusted hands. If you notice that your child is becoming increasingly more distressed, you're finding that you and your child are having difficulty establishing trust with the provider or there are ongoing challenges around communication, it is okay to take a step back and find someone else—if you have that option.

You may feel that you have absolutely no choice but to continue your relationship with the provider. Maybe they are the only one who takes your insurance or the only one with an opening. Maybe this person was recommended to you as being "the best of the best." But trust your gut. If you've given it a fair chance and it becomes clear that a therapist is not a good fit for your child, it is okay to move on. If it still doesn't feel right, it probably isn't right.

Remaining vigilant does not mean anticipating that the provider will fail to connect with your child, or becoming confrontational at the first appearance of misgivings about the provider's approach. It just means to keep a watchful eye to see if your child is becoming more comfortable with this relationship. Create a space for your child to talk openly with you about how they feel about their provider, without interrogating them, dismissing their feelings, or defending the provider. You can acknowledge that it is hard to be vulnerable with a new person and to start the process of improving their mental health. Both you and your child are on this journey that does not always have a clear path.

It can also happen that a therapeutic relationship that was a good fit for a long time stops being one. Your child is a work in progress. On their journey to adulthood, their needs evolve, and their relationship with their provider may change too. For example, a child going through puberty may no longer feel quite as comfortable as they once did with a provider of a different gender, or may want to explore their cultural or sexual identity with someone who shares that identity. Or your child has formed a therapeutic bond with some other professional they've met in the course of their care—the clinician who leads their dialectical behavioral therapy (DBT) group, a school counselor—and feels they are getting somewhere new in that relationship.

. . .

Your child's mental health journey may ultimately involve interacting with one or more different kinds of mental health professionals. Wherever the journey begins, that therapist, psychologist, or psychiatrist may initially want to evaluate your child before beginning treatment, in part to determine whether the child "meets the criteria" for a mental health diagnosis as defined in the *Diagnostic and Statistical Manual of Mental Disorders* (DSM), the standard classification that mental health professionals use to guide diagnosis in the United States. If your child does have a mental health disorder, having a diagnosis is important in helping target the best treatments, obtain support services, and secure insurance coverage. However, particularly when it comes to children, diagnosis is a process, not a fixed point; it's an art as much as it is a science. A diagnosis may change, or no longer be warranted, as your child grows. In the next chapter, I'll talk about what the evaluation process involves and what a diagnosis means and doesn't mean. Mental health professionals can be an important part of your child's mental health journey, providing much-needed support and resources such as therapy and medication. However, the amount of time that your child will spend with a mental health professional pales in comparison to the amount of time your child will spend with you. The reality is that most of the time, your child will likely not be in the hands of the designated expert. They will be spending time with you and your family at home or filling their days with school and extracurricular activities and hanging out with friends. The challenge most parents face is what to do when the appointment is over, and the child is still acting out, or still depressed, or still anxious.

You are still the most important person in your child's healing journey, and the most important skills you need to support your kid have to do with communication. Don't underestimate the tremendous value of possessing those skills. The communication between you and your child is ultimately more vital than the connection between your child and any particular mental health provider. You have something to bring to the table and it is important to leverage that for the sake of your child.

FOUR

Getting and Understanding a Mental Health Diagnosis

I f and when you decide you need to have your child evaluated by a mental health professional—whether that be with a psychiatrist to determine if medication is warranted, a therapist to determine if ongoing therapy would be beneficial, or a neuropsychologist to explore issues affecting a child's ability to learn—it can be helpful for both you and your child to have a basic understanding of what to expect from the evaluation process. Once the evaluation has been completed and your child receives a diagnosis, many caregivers are left asking themselves, "What now?" or "What does this mean for my child and my family?" This chapter will provide a general outline of what to expect during the evaluation and diagnosis stage of your child's mental health journey.

When you reach out to a mental health professional, they will schedule your child for what is often called an "intake" appointment. The purpose of an intake or evaluation is to obtain a clear picture of what is going on with your kid at this moment in time, and the factors that may be contributing to their distress, so clinicians and other professionals know how best to begin providing help.

During most mental health evaluations involving children, the mental health professional will need to spend some time talking to you, but most importantly they need to interact directly with your child. It isn't uncommon for caregivers who bring their child to an evaluation with me to be concerned about how that interaction will go. They may wonder, "If my child isn't talking to me, why would they talk to a complete stranger?" They may have concerns that the child is too young to have any insight regarding their mood and behavior and may not possess the language to clearly articulate their internal experience. Some caregivers may even delay bringing their kid in to be evaluated because of these concerns. I want to reassure you that mental health professionals who work with children have been trained on how to navigate an evaluation with children who respond in a variety of ways. Do not let that concern deter you from having someone meet with your child.

It is also important to mention that every mental health professional who is new to working with your child may re-ask some of the questions that were asked in the first evaluation. One of the reasons this happens is because each professional wants to form their own impressions by hearing both your answers and your child's while interacting with both of you directly. The reality is that things change over time and people look different over time. An evaluation done by a psychologist immediately following a major stressor in the child's life may reflect a picture of your child very different than the one that might develop from an evaluation done six months after the stressor is gone. Children change and situations change, so it is helpful for there to be ongoing assessment.

The mental health professional's approach toward the evaluation will largely depend on the age of the child. Most school-aged children (ages five to eleven) will be interviewed with the caregiver present in the room, and preteens (age twelve) and teens will be interviewed separately from the caregiver. There may be situations in which a mental health professional interviews a school-aged child individually. Some school-aged children may express a preference to be interviewed alone, particularly if there are concerns about trauma or other topics that the child finds challenging to talk about comfortably.

There are caregivers of teenagers who feel more comfortable remaining present in the room for the interview with their child. If that is the case for you, it can be incredibly helpful to explain why you want to do so with the mental health professional. Your reasoning will provide information about existing dynamics between you and your child that gives the mental health professional some perspective on the child's daily experience. However, if a mental health professional does ask for a few moments alone to meet with your child, do consider how valuable it may be for your teen to be able to speak openly about their emotional experience in a way they may feel unable to do in your presence. That does not necessarily mean your child wants to talk to the therapist about you or share their views on your flaws as a parent. Children and teens are aware of the impact that their moods and behavior have on their caregivers, and sometimes that can be quite painful and hard for them. They may not want to hurt, disappoint, or worry you. It can also be hard for them to talk about how existing dynamics at home, school, and elsewhere may be impacting their mental health with you in the room. Providing children of this age the space and privacy to discuss their emotional experience will be incredibly beneficial for them, since the mental health professional will have access to information that will allow them to make a more accurate diagnosis.

While it can also be painful and hard as a caregiver not to know everything about their child's experiences and feelings, it is important to know that mental health professionals maintain a certain level of what could be described as therapeutic confidentiality about the details of what a child shares with them during a private interaction. If for example your child discusses their sexual experiences or drug use, professional ethics require the therapist to maintain confidentiality unless the child expressly permits them to share those facts. However, the mental health professional is also ethically obligated to share information that is relevant to a child's mental health. For example, if you bring your teen in for an evaluation or therapy because they have been experiencing anxiety and the mental health professional determines that those symptoms appear to be related to the use of stimulants that have been prescribed to treat their sibling's ADHD, that would certainly be important information for the caregiver to have. Additionally, if there are concerns around safety, such that your child is having thoughts about self-harm or is using drugs in a way that could cause imminent harm, then you need to know all the details. If, however, your teen shares information with the therapist about their sexual experiences within a romantic relationship, and the therapist determines that the relationship is not abusive or exploitative, then they will not share the information with you even though your child is not abiding by your values. Generally speaking, a therapist may summarize key themes that have emerged during the interaction rather than providing you with a detailed account of the conversation.

When I meet with children and adolescents, I always like to start off by asking them questions about their social history: where they live, who they live with, their relationships with family members and friends, their engagement with academics and extracurricular activities, romantic relationships, bullying, hobbies, and where they see themselves "when they're old like me" (that's how I phrase my "what do you want to be when you grow up?" question). I like having the kid talk about things that are fairly easy to talk about with a complete stranger, rather than just starting with "Why are you so sad?" Throughout the interview, I'm watching the child and how they are interacting with the environment: Are they pacing around the room? Are they playing with one of the fidget spinners? Did they dump the entire box of Legos out on the floor and then quickly go over to play with the toy cars? Are they avoiding eye contact with me and just providing one-word answers? Are they talking incredibly fast, frantically describing an amazing art project that they've been working on over the past week including throughout the night? I'm noticing all of these things as part of what is termed in the mental health field a "mental status exam." Beyond the specific questions that I ask, my exam also involves my observations of a child's behavior, which can be a window into their mental health.

Similar to the way some adults get nervous at the doctor's and then chalk up their high blood pressure reading to anxiety, I know that when a child meets with a psychiatrist or another mental health professional, it can produce a lot of anxiety that may affect the evaluation. That is why we spend time talking to the caregivers who can tell us how their kid typically looks and acts. If children struggle to communicate with a mental health provider during an evaluation because of anxiety or are reluctant or resistant to talking for other reasons, that's okay. Their general behavior and response to the evaluation provide helpful information, and they will provide more information during future visits and over time. Mental health professionals who work with kids are like detectives; they can also (with your written consent) get information from primary care providers and schools. And most importantly they gather information from you, the caregiver.

Sometimes caregivers bring their child in for an evaluation thinking that the mental health professional will direct all of their attention to the child while they simply just sit and watch the evaluation take place. But caregivers are integral to the evaluation. Because I've met with families who aren't familiar with what this process involves or who have found it disconcerting or intrusive, I want to spend some time explaining what happens and why, so that you aren't surprised and understand that you, your child, and your clinician are all on the same team. Being caught off guard is never a good feeling, especially when you're being asked pointed questions about your child.

Having anxiety about taking your child to be evaluated is normal. It can feel as though you, too, are going to be evaluated as a caregiver. Please do keep in mind that the purpose of exploring your history and your relationship with your child is not to assign blame for what your child is experiencing, but to fully understand the world in which your child lives. You can provide not only critical background information, but information that allows the clinician to appreciate who your child is in the world beyond an hour-long evaluation with a professional they are likely meeting for the first time.

The person conducting the evaluation will ask questions not only about the concerns that led to the appointment being scheduled, but about the larger context of your child's life, and how it is that their distress manifests within that context. Mental health professionals have come to realize that the story behind what is happening now is often related to a story about what has happened in the past. The clinician is likely to ask about major events that have taken place and any significant stressors that have impacted the family throughout your child's life, as well as more recently. Examples of major life events could include a death in the family, divorce, a change in the child's living situation, the child or a family member experiencing a significant medical illness, and notable stressors related to school. Come prepared to discuss these types of life events, but know that you can be honest with the provider if going into extensive details about a particular event is too difficult for you. That, too, is helpful information for the provider to have.

The mental health professional may explore other experiences during your initial visit that may seem totally unrelated to your child's current struggles, and ask questions that could potentially be experienced as intrusive or voyeuristic. They will want to know about your relationship with your child over the years and about any trauma that you have experienced that your child might have witnessed, such as domestic violence. You will be asked about your mental health history, including any history of substance use, prior psychiatric diagnosis, hospitalizations, and suicide attempts. The clinician may also ask questions about other family members during the evaluation, mainly having to do with their psychiatric history. These questions are asked because your own mental health and previous trauma that you've experienced can influence how you relate and connect to your child, and the mental health provider wants to better understand whether any of your experiences may be connected to your child's current emotional and behavioral state. Information about family history is helpful to the provider because, given that certain mental health conditions do have a genetic component, it can help to shed light on any potential vulnerabilities or genetic predispositions for certain mental health conditions.

Again, I encourage you to share with the provider if the questions being asked of you make you uncomfortable. Knowing that you are free to discuss your feelings and concerns about the type of information that is gathered in the evaluation may reduce any reluctance you have about bringing your child to be evaluated. And your own feelings about the questions can be just as valuable to the evaluation as the answers.

I have noticed that caregivers often have a difficult time remembering information about the past at the time of the evaluation. Perhaps this is a by-product of being focused on what is currently happening with their child. It can be hard to look backward when you're struggling to deal with what's happening right in front of you. Coming to the evaluation prepared with a general sense as to how best to answer these types of questions will not only ensure that your clinician has the information that they need to best determine what is happening with your child, but can help to mitigate any anticipatory anxiety that you may have about what will happen during the session.

Key Areas of the Evaluation

The following is an overview of some of the areas of the evaluation that you may be asked to provide as a caregiver. Consider reviewing the following questions mentioned in this section in advance of the appointment with the mental health professional and think about your responses ahead of time.

Previous Mental Health History

The mental health professional will be interested to learn about previous discussions around your child's mental health. Typically, they will ask if your child has ever received a mental health diagnosis and what type of treatment they received. Information about previous medications that your child might have tried in the past is helpful, particularly if your child started and later stopped the medication due to side effects. Questions around whether your child required hospitalization due to significant concerns about their mood and behavior provide further insight into the severity of your child's mental health symptoms in the past.

Past Medical History

The clinician will inquire about any medical problems that your child has experienced. Medical conditions important to mention are typically those that are chronic or have, or have had, an impact on your child's daily activities. Chronic conditions include diabetes, asthma, seizure disorders, food allergies, heart and thyroid problems. Any significant injuries involving head trauma or loss of consciousness would be important to note. Children who have experienced significant medical issues throughout their lifetime may also have mental health conditions that stem from their longstanding history of struggling with the symptoms and the physical, social, and emotional consequences of those medical conditions. Knowing about a child's medical history may help the mental health professional better understand factors that may contribute to their current mood state.

Family History

The clinician will typically ask about immediate family members including siblings and parents as well as grandparents, uncles, and aunts who have experienced a mental health condition. They may ask about a specific diagnosis but if you're unsure, you can just briefly describe what it is that you observed about your family member's behavior or what you know about any mental health treatment they received. As I mentioned, certain mental health conditions can run in the family, and having this information up front will alert the clinician if the child is at increased risk for a certain condition. You may be asked whether anyone in the family has been psychiatrically hospitalized, attempted suicide, or died by suicide. This is important for your mental health care provider to know since studies have found that patients who had a family history of suicide were more likely to have a history of depression, bipolar disorder, and/or substance use disorder. Additionally, people who have a family history of suicide tend to first experience symptoms of depression at an earlier age.

Developmental History

The clinician will ask you questions related to your child's first few years of life to better understand their developmental history. This information will help the mental health professional determine if there were any delays or challenges during the child's first five years of life. Even if your child is a teenager, this information will be helpful to know. Typical questions that may come up during this part of the evaluation include:

- Pregnancy history: Was it a planned pregnancy? Were there any complications during the pregnancy? Any significant stressors or trauma experienced while pregnant with the child? Was there any known substance use during the pregnancy? How far along into the pregnancy was the child delivered— full-term or premature? Were there any complications during the delivery?

- Developmental milestones: Questions will explore the child's speech development during the early years; their physical development in terms of their ability to walk, run, and jump as well as fine motor skills such as being able to use utensils, hold a crayon, or fasten a button; and the development of cognitive skills such as their ability to problem-solve or understand information that is being communicated to them. Questions about their social and emotional development will help the clinician better understand how the child interacted with others and identify patterns in their behavior during those younger years. The mental health professional may ask if your child has ever been enrolled in Early Intervention, a national program available for children from birth to age three who may have delays in achieving some of their developmental milestones. If in advance of your child's scheduled intake session, you happen to have an appointment with their primary care provider or pediatrician, you can also ask them if there is any documentation of concerns regarding developmental milestones within the medical record.

Although answers to these questions may yield important information, don't worry if you can't recall all the details about all these aspects of your child's history. Providing rough approximations is okay when that's the best you can do. There may be situations in which you have no or little information about the first few years of a child's life, whether because you are a foster or adoptive parent or caregiver who is not the biological parent, because of changes in primary caregiver roles, or for other reasons. Do not hesitate to share with the mental health professional that you're limited in the information that you're able to provide and inform them when you entered the child's life.

The information regarding pregnancy and developmental history can provide critical information about factors that were observed in the child's first few years of life that may be connected to specific mental health conditions. It is known that exposure to certain substances during pregnancy can impact the child's mental health in later years. Fetal exposure to alcohol and other drugs during pregnancy has been associated with cognitive issues, social and communication challenges, impulsivity, hyperactivity, as well as difficulty sustaining focus. Children exposed to alcohol in utero may develop certain learning disabilities that can make learning in a traditional school environment difficult for them, which can have a negative impact on their self-esteem and overall mood, lead to disruptive behavior in the classroom, and/or result in poor academic performance. Understandably, you may be hesitant to disclose information about drug use during pregnancy to the mental health professional performing the evaluation out of fear of being negatively judged. I get it. However, the main goal of the mental health professional is to have a complete understanding of all the factors that may be contributing to your child's current state of mental health. Their focus is on helping your child, rather than assigning blame. If a provider makes you feel judged or shamed, know that this is inappropriate on their part and that you are deserving of respect and kindness from any health care provider.

Social History

Understanding the family dynamics and environment in which a child lives sheds light on the factors that influence their mood and behavior. The mental health professional may ask questions about where you live, the safety of your community, and the type of housing that you reside in. They may also ask questions to understand who lives in or regularly visits the home since these individuals may be influential in your child's life. Questions around the involvement of Child Protection Services may be asked, not to assign blame but to have a full picture of all the experiences that might have been significant to the child. The clinician may ask questions to better assess safety within the home, which may include questions about domestic violence or access to guns within the home.

Evaluating the Evaluator

As you can see, the evaluation certainly provides an opportunity for the mental health professional to learn about your child's mood and behavior as well as to gain a better appreciation for the context in which your child exists. However, if the mental health professional evaluating your child is doing so preparatory to providing ongoing mental health care for your child, the evaluation is also an opportunity for you to learn about them, and to ask your own questions. You want to make sure that you leave this session with a basic understanding of the following points:

- What is the provider's particular approach to providing mental health care?
- How do they typically communicate information about the child to families?
- Do they typically have caregivers present for all therapy sessions or only at certain time points during treatment?
- What is the best way for you to share new information about your child with them?

Over the course of the evaluation, make sure to listen to your gut when it comes to your initial impressions of the mental health professional. It is important that you feel comfortable communicating with this individual, but it's equally as important that your child feels comfortable. View the evaluation or any initial session with a therapist as an opportunity to explore whether the person is an appropriate fit for you and your child. It is not uncommon for families to meet with a mental health professional for one session and then decide not to follow up with that person because it just did not feel right. That is okay.

From Evaluation to Treatment Plan

You may have been anxiously awaiting your child's first appointment with a mental health professional in hopes that the interaction would answer all of your questions or that the clinician would make a breakthrough with your child. The challenging thing about an evaluation is that your child most likely will not leave the evaluation a changed person. The evaluation does, however, open the door to the potential for change. It's an important step in gaining clarity about what may be driving some of the moods and behaviors that you've noticed in your child, and in establishing a relationship with your provider. It may also yield a diagnosis, and suggest a treatment plan, both of which will be crucial in addressing your child's distress.

The diagnosis and the recommendations provided are tools that can be used to support your child's emotional well-being. You have the power to access and use these tools in the manner that you see fit. If you're unsure as to how to implement these tools at school and at home to support your child, make sure to talk to your mental health professionals about how to do so, and for help navigating any barriers to doing so.

Once the mental health evaluation is completed, the clinician should inform you about the next steps of the process. Those next steps may differ depending upon the kind of professional who conducted the evaluation, and whether that person is also the person who will serve as your child's therapist or psychiatric provider. In any case, the person who did the evaluation and determined what factors may be influencing your child's mood and behavior is the one who will help guide your next steps toward mental health treatment.

You may not get instant feedback after this initial evaluation. Sometimes, the person conducting the evaluation will want to gather more information, schedule another evaluation appointment, or think about the information they've gathered, before making a diagnosis or outlining a treatment plan. If a neuropsychologist or a child psychologist does the evaluation, they will also utilize various standardized tests that provide detailed information about your child's strengths and struggles with specific learning skills and processes, and they will summarize their findings in a formal report. This report can be helpful if you are seeking more support for your child in school. Most mental health professionals do not prepare formal reports, but you can ask the person who evaluated your child to write a letter summarizing their findings. A report can provide an incisive snapshot of your child at a particular moment in time, which may be valuable in interactions with other mental health and education professionals as your child grows.

If the evaluation is performed by a psychiatric prescriber such as a psychiatrist or a psychiatric nurse practitioner, they may suggest that your child undergo certain blood tests to rule out the possibility of an underlying medical issue that may be contributing to their mood and behavior. Examples of blood work that the psychiatric prescriber may want to obtain from your child would include a complete blood count to rule out different types of anemia, particularly iron deficiency anemia, which could contribute to low mood, fatigue, anxiety, irritability, and difficulty; labs to detect overall thyroid, kidney, and liver function; evaluation of vitamin deficiencies including vitamin D, vitamin B12, and folate.

There are times that the psychiatric prescriber may recommend medications to be started following that first initial visit if there are more immediate concerns about the distress signals that were shared during the time of the evaluation. If it has been determined that the distress signals indicate that the child's overall functioning is impaired, they may recommend medications to help with overall bodily functions such as improving sleep and appetite as well as to improve certain behaviors such as aggression, irritability, and more severe symptoms such as debilitating anxiety, depression, erratic mood swings, and psychosis. The prescriber should review the risks and benefits that are associated with starting these medications in children, particularly when it comes to the use of antidepressants. There's more information on psychiatric medications approved for use in children, throughout this book, in chapters discussing the particular mental health disorders they are used to treat.

When a clinician evaluates your child in preparation to become the child's therapist, they should provide you with an overview of how they approach individual therapy, including an overview of the type or types of therapy that they typically use with the children they work with. Ask them to explain why they may use a certain therapeutic approach rather than another to address your child's unique needs. Examples of types of therapy that clinicians offer include forms of cognitive behavioral therapy (CBT), dialectical behavioral therapy (DBT), play therapy, and psychodynamic psychotherapy, just to name a few; others are discussed in the chapters in part II that focus on particular mental health conditions. The clinician should inform you about the frequency of the therapy session with your child as well as the frequency with which they will meet with you to discuss your child's progress in therapy. You can also ask the therapist how it is that they monitor progress. Will they have you complete questionnaires at certain intervals to assess your child's mood and behavior outside of session? Or will they send questionnaires to your child's school to complete?

Therapists are often in contact with a child's school over the phone or via email to receive updates on how the child is doing in the school environment. The therapist should ask you to sign a release to permit them to contact the school. I highly recommend that you grant this permission, since the information they'll be able to obtain will help them continue to refine their treatment plan. The evaluation may also yield information about certain interventions that the child's school could put into place. If the diagnosis received during the evaluation reveals or confirms that the child's cognitive and emotional state may interfere with the child's ability to learn material in the traditional classroom setting, possible recommendations could include placing the child in special education programs such as an Individualized Educational Plan (IEP) or 504 accommodations. I provide more information on IEPs and accommodations in chapter 6, "Neurodevelopmental Disorders." You can choose to share information in the written evaluation provided by the mental health professional with the school, but please do keep in mind that you are not obligated to do so.

The Meaning of a Diagnosis

The clinician who conducts the evaluation will determine whether your child meets the criteria for a specific mental health diagnosis. For many caregivers, a diagnosis can, on the one hand, be sad or upsetting. Your child's distress has a name, a cause, a label, that may seem to make it real, or official: There is something wrong, such that your child is experiencing distress. This distress, this diagnosis, is not something you ever imagined affecting your child's experience of childhood.

On the other hand, getting a diagnosis may feel like a relief. If you know exactly what's wrong, then you'll know exactly how to solve the problem, right? In most situations that is the case. You bring your car to the mechanic, and they do an evaluation, determine what's wrong, and tell you which parts are needed to repair the car to make it function again. When we know that there is a problem with our bodies, we go to a medical provider, they assess the situation by performing a physical examination, doing blood tests, and doing imaging studies such as an X-ray, ultrasound, or MRI to get a visual of what is happening. It may be an expensive process and it may take a while, but when it comes to repairing something broken, there is usually a process involved of undergoing a diagnostic assessment to determine what the problem is and how to fix it.

However, when it comes to assessing and diagnosing mental health conditions, this process is not so clear-cut.

Simply defined, a diagnosis is a categorization of the signs and symptoms that are causing an individual to have a particular set of problems. Particularly when it comes to children, the signs and symptoms—the distress signals—that they exhibit reflect the current status of their mental health, which can change over time. Kids grow up and experience various challenges, and their capacity for navigating those challenges changes. A diagnosis is not set in stone because our children are continuously evolving and growing every day. Their strengths, resilience, and ability to tolerate distress (which we refer to throughout this book as distress tolerance) expand over time, supported by your guidance as a caregiver and the help and guidance of other people who are a part of their community.

I frequently encounter families who experience frustration when each evaluation of their child by each mental health professional that they encounter results in a different diagnosis. Frustration in the diagnostic process is common and understandable, as the fast-paced and often turbulent nature of child development means diagnosis during these years is like aiming at a moving target. Any diagnosis your child does receive, even into their early twenties, is not necessarily permanent and may change. It's important to think of a diagnosis as a tool for understanding behaviors and finding effective supports, rather than as a definitive prognosis for how the child will develop. And because diagnosis is an imperfect science, thinking of it as an approximation that will help identify supports, and not the key to unlocking the puzzle, can alleviate some of the frustration you experience as a caregiver.

If a diagnosis is just an approximation, a label describing what is happening at a given moment that will likely evolve as a child develops, you may wonder: What's the point of getting one?

There are several functions that the evaluation process can serve in your child's mental health journey. From a purely practical standpoint, a diagnosis helps guide what initial steps to take in accessing the tools, resources, and support your child needs right now. Having a diagnosis may make it easier to receive insurance coverage for specific types of services, and may allow your child to receive special accommodations and mental health resources at school. Think of the diagnosis as one tool in your toolbox that you can use to support your child, one you can use to advocate more effectively for what your child needs.

Learning the Shared Language of Mental Health

A diagnosis also generates a shared language for communicating about your child's mental health. We use language as a way to connect, to ensure that we're able to gain insights into another person's perspective. In the mental health world, there is a shared language professionals use to communicate with each other about their clients and patients. A diagnosis is "written" in that language. It captures some general trends in your child's mood and behavior in a way that can be quickly accessed and understood by others. It's almost like the diagnosis is a flash drive in which information about the child's mental health at that moment has been stored, available to be quickly downloaded by another professional to establish a mutual understanding of what is going on with your child.

As a caregiver, if you're not a part of that world already, this language may be completely new to you. A diagnosis may serve as an introduction to that language and to the way of thinking that it represents. Being aware of the language that mental health professionals use can also provide you with the confidence to enter conversations better informed of how they are conceptualizing your child's struggles. Having a diagnosis serves not only as a way to efficiently communicate other aspects of your child's mental health, but can also provide a framework for how people who aren't mental health providers can better understand your child's behavior. Sometimes it can be challenging to communicate with others about some of the emotional and behavioral difficulties that your child may be experiencing. The diagnosis can provide an opportunity for you to frame those behaviors and mood states for other people in your community.

Marie is a fifty-six-year-old woman from Massachusetts, the mother of two adult children, and currently serves on the board of her local NAMI affiliate. She shared with me during her interview that receiving the diagnosis of bipolar disorder for her elementary-age daughter Jillian helped create a path for better educating herself about her child's emotional and behavioral state. Having that diagnosis in hand gave her a starting point for seeking out community resources, support groups, and mental health providers who had expertise in pediatric bipolar disorder. It also allowed her to better communicate with teachers about the symptoms of depression and irritability that could sometimes affect Jillian's behavior in school:

> I was not embarrassed by her diagnosis. I didn't want her to be embarrassed by her diagnosis . . . I let the teachers know right away, asked for a meeting with them, and then I kind of laid out the things that would help her. I had a template email that I'd send to all of the teachers so they would understand Jillian's background. She loved school, she loved her teachers, she loved her friends, but school also was one of the biggest stressors for her because of just the nature of what it demands.

In a way, Marie generated a flash drive of information about her child, which included the diagnosis, that she was able to share with her daughter's school community. Giving teachers the information they needed to better understand and connect with Jillian was vitally important in nurturing Jillian's love for school and getting her the appropriate supports she needed to successfully navigate the school environment.

Diagnosis Is Not Prognosis

The tools that mental health professionals use to assess your child's mental health allow them to understand what your child is experiencing at this moment in time based on the information that they have. I often encounter families and caregivers in my office whose mental health professionals have given them a variety of explanations for why the child is behaving a certain way. They share with me that they leave each evaluation believing that they understand what is wrong, but then become confused when things evolve over time. They often feel that if a professional diagnosed their child with a particular condition, and has outlined what the course of the condition looks like with treatment, then it must be true. Caregivers hold on to the idea of how things will evolve based on what the professional has shared with them previously.

However, a diagnosis is not a definitive prognosis, and should not be thought of as such. The information provided by an evaluation, which serves as the basis for a diagnosis, is based in large part on people's ability to recall details and to provide their perspectives and observations of your child's mental health. As you can imagine, this is an imperfect science. Clinicians cannot 100 percent guarantee that your child is sharing the full extent of their mental health challenges, and we also cannot eliminate the role of bias in the reports of observations of the child's behaviors by others. It is not a perfect process. However, everyone involved should assume that we are all trying our best: The provider is trying their best to collect information about your child and to categorize their mood and behavior, your child is trying their best to articulate their experience over time, and you're trying your best to recall specific details of your child's history as well as provide information about things that you may feel ill-prepared to report.

With all that said, the diagnosis that is used to categorize your child's mood and mental health will certainly change over time, and that is okay. Most families don't realize that fact when they first start on their journey to support their child's mental health. The diagnosis does not need to be seen as a permanent truth. Your child will evolve over time. The information that your mental health provider is able to gather and to learn from your child changes over time and will help better inform the appropriate diagnosis. The diagnosis remains a type of language that is used to describe and categorize your child's mental health at a specific moment in time.

Lastly, we can't forget that kids should be allowed to just be kids. There can be a tendency to label certain behaviors and moods exhibited by youth as being problematic and in need of immediate mental health intervention. However, we should create space for our children to experience the wide range of emotions that can be elicited by various situations because our kids are facing these moments in their lives for the first time. They are learning how to manage and navigate big emotions for the very first time, and that's hard to do! They are still learning about themselves, their emotions, and the tools that best help them to cope and tolerate a given situation. Sierra Grandy, the law student from Minnesota we met in chapter 3, said it best when she urged us to maintain "empathy, compassion, the understanding that children are human and they're going through complex and intense emotions that are brand new for them."

There may be significant stressors, or major changes in your child's life, which may elicit particular reactions. That doesn't necessarily mean that those reactions, or their behaviors, are going to remain fixed over time. You may bring your child to be evaluated by a mental health professional shortly after they might have experienced a significant stressor— whether that be experiencing a major life change such as divorce, switching schools, moving in with new family members, separation from their primary caregiver, bullying, academic disappointment—and the child may look and behave a certain way in the context of those stressors. And what we see is that as time goes on, the child changes; they evolve, they look different. A diagnosis that was previously made may not hold up over time. Kids are sponges; they constantly absorb information from us, their teachers and other adults in their lives, and their friends about how to adapt and respond to stressful situations. The child may need time to make meaning of the stressor and to find the language to communicate what it is that they've experienced and how that has impacted them. They may need time to find different activities, strategies, or even people to help cope with the distress. Let's give kids the time and the space to soak up all of our support and make sense of these big feelings as they learn to navigate them for the first time.

Bringing your child in to be evaluated will never be a waste of time, even if the solution to alleviating their distress is ultimately just your support and the passage of time. You are communicating to your child that you recognize their distress and want to hear their perspective. You are taking the steps to lock in supports that they need such that the distress that they are experiencing does not radiate out to impact other areas of their life. You are looking, listening, and locking in.

A Diagnosis Is Not a Deficit

Don't let a diagnosis overshadow your kid's strengths. Although diagnoses are often sought during difficult times, getting one does not imply that a child lacks strengths or has a deficit of some kind. Many of the young adults and children we interviewed for this book expressed concerns that having a mental health diagnosis not only meant they were different from others who did not have a diagnosis, but that they were flawed in some way. The truth of the matter, once again, is that the diagnosis is just a way to effectively describe and share information about an individual's experience.

Make sure to highlight to your child their unique characteristics and strengths. Remind them that they are first and foremost a human being who is loved. They are not a patient, a client, or the sum of their problems. Empower your child by noticing, pointing to, and drawing out their strengths, continuously reminding them that they are a unique and miraculous human being, not their mental health diagnosis.

FIVE

Assembling the Team

Things get exponentially better when my son can be surrounded by a
team of people, and he is not just relying on me for all of these needs.

—BETH,

Illinois, mother of a preteen diagnosed with bipolar disorder

· · ·

We think of a team as a group of individual players who each
have a specific role and skill set. Let's use basketball as an example: You have your point guard, center, shooting guard, small forward,
and power forward. Some players are good at defending the basket,
some good at getting the ball to the person with the open shot, and
others especially good at shooting. In addition to the individual players, you have the head coach, assistant coaches, and the manager of the
team. The manager is usually not directly instructing the coaches and
players on how they should play, nor do they provide minute-to-minute
feedback during the game. In fact, the team manager may not have any
skills relevant to the sport of basketball. But that doesn't matter, because the team manager's role is to make critical decisions that affect
the overall trajectory of the team over the whole season and year to
year. The athletes report to the coach and the coach reports to the manager, who is charged with making decisions about the team as a whole.
As the parent or caregiver of a child with a mental or emotional health

concern, you will want to assemble a team of people to help your child continue to grow, develop, and learn the skills they need to manage or recover from the distress they've been experiencing. You are the team manager—the person making all the operational decisions. In this chapter, we'll discuss how to discern who should be on your team and the roles the members play.

A team can be a complex organization. For that complex structure to be reliably strong and sustainable, a steady foundation is key. That foundation is your relationship with your child. The communication skills that we explored in the previous chapter are the tools that will enable you to maintain this strong foundation as you add on the necessary layers of support from mental health professionals, educators, and others who are a part of your child's community. I encourage you to visualize this process of supporting your child as a circle that is gradually expanding its radius, growing to encompass all the people whose knowledge, skills, and abilities will be necessary to address your child's mental health concern as your child grows and develops. As you strengthen the lines of communication with your child and develop a better understanding of what they are struggling with, you are also gathering information about what kinds of support are necessary. Then you can expand outward to assemble team members with the particular skills to best help support you and your child along this mental health journey.

It may not always be clear where you should start in terms of figuring out who should be supporting your child. Even though there are many mental health experts out there in the world, it can be incredibly overwhelming to know exactly who you want on your child's team, and the pressure to determine the best course of action is tremendous. Who do you start with? Who is most important? Let's go back to the distress radius framework for guidance on how best to navigate the process of assembling the team.

Having used the distress radius framework to discern the depth and breadth of the symptoms your child is experiencing in various domains of life, you now want to think about how to mitigate the distress experienced in each of those domains. You also have hopefully had an opportunity to initiate a conversation with your child about the changes that you've noticed in them, and created space for them to share their thoughts and perspectives on their emotional state. Now you want to lock in by forming a network of support around them, containing their distress so that it does not continue to radiate outward and interfere with other domains in their life.

Ideally, a strong support network includes you and your child, your child's health care providers, and members of the community, including teachers, neighbors, and friends. Many of the families we interviewed described their optimal support system as one that included people from all these domains.

We'll first discuss the most critical players: you and your child. This relationship comprises the inner ring of your child's wellness team. Then, we'll move on to the middle ring—health care providers—and how to assess whether your child's providers and therapists are working together and if any changes are needed. Last, but certainly not least, we'll discuss how the community surrounding a child—the outer ring—can play a critical role in supporting them (and also you!).

The Inner Ring

At the innermost ring of the distress radius is your relationship with the child, which needs to be the priority. It is always first and foremost. This sounds obvious, but it is amazing how often we forget. For many families who begin to suspect that their child may have a problem, the first automatic thought is to look into external sources of support and expertise to potentially solve that problem. But by immediately rushing to find the "best" program or provider out there for their kid, they end up giving a lot of energy to this process rather than centering that energy on what is important: their child and their relationship with their child.

It's not that we truly forget about our relationship with our child when they are experiencing distress; it's just that it is too painful at times to bear witness to that distress. As a result, we go into fix-it mode. Rather than sit with the discomfort, we want to DO something, immediately drawing upon external resources to kick-start the problem-solving process. However, the majority of youth and young adults that we spoke to in our interviews mentioned that what they wanted and needed the most at the onset of their mental health journey was to be able to connect with their caregivers—to feel heard and seen by the ones they love.

Establishing support has to start with the partnership between you and your child. Having conversations with your child around assembling a team to help support their mental health keeps them engaged in the process of supporting their well-being and helps ensure that your child trusts you to select the right people. Your child does not have the ability to determine the exact best players to be on the team, but they need to know that their thoughts and opinions are being heard. It is important to remember that the point of these conversations is not just to inform or reassure your child about what you are doing, but to continue to ask open-ended questions, and to let them know you are listening to their answers.

As you're adding people with specific areas of expertise and skills to the team, always keep in mind that you are working in service of your child and that all moves and operations by the people you choose to be on the team should be centered around your child and your child's treatment goals. To extend our team metaphor, think of your child as the team's owner. Your child does not possess all the skills or knowledge to dictate what it is that they need and don't need as part of their treatment, or who is best qualified to provide care. The child may, however, understand, at least in part, what they are struggling with and what their goals are, and collaborating with your child to develop their treatment plan is an important component of constructing a functioning care team.

How do you use the communication skills we discussed in the last chapter to build and strengthen the connection between you and the child? I often say to the parents that I work with who are navigating challenges when trying to connect with their kid that you have to continuously provide the relational groundwork that will allow them to connect with you when they are finally ready.

To lay down tracks for a strong connection, use these tools:

- Maintain unconditional positive regard.
- Provide space and remain close.
- Keep the child's strengths in mind.
- Keep yourself in mind.

Maintain unconditional positive regard.

Psychologist Carl Rogers coined the phrase *unconditional positive regard* in the 1950s to describe a phenomenon that is innate and natural and at the same time perplexing. Think about the days when you come home from work, exhausted after a long day, and what you really want to do is order a pizza and call it a night. Instead, you head off into the kitchen and prepare a delicious, healthy meal for you and your kids. And then your toddler, in a hungry rage that you're not having pizza, throws the beautifully prepared meal to the floor. Despite the frustration that you experience, despite any irritation or anger you may express in the heat of that moment, when you finally get the child fed and to bed and down for the night you look at their sleeping face and think, "What a beautiful child." You still love that child and are willing to accept them for all of their faults. That's unconditional positive regard.

Due to the nature of a child's mental health condition, they may say or do things that are infuriating, but we continue to accept our children for who they are and remain supportive no matter how badly they may treat us. If your child's hurtful behavior continues over time, it can become a significant challenge. But demonstrating to your child that you still accept them for who they are and support them no matter what is essential to maintaining that connection with your child. Supporting and accepting them unconditionally, despite their short-comings, provides them with the grace to learn and grow.

Provide Space and Remain Close

Although you want to give your child the space to figure out their feelings and behavioral responses, and to learn for themselves what they need to navigate those feelings in the moment, you also want to stay close, to observe what your child is experiencing and be available for your child to reach out to for support and guidance. You're close enough to step in if it seems as though your child is unable to access tools on their own to cope—and that's okay. Envision yourself as a lighthouse, providing guidance, direction, and a source of light for your child throughout this journey. Providing your child with the space that they need conveys your confidence that they are capable of understanding and navigating their emotional journey. You're communicating that you're not going to come in and do all the work for them but will be there to support them as needed.

Keep the Child's Strengths in Mind

The relationship between you and your child is the core foundation, the innermost ring of support. However, this relationship cannot be dominated by the ongoing narrative that the child has certain deficits, shortcomings, and challenges that create problems. You want to avoid setting up a situation in which the relationship is primarily focused on the child's struggles. Nobody, including children, wants to be viewed as a "problem"—everyone wants to be seen for their strengths. For your relationship with your child to serve as the foundational core of the team that you are assembling, you want to make it a priority to enhance your child's ability to demonstrate their strengths and keep those strengths in mind when identifying the layers of support that would be most helpful to the child.

Kids want to know that you see them for all of who they are, not just their mental health struggles. Demonstrate that by pointing out their strengths, encouraging their interests, and helping them develop their talents. These are all the things that we do when we connect with other people in our lives; don't forget to keep them in mind while connecting with your child.

Keep Yourself in Mind

Your relationship with your child is affected by your relationship with yourself. If your relationship with yourself is not good, it is going to be quite challenging to strengthen your existing bond with your child while also trying to form connections with a whole host of people that you'll be working closely with to support your child. Having a child with mental health challenges or other special needs requires caregivers to devote a lot of time and energy to support that child. Caregivers can find themselves in a position in which they are constantly giving without any resources in place to replenish themselves. If you are not in a good place mentally or emotionally, such that it is hard to be fully present for your child in the way that they need you, then it will be difficult for your relationship with your child to serve as a foundation for, and guide you in, assembling the rest of the team.

Rachel Murray is a forty-six-year-old white woman living in Michigan. She cofounded Advocates for Mental Health for MI Youth to improve the mental health system after experiencing gaps in the system. She spoke to us about the importance of caring for yourself and giving yourself time and space to process what's happening with your child:

I think what I've learned is that the place to start is with taking care of yourself. I need to go into that conversation ready to be their support. I cannot go in there and, even inadvertently, expect their support. I think a lot of times we don't even know that's what we're doing as parents, but if we're feeling sad or upset when we go into the conversation, they're going to pick up on that, and then they're going to have to switch into caretaker role for us. We don't want to do that to our kids.

First things first is: Take care of myself before I go into the conversation so that I'm ready for whatever it is they bring to me. Just approaching it with compassion and attunement and understanding where they're trying to come from, so that I can just be the support and let them work through it on their own. Because I don't actually have to have advice for them. I don't have to have an answer. I can be confused with them and let them work through it. But as long as they know they're safe doing it with me, then they don't have to worry about anything else but doing that process.

Preparing yourself mentally and physically for enduring this journey with your child will better allow you to do exactly what was prescribed previously: maintain unconditional positive regard, provide space and remain close, and keep the child's strengths in mind. Preparing yourself involves identifying the resources and strategies that are essential for you to be able to fill up your own cup, so your child can consistently rely on you for safety and support. Filling your own cup might involve going to support groups, maintaining hobbies outside of your family life, and having places you can go where you can decompress and prevent burnout.

Keeping yourself in mind, and using the three steps to enhance the bond between you and your child, will help create that core and foundation so key to assembling the team of players necessary to support your child. You, and your bond with your child, are the things that will remain constant over the years. The diagnosis, the treatment plan, and the team members will likely all change over time, but what will not change is your love for your child. Although it is important to acknowledge the fact that the love you have for your child and the nature of your relationship may *look* different over time, as your child grows and you have different experiences both together and individually, keep in mind that the decisions that you make for and with your child along this mental health journey are rooted in love and nothing else.

I say this because often I meet parents who are so focused and preoccupied with determining what's wrong with the child, receiving a diagnosis, determining a plan for how they are going to solve the problem, assembling the treatment team, transporting the child to appointments and different programs, selecting the right school, ensuring the IEP is perfect, and fighting with the insurance companies to obtain coverage for services, that they lose sight of what is ultimately important. Once you lose sight of your connection to yourself by entering problem-solving mode, autopilot, attack mode—whatever it may be to cover up and distract you from your inner feelings about the whole situation—you're getting further away from the core so essential to your child's long-term recovery and well-being. The less that you're checking in on your child and returning to your relationship with them, again, the less attention that is being paid to the strength of that foundation.

You may not always get it right when it comes to connecting with your child, and there will be missteps along the way. You'll say the wrong thing or miss an opportunity in which you should have said something. You might jump to certain conclusions about your child, or completely miss a change in your child's behavior and mood. When these things happen, parents often resort to self-blame or wonder, "What if that was my fault?" However, that type of thinking can lead us astray, and once again distract us from just simply being there for our children. It is enough to be a fallible human being, so long as you are fully present and doing the best you can to listen, acknowledge, and love your child for who they are. At the onset of your mental health journey with your child, there are a few absolute truths that you should keep in mind:

- You should not and cannot do this alone.
- You are not expected to be perfect.
- Your love for your child will endure.

The Middle Ring

We are now going to move on to talk about the other members of the team you want to assemble around you and your child—people who have certain expertise and skill sets that allow them to provide additional layers of support. Mental health professionals such as therapists, social workers, psychiatrists, psychologists, and primary care providers are the people who have dedicated expertise in child development and who will join the team to work individually with your child to support their emotional well-being. Together with your child, you can make decisions on which providers are or aren't a good fit. You'll decide if and when to add someone to the team, and if and when to move on. It's important for you to feel comfortable communicating with these professionals about their progress with your child, and asking for a change in treatment plan if necessary.

If something doesn't feel right in your interaction with the provider or your child's experience engaging with the provider during visits, it's okay to listen to that even if you can't name it. It is important for any mental health provider that you work with to know your concerns about your interactions and how information is being communicated. Sharing those feelings with them will provide an opportunity to engage in a conversation about how things can be changed. Rather than walking away, mention your concerns to your provider and explore options with them on how best to move forward. You possess the power to make that change. Know that your voice and feedback can make a difference.

I often have parents ask me how they will know that treatment is working. The easiest way to measure your child's progress is by looking at their overall functioning in different domains of life. We can return to the distress radius for this—if they weren't getting out of bed at the beginning of treatment, are they better able to do that now? Are they eating three meals a day, whereas before they were only eating one? When it comes to measuring progress, it often boils down to small, measurable elements of day-to-day functioning.

In my own work, and from the families we spoke with for the book, remembering where their child was when they started treatment was an important thing to keep in mind when evaluating progress. We aren't striving for perfection, just improvement. If your child is able to get out of bed four days a week, that might not seem like evidence of success, but if three months ago, they were getting out of bed only twice a week, this is progress.

Another common question relates to the timeline of improvement. As pressing as this feels, it's often very difficult to pinpoint an exact answer. As much as we might want to have a fixed number of weeks, months, or sessions, everyone's timeline is different. That being said, if you haven't seen any improvement in day-to-day functioning and the distress radius is expanding, it's worth considering whether a change of approach is needed.

One of the biggest challenges around timelines for treatment has to do with the length of time that a child should remain in therapy. In part, that's because therapy often feels like a mystery. Your child will meet with their therapist individually behind closed doors and you don't really know what is being said in your absence—which can be hard for some caregivers to tolerate. You may want to immediately check in with your child after a therapy session to know what they talked about or how it went and chances are they won't go into details. You're still left wondering, *Is therapy even working? What are they doing in there?*

If you begin feeling uneasy about the progress that is being made in therapy, either because you can't tell if your child has made an improvement or because you notice that the child has even gotten worse over the course of therapy, contact the therapist to set up a time to discuss how therapy is progressing. There are some therapists who would schedule a separate session with you, or they may split the time during one of your child's regularly scheduled sessions to meet with you individually. Please note that the therapist will not be able to share with you all the specific details about what your child has shared (unless there are immediate safety concerns) because there remains a certain level of confidentiality that needs to be preserved to maintain the integrity of the therapist/patient relationship. But the therapist can summarize key themes that are coming up during their sessions and major areas that they are working through, or share some language and tools for how to better navigate some emotional and behavioral challenges that may arise. This conversation with the therapist could also provide you with some insight into how you can reinforce the use of some of the skills that they've learned during their therapy sessions. Supporting your child in using skills learned during therapy while at home and in other areas of their life could help the child better appreciate the utility of ongoing therapy.

The conversation with the therapist could also provide you with a sense of how the therapist is measuring progress. Are they taking note of how the child is better able to label their emotions and to identify triggers or changes in their thinking that tend to precede alterations in their mood and behavioral state? Some therapists use validated questionnaires to assess the severity of symptoms of depression, anxiety, and other significant emotional states. Understanding the metrics that are being used to assess progress will also provide you with a better understanding of the utility of therapy.

Additionally, if you're noticing that the child seems to be experiencing an increase in some emotional and behavioral difficulties, it is important to bring that up to the therapist to gain their insights as to why that may be the case. They could potentially provide you with some reassurance that the nature of the work that they are doing in therapy, particularly some specific trauma therapies and some forms of exposure therapy for types of anxiety disorders, can make kids appear worse for a brief period. Alternatively, it may be helpful to share your observations of your child outside of therapy sessions since the therapist may not even be aware of the fact that things have been challenging for the child outside of the session. This should hopefully lead to a conversation about how to move forward in a way to better support the child during and outside of sessions.

Forming relationships with providers can also lead to the expansion of your team of professional supports—your middle ring. The mental health field is a highly interdisciplinary field in which social workers, therapists, and prescribers all work closely with each other to support one individual's mental health, but they also collaborate with experts in other disciplines whose skill sets can also support the mental health of children. It is not uncommon for a therapist to make a recommendation for the child to see a psychiatrist or a psychiatric prescriber if they believe that the emotional and behavioral challenges are interfering with the child's ability to fully engage in therapy, and that the child may be struggling to function in their everyday life or experiencing more significant mental health symptoms. Conversely, a psychiatric prescriber will routinely recommend therapy to happen alongside medication management, which has proven to be a highly effective combination yielding the best results for the resolution of some mental health symptoms. Therapy is recommended not only to help ensure that the child can acquire skills to navigate potentially triggering and stressful situations but also to help them better understand their own mood and behavioral state so they can be more proactive in maintaining their mental health as they grow.

An instrumental form of support that a mental health provider could refer your child to is a certified peer specialist. These are individuals with lived experience of mental health–related issues who can serve as a resource and advocate for the child. The peer specialist can appreciate the unique challenges of living with emotional and behavioral struggles and can share ideas for managing them with the child or adolescent so that they do not feel alone in their experience. They can also offer hope and encouragement that these struggles can be overcome. It can also be helpful for you as a caregiver to learn from someone who has experienced similar challenges as your child so that you, too, can remain hopeful that they will learn to navigate these difficult moments.

One of the challenging things about assembling your middle ring team of support is that you don't just have to identify the right team members but also figure out how you're going to pay for these resources. During my interviews with caregivers, I met with many people who talked about the significant challenges that they faced trying to find a mental health provider who was available and took their insurance. Unfortunately, given the limited number of mental health professionals who accept insurance, a lot of families are having to pay out of pocket by bringing their kid to see a mental health professional in private practice. Although some people can submit a copy of the invoice for the service to the insurance company for some reimbursement, it can still take weeks, if not months, to finally receive even that. Many families do not have the option to wait months to be reimbursed and therefore a private practice provider is not within reach. Some families are on Medicaid, which is insurance provided through the state for people with limited income. Unfortunately, those families don't have the option of being reimbursed for seeing a provider outside the network of approved providers. This is a strong reason why it can be helpful to ask your PCP about mental health providers to whom they commonly refer their patients. You can also reach out to others through NAMI support groups or through the NAMI Basics program, where you would have an opportunity to meet other families who have also navigated the mental health system and can learn from them how they were able to establish care for their child.

Another option to explore for establishing care for your child with a mental health provider is to see if your child's school has embedded mental health supports. There are a number of school districts across the country, though not nearly enough, that have school psychologists, licensed clinical social workers, and licensed mental health counselors who can provide ongoing individual therapy to their students inside of the school. This is an incredible resource given that the school-based mental health professional has a working understanding of some of the unique challenges within a given school, with awareness of some of the academic and cultural challenges within that environment. Being located within the school makes it so much easier for the child to remain engaged in ongoing care.

Flexibility in terms of where you can access a mental health professional is critical when trying to keep kids engaged in mental health supports. Since the Covid-19 pandemic, there has been an explosion of virtual options that have become available that provide individual therapy and medication management. This is a great opportunity for families who may have challenges with transportation or busy schedules that make it difficult to bring their child in for ongoing in-person services. The hospital where I currently see patients, Boston Medical Center, even has the option of children and adolescents using libraries and community sites as "telehubs" from which to conduct their virtual visits with their therapist. This provides youth with a safe, private, and quiet space to meet with their provider when coming in person would be problematic. Charlie Health (www.charliehealth.com) is another online resource that provides intensive outpatient support in a nine- to twelve-week program, offering access to mental health providers for youth with more immediate mental health needs. InStride Health (instride.health) also provides virtual mental health care specifically for children and adolescents who are experiencing significant symptoms of anxiety.

Once your child has established care with a mental health provider, it can come as a relief that all the hard work to find someone has finally paid off. However, there are times in which you may need to change the lineup of mental health providers within the middle ring of support. Children and teens are continuously growing and evolving and so are their individual mental health needs. Some therapists may be more skilled in addressing one particular set of mental health challenges compared to others. For example, you could have a child who during their elementary school years appears to be struggling with anxiety, but as they get older and enter middle school they develop an eating disorder as a way to establish a sense of control to mitigate uncertainty in other areas of their life; then you may need to seek out professionals who specialize in the treatment of eating disorders. Youth may want to be with a therapist who represents a specific religious, cultural, ethnic, racial, or gender identity that more closely aligns with their own, in order to feel more comfortable discussing certain issues. And just in general: We want our youth to feel connected to their therapist and to have a strong therapeutic alliance. If the alliance isn't there despite there being a reasonable effort to foster that connection, we should provide our youth with the option to find another therapist if at all possible.

The Outer Ring

Countless caregivers we interviewed mentioned that it really does take a whole village to support a child and their mental health. Think about the people that you rely on for support; the people outside of your home and family that your child interacts with. All these people make up your community, your extended social network. Their power and influence on shaping the mental health journey of your child simply cannot be ignored. These people and the communities they represent are able to see your child for the *whole* person that they are outside of their having a mental health concern. This is important because we do not want your child (or you, for that matter) to lose a fully rounded sense of self along this journey. Leaning into community supports will provide you and your child with the fuel necessary to navigate this mental health journey.

In our interviews, community support came in a multitude of different forms. From within the educational system, teachers, school administrators, guidance counselors, and school psychologists were just a few of the possible pillars of support available. Outside of the school system, we heard from families about faith communities and scout leaders, athletic coaches, and sports leagues, music and art teachers, community theater organizations, camp directors and camp counselors, informal mentors, support groups, online gaming networks, other parents, friends, and extended family. The outer ring is going to look different for everyone. What's important is that you as a caregiver recognize the community around you as a means of support for your child.

Of course, interacting with your community and building that outer ring of support for your child is not always as seamless a process as we wish it were, and it can require us to stretch in ways we may not always be comfortable with. One of the challenges caregivers face is getting feedback about their child from the outside world that doesn't always sit easily. I can tell you that as a parent, I tend to have a physical response to anyone making any sort of comment about my child. I notice that my chest gets tight, my brow may begin to furrow, and my ears perk up. These are some of the physical signals that convey how deeply you care about your child. For some, thoughts such as "Who do they think they are? What do they know about my child?" start to flood the mind. It is common to hold on to the belief that no one knows your child better than you and to experience a level of distrust or skepticism when another adult who does not live in your house and maybe has interacted with your child for only minutes, days, or weeks rather than years comments on your child's mood and behaviors.

I completely understand those initial reactions and they are totally valid. However, I also want to acknowledge the fact that your child is a citizen of the world. Their presence and existence will touch the lives of others. They will interact with peers and adults and through those interactions, people will have their own thoughts and opinions about your child, especially those who work in a profession in which they have exposure to a variety of different kids.

During these interactions with other adults whose expertise informs their thoughts about our child, we must consciously start from a place of wanting to better understand their observations and their rationale for making particular comments or expressing particular concerns. Sometimes it can be challenging to maintain that perspective in the moment when automatic protective thoughts and physical responses kick into gear, but it is important to stay open to the possibility that hearing feedback on how your child is perceived by others can ultimately be helpful. Often we can be quick to make a judgment about the person who provided the feedback or to direct that judgment toward ourselves, both of which can get in the way of truly listening and receiving the feedback. Instead, we should receive the feedback as a way to better understand our children and to develop an understanding of how they interact with others.

In the clinic, I've had parents share with me that their child's teacher has called them stating that their child is misbehaving during class, describing the child's behavior as disruptive, problematic, or disrespectful. For many of the parents I work with, this is difficult to hear. It might not align with how they know their child to be at home, or it might mean that behavioral issues they're seeing at home are starting to appear in other areas of life. Either way, no one likes hearing negative feedback about their child's behavior. We don't have to immediately accept these comments from others, but try to be curious about what behaviors led the person to draw the conclusions that they may be sharing with you.

The teachers in your children's school are uniquely positioned to recognize potential concerns in your child. Given their professional role and experience, they have exposure to many kids of a similar age and have a sense of moods and behaviors typical to children of that age. Teachers may be the first to bring up a concern about your child's mental health since they see your kid five days a week for many hours at a given time. Sharing information with your child's teachers and school team about how your child functions before and after school is essential since educators do not share that same perspective of your child. Over the six or eight hours that a child is in school, they may act and behave very differently from what you've observed at home.

The team of support that surrounds your child with love, care, and guidance while on this mental health journey may look different over time depending on your child's evolving needs as well as the ever-present reality that members of the team may come and go for a variety of reasons. The thing that will always remain a constant presence on this team is both you and your child. Even if there are times in which you may feel less involved or feel as though your child is trying to sideline you, no matter what, you'll always be on the team. You are essential even during times in which you may feel otherwise—please do keep that in mind.

SIX

Neurodevelopmental Disorders

I n every society, people come to have certain expectations for how children should think and act at various ages or phases of their development. Pediatricians and parenting books often provide caregivers with basic guidelines on when to expect their children to meet certain developmental milestones such as walking, talking, and becoming toilet trained. When children reach school age, there are certain academic benchmarks they are expected to achieve in certain grades, and they are examined to determine where they stand relative to their peers in terms of academic performance. There also seems to be a set of unwritten expectations for things that children should be doing socially across their early years—that they will forge friendships, have an interest in joining sports teams or other extracurricular activities, and become interested in dating, working, going to college, and branching out on their own. These societal expectations that kids will be similar to their peers are so pervasive that when adults encounter a child who is not like their peers, they often become concerned that something is wrong with the child; that they are not developing "normally."

Fortunately, over the past few decades, we have come to realize that children don't necessarily experience the world in a similar way, given their differences in cognitive ability, social communication skill, sensory processing, impulse control, and ability to regulate their physical and mental state. These individual differences provide children with unique individual perspectives through which they see and experience the world. As caregivers, we do our best to support our children based on what we know from our own experience of having been a child, what we have learned over the years through observations of other children, and whatever knowledge we have gleaned from our own education. But there is no user's manual for any specific child. Every child is their own unique and distinct model.

For some children, individual differences in how they experience the world cognitively, socially, and emotionally may, if these differences interfere with the ease with which they can navigate the world, contribute to creating distress. The distress that may emerge as a consequence of these differences may be reflected in behavioral changes or emotional disturbances that resemble certain mental health symptoms. Having an appreciation early on for a child's individual differences can help ensure they can receive appropriate supports—meaning care and education better tailored to the unique way in which their brain works. We talk a lot about diversity when it comes to race and ethnicity, gender identity, religion, and sexual orientation, but there is also diversity in how people's brains function. We call this neurodiversity.

Neurodiversity can be a result of what clinicians term a neurodevelopmental disorder. Neurodevelopmental disorders affect the growth and development of the brain and have cognitive, social, and emotional impacts. This chapter will review conditions included in the *Diagnostic and Statistical Manual of Mental Disorders* (DSM) that are secondary to alterations in brain development during early childhood, and that have an impact on key domains of functioning into adolescence and potentially into adulthood. "Neurodevelopmental disorders" was introduced as an overarching category of disorders for the first time in the fifth edition of the DSM, in 2013. As scientific research continues to reveal more about genetics and brain development, the specific conditions included in the DSM, and the way they are classified and diagnosed, will very likely evolve. For this book, I will discuss the disorders specifically mentioned in the DSM, but much of the information will also be relevant for caregivers of children with other neurodevelopmental conditions and differences.

We often misunderstand behavior (or distress) that stems from a child's neurodivergence and don't see that it reflects underlying differences in how that particular child's brain functions and signifies the need for specialized supports to enhance that child's neurodevelopment and growth. I will also discuss the different conditions that often contribute to the neurodiversity that we see in children and the specialized supports that are beneficial to access if a child has these conditions. My hope is that this overview of what are referred to as neurodevelopmental disorders will help you begin to explore and better understand how your child's brain functions, and equip you to begin seeking the appropriate supports.

Children who have a neurodevelopmental disorder can manifest a wide range of emotional and behavioral responses, but understanding the unique aspects of your own child's brain development that may predispose them to a certain pattern of behavior can better guide you on how best to support your child. You can also keep some of this information in mind as you read about specific mental health–related symptoms discussed in part II of this book. Appreciating underlying neurodevelopmental factors first can provide insight into what may be driving some of your child's feelings and behaviors.

What Is a Neurodevelopmental Disorder?

Neurodevelopmental disorders are a group of conditions that reflect disruptions in typical brain development in children that can affect cognition, intelligence, learning, memory, and language, as well as physical and sensory abilities. The neurodevelopmental conditions included in the DSM are autism spectrum disorder (ASD), attention-deficit/hyperactivity disorder (ADHD), intellectual disability, specific learning disorders, motor disorders, and communication disorders. There has been extensive research in the field to better understand the key factors that contribute to the onset of neurodevelopmental disorders and to determine what treatments and other forms of supports can reduce their impact on a child's ability to function. Given how much information about specific neurodevelopmental conditions there is in other books and resources, I will not go into extensive detail about every single one. What follows is a general overview intended to give you a basic understanding of these conditions and their significance.

Currently, there are no specific biomarkers that can be used to identify whether a child has a neurodevelopmental disorder, or the extent to which a neurodevelopmental condition will affect a child's life. What research shows to be true so far is that a number of these disorders are highly heritable—meaning they tend to run in families—which supports the fact that genetics certainly play a role in whether a child develops some of these conditions. Researchers have begun looking into various genes that could be implicated. However, there are people born into families in which certain neurodevelopmental disorders are present, but those individuals do not go on to develop the condition. Certain environmental exposures and stressors make it such that one person develops a particular condition while others with the same set of genes do not. The environmental stressor that resulted in an individual developing the condition could include an adverse exposure during the prenatal period, a complication at birth that might have resulted in some injury that impacted the brain such as lack of oxygen and blood flow during the delivery, or a specific traumatic injury that impacted the child later on in life. There have also been studies looking at certain infections during pregnancy that could also be linked to neurodevelopmental disorders.

For many caregivers, it can be difficult to recognize that your child may have a neurodevelopmental disorder or condition. In your eyes, they are just your kid. Kids develop differently from one another and have different personalities, and especially if the child is your first, you don't know what does or doesn't constitute "ordinary" development. Some caregivers may detect certain individual differences during the first few years of their child's life, as the child does not meet certain developmental milestones. You or your child's primary care provider may have noticed delays in speaking or walking, challenges related to feeding, acute sensitivity to sound or other sensory stimulation, or other physical concerns impacting their functioning. These deviations from the developmental milestones are easier to detect since there is such clear guidance on screening for certain neurodevelopmental conditions and because your child's primary care provider performs developmental screenings at "well child" checkups during your child's first several years of life. There are also a handful of charts often included in parenting guides that give you a general idea of where most neurotypical kids are in terms of certain cognitive measures, social and emotional milestones, language and communication, and overall physical development. Sometimes, however, caregivers and even primary care providers may miss signs of neurodivergence because they manifest in what seems like unusual intelligence or an unusually early development of a particular skill. For example, hyperlexia—an early fascination with letters and numbers that results in a child reading at a very early age—may be an early indicator that a child has ASD. Children with neurodevelopmental conditions may in fact be unusually intelligent or gifted in some way, but still diverge from their age peers in other aspects of development considered normative in the neurotypical world.

If you or a primary care provider, daycare provider, or preschool teacher recognizes a developmental delay when your child is under the age of three, your child may gain access to an early intervention program. Early intervention programs, available in every state, provide in-home support to children under age three who have a developmental delay. Sometimes, supplemental support is also offered in early intervention centers or by early intervention providers working in daycare or preschool settings. Not all children identified for Early Intervention will later be identified as having a neurodevelopmental disorder. However, if your child qualifies for additional supports to aid in their development early on, that may be a clue that some unique differences in key regions of their brain may have implications for how they learn, grow, and function socially and emotionally in the future. It is also true that not every child with a neurodevelopmental disorder is identified for Early Intervention. Sometimes brain differences do not manifest in noticeable delays in early development but become evident later on, when a child begins to struggle with more complex academic or social expectations.

Sometimes, the signs and symptoms indicative of a neuro-developmental disorder are first recognized by teachers, given that they have a lot of experience working with kids of a certain developmental stage and a good idea of where most kids are at, socially and academically. Angelina Hudson is a fifty-three-year-old African American woman from Houston, Texas. Married for thirty years, Angelina and her husband, Keith, have raised three children to adulthood diagnosed with autism, anxiety, ADHD, and depression, collectively. In our interview, Angelina described her surprise and initial hesitancy to get her child evaluated at age six, when her teacher noticed that she was not responding to her name and tended to keep to herself rather than interact with the other kids. Angelina did not want to believe the teacher, despite her twenty-eight years of teaching experience; she had hoped that there wasn't anything wrong with her child. She was relieved to discover NAMI, where the support of other caregivers helped her navigate a new diagnosis of autism in her child. "NAMI helps us face what we've got to face, endure what we've got to endure," she told me. "Then it gives us the idea or the notion that we can overcome. And then it happens."

Caregivers who have a child with a neurodevelopmental disorder may question whether their child's condition has anything to do with the choices they may have made during pregnancy or in their home life postpartum. We do know that certain environmental exposures have a direct impact on the development of a child's brain that can result in long-term emotional, behavioral, and cognitive challenges. Contaminants such as lead and polychlorinated biphenyls (PCBs) have been implicated in a number of conditions that affect a child's intelligence and decrease function in the areas of language, attention, and memory. Since the late 1970s, tremendous efforts have been made to eliminate lead from products it was once used to manufacture, such as gasoline and paint. However, despite changes in public policy and law, there are still places where children are exposed to lead. In homes and apartment buildings built prior to 1978, there may be lead-based paint on the walls, lead pipes used for plumbing, and lead in the soil under or around the structure. It is typically recommended that children be tested for the presence of lead in their bodies between the ages of one and two, but a child can be exposed to lead outside of that time frame. Children exposed to lead can have a low IQ, low academic achievement, problems with speech and learning, and decreased ability to pay attention.

A child's prenatal exposure to what are referred to as PCBs has been associated with future deficits in learning, memory, and general intelligence, as well as problems with inattention and impulsive behavior. Beyond the behavioral and cognitive concerns linked to exposure prenatally, studies have found that infants and children who consume PCBs are at risk of altered neurological development. PCBs are found in old fluorescent lighting fixtures and electrical appliances that were made prior to the 1970s. When these devices get hot during operation, they can leak small amounts of PCBs into the air. Also, people can be exposed to PCBs by eating contaminated food, fish caught (largely during sportfishing, not commercially) from contaminated waters, and drinking contaminated well water.

Synthetic dyes such as Red No. 3, Red No. 40, Yellow No. 5, Blue No. 1, and Blue No. 2 have also been associated with adverse neurobehavioral outcomes such as hyperactivity and inattention. The most common foods in which these types of synthetic dyes have been used include fruit-flavored juice drinks, soft drinks, and breakfast cereals as well as candies and fruit-flavored snacks. The majority of the studies that tested the behavioral effects of synthetic dyes placed kids on a dye-free diet for several weeks and then placed them on a diet that exposed them to food containing synthetic dyes. On days children consumed synthetic food dyes, there was a notable change in their behavior, manifesting in increased inattentiveness, hyperactivity, and restlessness.

The takeaway is that there are children who may be exhibiting significant behavioral and mood-related issues that are not their fault. Due to factors beyond their control, their brain has developed in such a way that they have difficulties changing their behavior in the moment responding to certain stressors in the same way many other children do. At the end of the day, kids are trying the best that they can with the brain that they have.

I'll now review some specific neurodevelopmental disorders and their signs and symptoms. If you are concerned that your child may be affected, you should seek to have them evaluated by a provider with expertise in these conditions and who can make a diagnosis. Pediatric neuropsychologists are clinicians who receive specialized training in diagnosing neurodevelopmental disorders as well as other conditions that may co-occur with them. The neuropsychologist will perform a series of assessments and conduct observations of your child to see if they meet the criteria for a specific disorder. Once the neuropsychologist has confirmed a diagnosis, your child can gain access to the specialized care that best meets their needs academically, supports their acquisition of language and communication skills, and provides them with other tools they need to learn and grow in a "neuronormative" world. Later, I'll discuss some of the subsequent steps involved in accessing services available through your school system.

Autism Spectrum Disorder

Children and adolescents who are neurodiverse possess a myriad of strengths as well as some challenges when it comes to navigating the world. Autism spectrum disorder (ASD) is a neurodevelopmental condition in which individuals differ in the ways they interact with others, experience various sensory inputs from the environment, and learn and behave. People who have autism can exhibit a wide range of differences that affect their functioning to varying degrees, which is why the condition is referred to as a spectrum disorder. As part of the spectrum of autism, there is a diagnosis previously known as Asperger Syndrome in which individuals evidence strong verbal language skills and intellectual ability, but may have some challenges related to social interactions and nonverbal communication. Some people with autism have been so successful at adapting to the "neurotypical" world that they are diagnosed with the disorder only as adults, though increased social awareness about the condition now makes it more likely that a child will be identified as autistic at school age, if not earlier. Most of the signs and symptoms are noticeable during a child's first two years of life.

The way ASD presents in youth varies greatly. However, in general, the condition is characterized by persistent challenges in social communication and restrictive, repetitive patterns of behavior, interests, and activities. Some early signs include delayed language skills, not responding to their name by age twelve months, not using pointing or other nonverbal cues to indicate their interest in something to others by age fourteen months, lack of pretend play by nineteen months, repetitive behavior, difficulty making eye contact, having unusual reactions to the way things sound, smell, taste, look, or feel, and difficulty tolerating minor changes.

ASD affects about one out of thirty-six children in the United States. It tends to be more common among those who were assigned male at birth (one in twenty-three) and less common in those who were assigned female at birth (one in eighty-eight). Prevalence rates have been increasing since the 1990s, reflecting the growing awareness of the condition and its signs and symptoms. Our ability to recognize and diagnose the signs and symptoms of ASD has certainly improved over time. For about 85 percent of children identified with ASD, caregivers had concerns about their development by the time they were three years old. The average age at which children with autism receive a diagnosis is about four, but some studies have indicated that Black children experience delays in receiving a diagnosis even though parents expressed their concerns early on.

Angelina Hudson from Houston, Texas, whom we met earlier, commented on her challenges advocating for an evaluation for her son who was exhibiting early signs of autism:

My son didn't talk, and he missed all the developmental milestones except for running, which he did very well. He skipped walking, went straight to running. I worked in an elementary school as a social worker and my son did not look like the other children. I knew at seven months that he had a problem. I raised the red flag because I had this little silly game where I'd blink my eyes and you blink your eyes, I smile and you smile, and . . . he couldn't do this. It was more than that. He didn't want to be touched and rocked and just so many different things. I said, "Something's wrong." I knew this was something much more serious than what they had been telling me at the doctor's office. At the doctor's office, they were saying, "Your son is just not like your daughter. You're overreacting. Why don't you give it another year?"

When he turned three, after hearing "give it another year," I told my pediatrician, "Look, I love you, Deborah, but if you don't get me a referral right now, I'm not coming back to this office. As much as I care about you, I'm not coming back." I had trusted her with the first delivery, the second delivery. I thought, this is somebody I've built a relationship with. Now, in all fairness, this is twenty-four years ago, and people didn't talk about autism, right? Right now, if I presented her with the same thing, I think she'd get a referral just like that.

Treatment and Support for Children with Autism Spectrum Disorder

Youth who have ASD benefit from working with a multidisciplinary team to address the unique challenges they may face. Occupational therapists help kids regulate their responses to different sensory inputs, whether they have difficulty tolerating loud sounds or different clothing textures, or have limited food preferences due to the way the food feels in their mouths. Speech therapy that addresses both verbal and nonverbal forms of communication is also a beneficial form of support for children who have difficulty effectively communicating with their peers. Psychotherapy can provide children with the tools they need to help improve their relationships with peers and to navigate challenging emotions. Some children may experience significant distress related to communication issues and present behavioral challenges that arise in response to sensory issues, rigidity around how things ought to be done, and encountering obstacles (like you saying "no") to engaging in their preferred activities. In these cases, it can be beneficial for the child to take medication in conjunction with forms of psychotherapy, occupational therapy, and speech therapy to mitigate the child's distress. Medications known as alpha agonists, including clonidine and guanfacine, help dampen the sympathetic nervous system so that kids feel calmer and less likely to act out, and for more extreme cases when a child's behavior becomes aggressive, antipsychotics may be helpful.

Specialized behavioral supports are also available to children who are living with autism. Some behaviors and communication limitations that children with autism have may make it quite challenging for them to remain engaged in certain social situations or may interfere with their learning. Applied behavioral analysis, also known as ABA, is an intervention that focuses on reinforcing certain behaviors linked to improved overall functioning. The primary goals of ABA include enhancing communication skills, improving age-appropriate social skills, decreasing incidents of inappropriate behaviors, and strengthening skills beneficial for success in the school environment. The ABA therapist identifies specific goal behaviors to target during these sessions. Some goal behaviors might include following instructions that require multiple steps, inhibiting aggressive behaviors triggered by certain situations or by having to perform certain routines, or specific social communication skills such as responding to their name when called. ABA uses the principles of positive reinforcement, providing a reward each time a certain behavior or skill is demonstrated. The reward typically is something that is highly motivating for the child such as praise, a toy, watching a video, or gaining more access to the playground. The therapist engages in this process through the use of repetition until the skill is completed successfully every time. A core component of ABA is for the therapist to develop a better understanding of what might be driving some of the child's behavioral responses, particularly when they occur in certain settings. This is accomplished by what are referred to as the ABCs of ABA: The ABA therapist takes detailed notes of what happens prior to an occurrence of a particular behavior, which is referred to as the **Antecedent**. This data can help determine whether there are particular things in a given environment that lead to a certain **Behavior**, for example, something sensory like a particular sound or smell, the texture of a couch or chair, or a change in how the furniture is arranged. The therapist takes detailed notes through each session describing the child's behaviors in response to certain antecedents and noting the **Consequence** of a particular behavior. Here is an example included in the description of ABA on the website of the nonprofit organization Autism Speaks:

- **ANTECEDENT:** The teacher says, "It's time to clean up your toys" at the end of the day.

- **BEHAVIOR:** The student yells, "No!"

- **CONSEQUENCE:** The teacher removes the toys and says, "Okay, toys are all done."

How could ABA help the student learn a more appropriate behavior in this situation?

- **ANTECEDENT**: At the end of the day, the teacher says, "Time to clean up."

- **BEHAVIOR**: The student is reminded to ask, "Can I have five more minutes?"

- **CONSEQUENCE**: The teacher says, "Of course you can have five more minutes!"

In this example, the ABA teacher/clinician is reinforcing the behavior of having the child ask for an additional five minutes; since he communicated that request, the positive reinforcement is the praise and honoring the request. With continued practice, the student will be able to replace the inappropriate behavior with one that is more helpful.

Although ABA is often recommended as a treatment option for children with autism, it may not be the best fit for every child. Critics of ABA argue that this form of therapy and the repetitive approach to reinforcing a certain set of behaviors is forcing children to act in a way that is considered to be "normal" and discouraging them from responding to certain situations in a manner that may feel more natural to them. Typically, it is recommended that children with autism engage in ABA therapy for at least twenty-five hours per week, especially if they are under the age of five, which can be a challenging amount of time for some kids. Given robust evidence-based literature touting its use in children with autism, and strong support from advocates in the education and treatment communities, ABA is also widely covered by insurance. For all these reasons, it is often recommended as the first-line treatment for children with autism—which limits the ability of caregivers to pursue alternative options unless they are paying out of pocket.

Another highly valuable therapeutic intervention that is beneficial for children with autism is the Greenspan Floortime Approach developed by renowned psychiatrist Stanley Greenspan and clinical psychologist Serena Wieder. Floortime is a relationship-based therapy that emphasizes the development of an emotional connection between the child and others, including peers, rather than just focusing on behavior, which can oftentimes be the case in ABA. The idea is that strengthening relationships between the child and others is not only valuable in and of itself, but also serves as a way to motivate and reinforce socially adaptive behaviors. Floortime focuses on having children expand their "circles of communication" as a way to facilitate and enhance two-way communication, broaden the child's interest in engaging with others, and expand the range of their play beyond activities they like to do on their own. The key milestones of Floortime include self-regulation, interest in the world, intimacy or engagement in relationships, two-way communication, complex communication, emotional ideas, and emotional thinking. Interestingly, Floortime can also be used to help children develop their speech, motor, and cognitive skills through the use of play. Some speech therapists and occupational therapists also become trained in Floortime therapy to incorporate not only its play-based approach but its focus on emotional development into the work that they do with children.

James J. Messina, PhD, and Constance Messina, PhD, wrote a helpful summary of the five steps of a Floortime session:

1. Observation: Therapists as well as caregivers—who are active participants in this form of therapy—notice the child's behavior, facial expressions, and postures to determine how best to approach the child. For example, do they appear excited, angry, more withdrawn, or relaxed?

2. Open circles of communication: The therapist or caregiver then approaches the child and builds engagement around whatever activity the child is doing in the present moment.

3. Follow the child's lead: The child sets the tone and directs the action for the play that they are engaged in. The adult follows the child and serves as their play partner. This gives the child a sense that they are being noticed and provides them with an opportunity to connect with the adult.

4. Extend and expand play: While engaged in a play activity, the adult may introduce some ideas to build off of the play themes initiated by the child. This helps to further expand upon the child's creativity and allows for the possibility of introducing some concepts that focus on emotional themes that could be incorporated into the play.

5. Child closes the circle of communication: This occurs when the child is able to build upon suggestions and comments the adult made during the play to create their own new ideas. The child is able to experience the impact that engaging with someone else's ideas has on their ability to generate new ideas. This helps enhance social connectedness and motivates the child to be socially communicative.

The Autism Speaks website provides an example of Floortime in action:

If the child is tapping a toy truck, the parent might tap a toy car in the same way. The parent might then put the car in front of the child's truck or add language to the game. This encourages the child to respond and interact.

As children grow, therapists and parents match the strategies with their child's developing interests. They encourage higher levels of interaction.

For example, instead of playing with toy trucks, parents can engage with model airplanes or even ideas and academic fields of special interest to their child.

Families are encouraged to use Floortime principles in their day-to-day lives.

While many more people lived through childhood years with symptoms of ASD that were never diagnosed or treated in the past, there are still children who are not identified early on who may struggle in peer interactions and have difficulty managing strong feelings. Over time, these individuals may be treated for other mental health conditions, but the underlying ASD is missed. It can be quite isolating to have these experiences and to feel alone in them without the appropriate supports. Sierra Grandy, whom we met earlier, was diagnosed with ASD and ADHD as an adult six months prior to my interview with her. She described her experience growing up, reflecting on her undiagnosed ASD and ADHD symptoms during her younger years.

I'm smart, clever, picky, sensitive. Sensitive is a really good one there. Not good at reading the room as most children are, but I just didn't grow out of it. That's how it was. I was friendly, adventurous. There's a story that my mom loves to tell where I was probably four or five, and I just left the house to go to the park because I wanted to go to the park. No adult knew where I was going, but they found me. And so that's a positive, but I was adventurous or bold.

I was very analytical, very rigid in my thinking. The way I played was unusual. I would ask my parents in elementary school to get me college textbooks so I could fill out the back questions and I would do puzzles upside down. I got bored with the puzzles. And so things like that, weird, odd types of play. My neurodivergent traits also showed up in the way I communicated with people, for example I still don't really understand authority super well. And so there was this expectation that you were supposed to respect authority, and it was really hard for me to do. So I would just treat adults like I wanted them to treat me, but then it was really hard to connect with my peers. Interpersonal relationships were really, really hard because there was never a clear understanding or explicitness. I think the theme of all of that is having clearer explicit words and rules to follow would've been a lot easier.

Some children who have ASD may experience difficulties in the classroom environment, whether that means tolerating transitions throughout the day or becoming distracted by various sensory stimuli. Children diagnosed with ASD are eligible for what is referred to as an Individualized Educational Plan, also known as an IEP. Accommodations can be put into place that reduce barriers to learning in the school environment. Examples of accommodations could include giving the child an opportunity to engage in sensory activities throughout the day to mitigate overstimulation, being in a smaller classroom setting, or having information from the curriculum delivered in a way more adapted to their skills, strengths, and learning style, such as including visual prompts, color-coding new information, using social stories to present new ideas, or ensuring that the child is prepared as far in advance as possible for any anticipated changes in their usual activities. There is more about IEPs at the end of this chapter.

ADHD

The impression many people have of the neurodevelopmental condition called ADHD—attention-deficit/hyperactivity disorder—is of children who have trouble sitting still in class. Or we may hear about college students using ADHD medication to complete big assignments at the last minute or pull all-nighters so that they can stay up and study. To be fully transparent, for many years, including my time in medical school and part of my residency, when I thought of child psychiatry, I always equated it with diagnosing and treating kids for ADHD. It seemed there was a lot of skeptical conversation in lay media about kids being overdiagnosed with ADHD or adults being diagnosed with it suspiciously late in life.

Some of the controversy that surrounds the diagnosis of ADHD is that psychiatric prescribers are using medication to treat what some people view as typical childhood behaviors. Others argue that the diagnosis of ADHD could lead young people to embrace the identity of this disorder as a crutch or use it as an excuse when they struggle to complete certain tasks. And it does seem to be commonplace on college campuses for some young adults to use ADHD medication strictly for performance enhancement, not as a treatment for a diagnosed condition.

Conversations have taken place for years regarding what may be contributing to the growing rates of ADHD: Is it a function of our growing dependence on the use of technology and exposing children to various stimulating devices with screens, where they access games and social media and a constant stream of ever-available entertainment designed to hijack attention, early on in their development? Or are caregivers so fixated on academic success and compliance that they may overreport symptoms so that their child receives ADHD treatment? It's really hard to say. What we do know to be true is that ADHD is a real condition that has a tremendous impact on child development and that influences how a child experiences the world around them.

ADHD is one of the most common childhood disorders. Between 9 and 15 percent of school-aged children are diagnosed with this condition. It tends to be more prevalent among people assigned male at birth; studies have found that the prevalence is 14 percent in males and 6 percent in females. Rates of ADHD have been trending upward since the late 1990s according to survey data collected by the Centers for Disease Control (CDC), but it's difficult to determine whether the trend reflects the fact that more kids are newly developing symptoms of ADHD, more kids are being arbitrarily diagnosed, or we're just better at identifying symptoms through screening and getting kids into treatment. In any case, what we do know to be true is that at least 6.1 million children in the United States carry a diagnosis of ADHD.

We also know that there is a genetic component to ADHD as studies show that heritability of the condition is 77 to 88 percent. Researchers have found there appears to be an imbalance in key neurotransmitters in certain parts of the brain. There are also structural differences in the brains of children who have ADHD; the size of their prefrontal cortex is smaller than those who do not have ADHD. There are also differences in activity levels in key areas of the brain. Studies show that areas in the brain that have reduced activity due to ADHD become activated when they take medication that is used to treat ADHD symptoms.

Some children may present with symptoms similar to those of ADHD—inattention, hyperactivity, and impulsivity—that could be secondary to exposures to certain substances during their mother's pregnancy, which is referred to as intrauterine drug exposure. Excessive alcohol use during pregnancy is known to be associated with fetal alcohol syndrome, which is marked by distinct facial features and can also have neurobehavioral consequences, resulting in issues such as lack of impulse control, executive functioning deficits, as well as problems with hyperactivity and inattention. These symptoms can manifest quite early in a child's life and can persist. Other drug exposures during pregnancy that can have lasting effects on brain development include exposure to cigarettes, cocaine, and marijuana, resulting in symptoms that present very similarly to those of ADHD.

The core constellation of symptoms that we see in children who have ADHD are inattention, hyperactivity, and impulsivity. Children with ADHD can have a combination of all three, or they can have symptoms that are predominantly inattentive or predominantly hyperactive and impulsive.

Children who have the predominantly inattentive subtype of ADHD tend to have difficulty sustaining attention on tasks, especially when it comes to non-preferred activities. Caregivers and teachers may describe these children as often appearing as though they are daydreaming or somewhat off task; that they can make careless mistakes, have difficulty organizing their belongings and often misplace items; that they tend to become easily distracted by things going on in their environment; that they may have difficulty following through on certain tasks and avoid tasks that require sustained mental effort, such as homework and per-forming certain chores. Caregivers are often surprised when their child meets the criteria for ADHD inattentive type since the child can play video games or practice playing their favorite musical instrument for hours at a time. And in fact, these children may have an ability to hy-perfocus in ways that can serve them well, if their preferred activity has academic, artistic, or athletic value. But they may nevertheless still struggle in other areas of life. The key thing to keep in mind is that children with ADHD inattentive type have difficulty sustaining atten-tion in non-preferred activities, which is why some of these signs and symptoms can become more apparent in the school environment or when caregivers ask them repeatedly to engage in mundane activities around the house, like doing chores or cleaning their room.

Kids who appear to be constantly on the go may also be manifesting symptoms suggestive of hyperactivity and impulsivity. Being energetic and physically active can of course be entirely developmentally appro-priate and aren't the same thing as hyperactivity. Hyperactivity in younger kids could include behaviors such as inappropriately climbing on things or running around in unsafe settings. Over time, as kids age into the adolescent years, they experience more restlessness, may have difficulty sitting still, and are often fidgety. Adolescents are less likely to exhibit hyperactive behavior and tend to minimize the significance of some of their behaviors that caregivers or other adults in their lives may find problematic. Impulsivity can be seen in kids who have diffi-culty waiting their turn, often blurt out answers in a classroom setting, are prone to interrupt others, or tend to invade other people's personal space. Adolescents with ADHD may engage in impulsive behavior that could result in sexual risk-taking, substance use, suicidal behav-iors, and self-harm behaviors such as cutting themselves or inflicting some other form of physical injury (hitting, burning, scratching) to themselves. However, symptoms of hyperactivity tend to appear by the age of four years and reach a peak severity when the child is seven to eight years old.

Pediatricians have grown increasingly adept at diagnosing and treating ADHD in the primary care setting. Many primary care providers use a particular set of questionnaires, referred to as the Vanderbilt Rating Scale, which includes questions to assess for the presence of ADHD symptoms; however, it also includes symptoms related to depression, anxiety, and other behavioral problems. This questionnaire is given both to the caregiver and to the child's teacher to complete. The idea is that for a child to receive a diagnosis of ADHD, the symptoms need to be present in at least two different settings. Those settings can include home, school, or wherever your child engages in extracurricular or community activities. The score the child receives from both questionnaires helps to determine whether or not the child meets the criteria for ADHD. It is important to note that ADHD is a clinical diagnosis, meaning that a medical or mental health care professional can diagnose it without necessarily using a rating scale such as the Vanderbilt. However, the Vanderbilt Rating Scale questionnaire is so frequently and widely used that many teachers are quite familiar with how to fill it out. Other questionnaires that assess for ADHD symptoms include the Conners Rating Scale and the ADHD Rating Scale, which also includes a preschool version.

Part of the criteria for diagnosing ADHD in children is that symptoms be present before the age of twelve. But it can sometimes be a challenge to differentiate between behavior typical to children at a given age versus behavior attributable to ADHD. Valerie Cantella, a mother as well as an author and advocate who shares her experience to help others, described her observations of her son's behavior over the years prior to him receiving a diagnosis.

He was a very happy toddler and early grade–schooler, full of life and energy. He just bounced with joy and searched the world for what he could learn and what he could explore and how he could do things that were fun and creative. And then when he started to realize that he learned differently, he started to look kind of stressed. He didn't want to go to school.

He could hyperfocus on anything he was interested in. So, he could spend eight hours a day trying to master a skate trick, or he could spend hours and hours trying to put together a Lego or a K'nex set to build these amazing creations. But when it was something he didn't want to do, like math, it was much harder for him to focus or to sit down to read a book. If it wasn't a book that was engaging, he didn't want to do it. So functionally on a day-to-day basis, I didn't see behaviors that were particularly concerning to me. I just thought he was a rambunctious boy and doing what he thought he should do.

One of the other important points that Valerie makes when she is describing her son's symptoms of ADHD is the amount of distress that he experienced going to school. Knowing as a kid that you are learning information in a way that differs from the other kids, or noticing that your ability to tolerate the classroom environment is challenged by how easily you become distracted, or experiencing an ongoing need to move your body or difficulty controlling the words that come out of your mouth, can be incredibly distressing. I've noticed children with undiagnosed ADHD have difficulty not only attaining good grades in light of their struggle to pay attention and absorb information, but also in connecting with their peers. They may constantly interrupt their peers during conversations or have difficulty controlling their impulses to invade another person's space. They can be the class clown, prone to getting in trouble in class and carrying the label of troublemaker.

Children with ADHD can experience significant anxiety. They can feel on edge about possibly making a careless mistake or worry about constantly misplacing items and forgetting important details. The distress that can come with symptoms of ADHD occurs not just in school but outside of it. It is critical as a growing child to be able to pay attention to the world around you, control your impulses, and regulate your energy level. Not being able to do that reliably can be incredibly stressful. That's why, if you're noticing ADHD symptoms in your child, you shouldn't just ignore them or brush them off as typical childhood behavior. If you notice that the symptoms are interfering with your child's ability to function at home, at school, and in their relationships, then getting your child diagnosed and eventually treated can enable them to navigate the world with a bit more ease.

Treatment for Children with ADHD

Most pediatric primary care providers are quite comfortable not only diagnosing ADHD but also treating it. There are behavioral strategies as well as medications that can help kids improve their overall functioning while living with ADHD, which is considered a chronic condition. However, clinicians other than your child's PCP can provide some treatment strategies for ADHD that have been proven to be beneficial, especially for younger children.

According to the American Academy of Pediatrics, parents of children ages four to six years who meet the criteria for ADHD should be referred to Parent Training in Behavioral Management. This type of training can provide tools to help you better manage and support your child at home. This training provides education for caregivers on "age-appropriate developmental expectations, behaviors that strengthen the parent-child relationship and specific management skills for problem behaviors." Taking this training won't cure your child of ADHD symptoms, but it will strengthen your ability to support your child and manage problematic behaviors that can emerge.

Behavioral classroom interventions—such as seating the child in the front of the class, or building in breaks so that the kid can get up and walk around—should also be put into place as first-line treatment. However, if the behavioral interventions don't lead to significant improvement and there are ongoing impairments in the child's ability to function, then starting medication would be warranted. Many caregivers understandably worry about starting children on medication at such a young age, but it's important to remember that delaying that treatment when best efforts at behavioral interventions aren't working can mean your child will experience significant continued distress. For children over the age of six, it is recommended that medication be prescribed concurrently with the initiation of behavioral interventions at school.

One option for providing extra support to a kid with ADHD is to enlist the help of an executive function coach. Executive function coaches help kids who struggle with time management, planning, problem-solving, and organization learn practical skills to improve their performance in these areas. They meet regularly with your kid to support them in and to hold them accountable for incorporating these skills into their daily activities. To learn more about executive functioning coaches you can check out adhdcoaches.org.

ADHD is a highly treatable condition and medications can yield significant improvements in ADHD symptoms in a relatively short period. The primary medications used to treat ADHD are called stimulants. They come in two different formulations: methylphenidate and amphetamine. Generally speaking, most children are started on methylphenidate formulations since they are better tolerated, meaning that children tend to experience fewer side effects while on them. Amphetamines are slightly more efficacious than methylphenidate, but the side effects may make it difficult for some people to remain on the medication. The free resource ADHDmedicationguide.com provides a summary of all the stimulant medications that are currently on the market. Other medications considered to be nonstimulants are helpful for mitigating ADHD symptoms. These medications include atomoxetine viloxazine, clonidine, and guanfacine.

The list of stimulants that your child's PCP or psychiatric prescriber can choose from can seem quite overwhelming. To select the best option for your child, the prescriber will consider factors like whether your child can swallow pills or would benefit from a patch or a capsule that could be opened and its contents sprinkled into juice or water; whether short-acting or long-acting formulations would be best; and

any side effects experienced by the child once they try a particular medication, such as insomnia, diminished appetite, or increased irritability.
The most common side effects from the use of stimulants to treat
ADHD include decreased appetite, abdominal pain, headaches, and
problems with sleep. There is also the possibility of elevated heart rate
and blood pressure while on a stimulant, which your child's prescriber
should monitor. When your child's prescriber recommends a specific
stimulant or any medication for ADHD, it is reasonable and important
to ask which factors influenced their choice, so you know that their
rationale wasn't just a random one.

I spoke with Dr. Oscar Bukstein, an ADHD researcher and expert
who is a child and adolescent psychiatrist at Boston Children's
Hospital, about some common questions caregivers ask when their
child is diagnosed with ADHD. One question caregivers often ask
when it comes to symptoms of ADHD is whether the child will simply grow out if it over time. "I can't tell parents for sure whether their
kid's going to grow out of it," Dr. Bukstein said. "We do have data to
indicate that not every kid who's diagnosed with ADHD has problems when they get older. Some drop off in adolescence. Many drop
off in adulthood, for a variety of reasons. In fact, it may be that they
still have ADHD symptoms, but no impairment, because they're able
to compensate."

Symptoms can also wane over the course of the child's development
since over time the brain's development could play catch-up, and connections could form in key regions of the brain that can mitigate
ADHD symptoms. Also, over time, the child can engage in various
activities, develop certain routines, and flourish with support from
loved ones such that the symptoms no longer interfere with their functioning in a significant way. For a child with the hyperactive/impulsive
subtype of ADHD, perhaps participation in a sport that really reso-
nated with them served to direct their symptoms such that what was
problematic in another setting proves itself to be beneficial in the sphere
of athletics.

Dr. Bukstein told me that some caregivers also express concerns about the potential for misuse of stimulant medication when treating ADHD, especially when it comes to adolescents:

> That is a very common question: "Is this addictive?" I say, "No, there's no evidence that this produces drug-seeking individuals either as children or as adolescents." But we still advocate for parents to exercise control and administration of the medicine, or adults in the case of when it has to be taken at school.
>
> We don't want the medication just to be readily available—not just for your child to misuse it, but for their friends to misuse it, to see pills lying around. The whole idea of misuse, of diversion, is a very serious discussion that we have initially with parents, and eventually with the children themselves once they're adolescents, that these are agents that admittedly can be abused, that your friends may ask you for it, and how to deal with that issue.

He also shares helpful guidance when it comes to talking to adolescents about the use of stimulants for performance enhancement:

> This idea of performance enhancement, rather than treating a disorder, is a difficult one because I can see where it's a slippery slope. When do you stop? What do you require? Most of the data seem to indicate that a majority of the kids who do misuse medication, many of them do have ADHD and they do have problems. They use it because it helps them. There's another group of individuals who are just using it recreationally.
>
> When a young adult goes away to college, we often have what people in the profession call "the talk": "These are to help you. These are your medications. They're not to share. In fact, we really advise you to keep quiet about it. Not that I'm worried about your roommate, not that I'm worried about your roommate's friend, but it's your roommate's friend's friend. People who would come in and go right away to your things, if

they see something like that, just as they might go to your family's med-icine cabinet when they go to the bathroom looking for medications like stimulants." We say, "Get a lockbox. Don't advertise that you're on medicine. If people do find out, resist the constant entreaties that you have to share your medicine with your friends."

Learning Disorders

There are a number of children who have neurologically based chal-lenges related to their ability to acquire specific academic skills in the areas of reading, writing, and math. Other children can experience learning disorders more specifically affecting language skills. These kids may be able to encode, decode, and print words as well as their peers, but not have the vocabulary, grammar, or narrative comprehension skills needed to comprehend text or write a composition at the level expected for their age or grade. Students with impaired language skills also may have difficulties with classroom participation. They may not be able to understand and follow teacher directions, follow or partici-pate in classroom discussion, and may even have difficulty communi-cating with peers in a social setting. These classroom participation behaviors are as important as reading and writing for the student's suc-cess at school. Other children may have what is referred to as nonverbal learning disorders in which they have not had any significant concerns related to their ability to acquire basic language skills but do experience challenges related to weakness in visual-spatial organization, difficulty in social reasoning, weakness in higher-order reading comprehension and written expression, weaknesses in attention and executive function, anxiety, and depression.

These conditions are typically recognized when children are of school age. Often, a teacher will recommend an evaluation when they notice that a child has hit a stumbling block that may be related to a learning disorder. Children may be referred to a neuropsychologist who will conduct a series of assessments to determine whether or not your child meets criteria for a learning disorder. These evaluations also pinpoint much more specifically the subskills a child lacks or is struggling with, and identify areas of strength that a child can draw upon as they learn to work around, compensate for, or develop in areas of weakness. If a learning disorder is diagnosed, the evaluation also helps identify appropriate interventions and accommodations that can be put in place in the school environment to help support your child's learning. These types of accommodations will be discussed later on in the chapter.

Intellectual Disability

Intellectual disability is a neurodevelopmental disorder characterized by challenges related to intellectual function as well as difficulty performing, without some form of assistance, tasks that are important for daily living. As with the other neurodevelopmental disorders, there can be a spectrum in terms of the degree of functional impairment and the need for assistance. The onset of challenges associated with intellectual disability begins prior to the age of eighteen and has a significant impact on a child's academic, social, and emotional growth and their trajectory in life generally. Technically, for a diagnosis of intellectual disability, the child would demonstrate both impaired intellectual and adaptive functioning. Adaptive functioning involves conceptual, social, and practical domains. The conceptual domain involves one's ability to communicate, read, and write, as well as processes like reasoning, memory, and judgment. The social domain includes skills involved in a person's ability to relate to peers, engage in social problem-solving, and respond empathically to others; and the practical domain includes activities such as eating, dressing, toileting, and mobility. Intellectual disability is framed in terms of levels of severity, meant to describe the impact of the symptoms and the extent of support and assistance the child needs to be able to complete various tasks.

Intellectual disability affects 1 to 3 percent of children and is mainly secondary to genetic conditions such as Down syndrome, DiGeorge syndrome, Williams syndrome, Smith-Magenis syndrome, Fragile X syndrome, Rett syndrome, and Angelman and Prader-Willi syndromes, just to name a few. About 28 percent of children who have autism also have intellectual disability. Children who show evidence of intellectual disability undergo an evaluation process to determine if there is a specific condition that may be contributing to it and whether there are comorbidities associated with that condition that may have some negative consequences on the child's overall physical and mental well-being. Your child's primary care provider may make a referral to a developmental pediatrician who would conduct a thorough medical and developmental history, family history, and a physical examination to determine if there are any particular features suggestive of a specific condition. The pediatrician may also connect you with a genetic counselor to discuss options for testing.

In addition to genetic causes of intellectual disability, there are also situations that may arise during pregnancy or the postnatal period that could contribute to the development of intellectual disability. These include infections such as rubella, herpes, or cytomegalovirus, or exposure to environmental toxins such as lead, mercury, and radiation. Children also may be born without any known concerns but later experience traumas such as lack of oxygen to the brain and exposures to toxins that affect the central nervous system and can result in intellectual disability.

Children with an intellectual disability also may have other mental health concerns. Other conditions associated with ID include ADHD, depression, anxiety, and substance use disorder. Children may engage in self-injurious behavior such as hitting themselves, possibly to express feelings they don't know how to manage otherwise because they possess limited communication skills. It is important to understand how a child's intellectual functioning impacts how they communicate their emotional needs, and how it can limit the range of their behavioral responses to certain situations. Your child's primary care provider or a psychiatric prescriber may recommend using medication to help mitigate some of the more challenging behaviors. There are also a number of training programs for caregivers designed to provide you with tools and strategies to best support your child.

School-Based Resources: Evaluation, IEPs, and 504 Plans

In the US public school system, children diagnosed with a condition considered to be a disability are eligible for additional support within the school environment under the Individuals with Disabilities Education Act (IDEA). IDEA is a federal law mandating that all children within the public school system be able to access free education regardless of any challenges they may have that interfere with their ability to learn in a traditional classroom setting. IDEA also requires schools to provide adequate resources for students with a disability to have a meaningful learning experience within the same school environment as students who do not have an identified set of challenges that interfere with their learning. To ensure the right of all kids to a free public education, the law provides resources for children to be evaluated for differences in the way in which children cognitively process information, and social and emotional conditions that may make it difficult for them to learn in a traditional classroom environment. Certain mental health conditions that are diagnosed in children also meet the criteria for being considered a disability according to IDEA and therefore make the child eligible to access special education resources.

Many caregivers are put off by the idea that their child's receiving a mental health diagnosis potentially labels the child as being disabled and are concerned about the ramifications of assigning the child that label within the school system. They worry that this label will follow their child and negatively impact both their academic experience and their ability to fit in and be just like the other kids. For some caregivers, there are also concerns that such a label will compromise their child's ability to reach their full potential, given that acknowledgment of a diagnosis implies that the child has certain limitations. For these reasons, caregivers may not want to have their child receive specialized supports within the school. Many of these concerns are legitimate, based on the caregivers' own experiences as children and on the long history of stigmatization, discrimination, and marginalization of people with both mental and physical disabilities that inspired IDEA in the first place. Today, however, in-school supports can often be invaluable in ensuring that your child has a fair shot educationally despite any intellectual, social, or emotional challenges they may be experiencing.

As I've already mentioned, children need to undergo an evaluation and be diagnosed with a condition that makes them eligible for special education under IDEA in order to access resources available within your public school system. From there, there are multiple options for support that you can advocate for as a caregiver.

There are multiple pathways to undergoing the school evaluation. If you have concerns about your child's academic performance or are worried about your child's behavior and emotional state within the school environment, as your child's parent or legal caregiver you can request the school perform an evaluation to determine if your child is eligible for an Individualized Educational Plan (IEP). An IEP will outline exactly what is meant by the more general term *special education* when it comes to your child. It contains specific recommendations about the interventions to be provided within a school setting in order for the child to access their education in light of the challenges interfering with their ability to learn in a mainstream classroom or from the standard curriculum. Once an evaluation identifies that a child meets eligibility for an IEP, and once an IEP has been put in place, a public, charter, or magnet school must by law provide the supports specified in that IEP.

The types of concerns that you or your child's teacher may have will determine the type of evaluation that the school will be willing to provide for your child. There is a psychoeducational evaluation, typically performed within the school, which is primarily focused on differences that impact a student's academic performance, including specific learning disorders like dyslexia and dyscalculia that affect their attainment of reading or math skills. A school psychologist often performs these types of assessments using several questionnaires that are completed by parents and teachers as well as specific tests administered to the child to determine how the child thinks and processes information. Some schools provide neuropsychological evaluations that also assess how the child's social functioning, behavior, and cognitive skills impact their ability to navigate the school environment and to learn. Your child's evaluation will also include recommendations about how to best support the child given their cognitive skills, any specific learning disorders, and any mental health issues. It's important to know that while a school-based evaluation may identify mental health issues, the purpose of the evaluation is only to identify resources that could help the child to succeed in the classroom. Evaluations can also be obtained through an outside neuropsychology clinic that conducts them, though they may or may not be covered by insurance.

All public schools that are engaged in the IEP process will set up a meeting with you and members of the special education team who were part of the evaluation process. At the meeting, the special education team will review the findings of the evaluation with you and present their recommendations about how they can best support your child within the school. This meeting can seem very intimidating because it will involve a group of people talking extensively about your child's challenges, which can be difficult for many caregivers to hear. Lots of information will be discussed, including possible conditions your child may have that could be interfering with their learning; they may even discuss the possibility of modifying the curriculum or putting them in a separate classroom. You may feel so overwhelmed by the experience that you have difficulty fully capturing and absorbing everything that is being said.

Many caregivers don't know this, and your child's school may or may not advise you beforehand, but you can bring someone with you to this meeting to advocate with you on behalf of your child. Trained educational advocates can help you better understand the IEP process before the meeting, and can be helpful at the meeting in reviewing the recommendations proposed by the school, assessing whether the recommendations are appropriate and adequate in light of your child's evaluation, and asking questions you might not think to ask. You can find an educational advocate by asking other parents in your community, talking to the people who performed the evaluation, or visiting your state's Parent Training and Information Center, which should have information about available educational advocates in the region. You can visit the following website to learn more about the Parent Training and Information Center near you: www.parentcenterhub.org/find-your-center/.

In addition to having an educational advocate attend the meeting with you, you can also invite family members, partners, and providers who have previously worked with your child. It is not uncommon for me as a child psychiatrist to participate in an IEP meeting for one of my patients if their mental health condition is interfering with their ability to learn in the school environment. In addition to being able to provide further clarity to caregivers about the IEP process and to discuss and review with them what was discussed at the meeting after it occurs, I also provide psychoeducation during the meeting about the nature of the child's mental health condition and how it may be interfering with the child's academic functioning. This can be especially helpful if the team at the school is unfamiliar with a particular diagnosis, and my insights can shed light on the need for more robust supports within the school.

When you attend the IEP meeting, please take notes. Write down the names of everyone who is in attendance as well as their role. Take your time in reviewing any paperwork/documentation that is provided to you during the time of the meeting, and do not feel compelled to sign anything right away. They will review the IEP with you, which outlines their recommendations, but you do not need to sign that document right away. You can take it home with you and review it, and/or consult with others, to make sure that it makes sense for your child. If you want to schedule another meeting to ask additional questions, please feel empowered to do so. It may feel as though you don't have much agency during this seemingly very formal process, but you should and can advocate for yourself—and thus for your child—in terms of the time that you need to review the material and discuss it with other people to better inform your decision-making.

Private schools are not required by law to provide evaluations for special education. Private schools can provide what are referred to as "individualized service plans" outlining some of the specific resources that they can provide for a child, but they may not be as robust as what is available in the public school setting since school districts are able to access tax dollars in order to meet the specific needs of children who have an IEP. On the other hand, private schools may offer smaller classroom sizes, more individualized attention, and a more intimate and less chaotic or sensorily intense environment that may well serve your child, if you have the resources to afford a private school or can access scholarship support. Depending on those resources and where you live, there are also some private schools dedicated specifically to serving the needs of kids with particular neurodevelopmental disorders.

If your school district does not offer the services that an evaluation indicates that your child needs, if you believe that the evaluation conducted by the school was inadequate, or if you disagree with the school's interpretation of the evaluation or with the extent or nature of the recommendations and accommodations the school has agreed to include in an IEP, you may want to find more help in advocating for your child. The National Disability Rights Network (NDRN) is the nonprofit member organization for the federally mandated Protection and Advocacy (P&A) Systems and Client Assistance Programs (CAP) providing legally based advocacy services to people with disabilities in the United States. There are P&A and CAP programs in every state

and US territory, as well as one serving the Native American population, and you can visit NDRN's website to locate the one in your
state (ndrn.org). There are also advocacy organizations for people with
certain neurodevelopmental disorders that might have suggestions
and resources to offer. The Arc, for example, is the largest national
community-based organization advocating for and supporting people
with developmental and intellectual disabilities (thearc.org).

Another type of accommodation that can be put in place for a child
with a neurodevelopmental disorder or a mental health condition is
called a 504 plan. The types of accommodations included in a 504 plan
are not considered part of special education and don't involve modifica-
tions to the academic curriculum. In a 504 plan, accommodations such
as extra test-taking time, completing exams in a quiet room, and having the teacher write down detailed instructions for homework assignments are some examples. If you believe that your child would benefit
from accommodations that would make it easier for them to complete
their work in the educational environment, speak to your child's teachers to discuss the process for putting that into place. Technically, students do not need to receive a neuropsychological evaluation in order
to qualify for a 504 plan. However, some schools may opt to perform a
full evaluation to determine whether your child is eligible for an IEP. If
not, then they will most likely decide to institute a 504 plan.

For children who need specific mental health supports, there are
some public school systems with the resources to fund mental health
resources within the school. For example, the Boston Public School
system has established health centers within a number of their schools
that provide not only expanded medical services but also mental health
services including individual and group therapy. Caregivers give consent at the beginning of the school year, granting permission for their
child to access any of the health center services whenever they want
without having to notify their caregiver every time. Students are able to
meet with an individual therapist weekly during the school day to learn
about effective coping strategies to navigate some of their mental health

struggles. Be sure to check whether your own public school system has mental health resources to offer.

Neurodevelopmental Differences and Mental Health

Understanding that there are individual differences in how children experience the world cognitively and sensorily, and in how they learn and process new information, is an important aspect of understanding your child's mental health. The neurodevelopmental conditions that develop as a consequence of brain-based differences can both resemble, and co-occur with, some of the mental health conditions that will be explored in detail in part II of this book. Learning more about how your child's brain works, and what neurodevelopmental differences may affect their intellectual, social, and emotional growth, is essential in identifying strategies to effectively support your child. As you read the chapters that follow, keep in mind that these individual differences in how your child's brain functions may play a significant role in their mental health challenges.

PART II

Exploring Mental Health Conditions in Children and Adolescents

SEVEN

The Impact of Trauma

There was a moment where I recognized the true impact that the divorce had on the children. People would say, "Oh, you got it. Nah, they'll be fine. Kids are resilient." You have that misnomer in your head. That's when I realized how fragile and how simple their needs were all at once. Just that simple connection that they needed from me, the reassurance they needed from me, the ability to speak about feelings.

—**MIKE LAMBERT,**
father and police officer of native Hawaiian heritage,
advocate for behavioral health services

• • •

T here are certain childhood memories that never fade. Certain places, smells, sounds, and people, when encountered during adulthood, can transport you back to youth. You may be able to recall with exquisite detail the home where you spent most of your childhood or the scent of your grandmother's perfume. These memories stay with us and serve as a reminder of the events, people, and places that have shaped our lives and our understanding of the world. The relationships we formed in childhood with other children and adults provide the blueprint for our understanding of how to form human connections into adulthood. The words others used when talking to you as a child, or the opinions and ideas others shared about you and around you, have an influence on how you view yourself today as an adult.

Although we want to ensure that our children find themselves in the types of environments and relationships that create long-lasting, positive memories that they can reflect on with fondness during their adult lives, there are times when despite our best intentions that may not be possible. Whether it be individual conflicts children have with peers, negative interactions with authority figures in or outside of the home, or shared global experiences like the Covid-19 pandemic, negative experiences are part of life. All of us experience pain, disappointment, and adversity in childhood; this is part of growing up. But certain childhood experiences can be so profoundly painful that they scar our memories—and continue to affect our brains and bodies—into adulthood. Some of these scars can even be passed along to future generations.

So, what experiences are we referring to when we talk about trauma? In the field of medicine, we have long understood trauma to mean injuries to the body: blunt force trauma, penetrating trauma, an injury that may be treated in a trauma unit. More recently, we've come to understand that there can be emotional and psychological trauma— injuries to the psyche and the soul—that can be just as life-altering as physical trauma. The types of experiences that "count" as traumatic vary drastically based on the individual and their environment, and there is a difference between experiencing trauma, being impacted negatively by it, and developing post-traumatic stress disorder (PTSD). We'll discuss the nuances of the definition of trauma, and why they are important for us to understand as caregivers, later in the chapter, but for now, our working definition can be this: *A traumatic event is one that severely impacts a child's developing sense of self in a way that feels threatening, unsafe, and uncontrollable.*

There are certainly children who have experienced trauma but did not develop significant mental health symptoms. However, the idea that *all* children are resilient to trauma, and that they simply just forget or get over negative events, is a myth. It has been well researched and documented that traumatic experiences have lasting impacts on the development of a child's brain and on their physical and emotional well-being and increase their likelihood of developing a mental health condition in adulthood.

If you suspect—or know—that your child has experienced trauma, it's important to take what clinicians now call a "trauma-informed approach" both to understanding their behavior and to providing the support they need. That means thinking about any disruptive behavior that affects their ability to function—at home, at school, or even on the playground—from a place of curiosity about what may be driving those behaviors. Recognizing specific reactions and behaviors that may be rooted in trauma, and understanding why and when they happen, is vital to helping your child grow and develop resilience. Sharing this understanding with other adults in your child's life will allow them to respond in a similarly supportive way.

In the past few decades, research on how trauma experienced in childhood can differ from trauma experienced in adulthood has flourished. Though we're far from fully understanding how trauma impacts the developing brain, and how best to mitigate the negative effects of traumatic stress, we've learned that certain "problem" behaviors often seen in children are frequently associated with an experience of trauma at some point in their developmental process.

Throughout this chapter, we'll review some of the behaviors associated with experiences of trauma in childhood and share stories from real families about how they learned about, understood, and responded to trauma. We'll also explore some of the most prevalent topics in child trauma research today, including our understanding of trauma's impact on the developing brain, and share options for supporting a child who has experienced trauma.

First Steps: Noticing Behaviors

You might already be aware that your child, or a child you care for, has experienced some form of trauma in their life and is exhibiting behaviors related to those experiences. If you don't think your child has had

traumatic experiences or aren't sure, but have noticed some of the behaviors discussed below, it's worth considering the possibility that your
child has experienced some form of trauma that is impacting their ability to feel safe in their surroundings. The list of behaviors I describe is
not exhaustive but covers some of the more prevalent behavior patterns
observed in children who have a history of traumatic stress.

Hypervigilance

One of the symptoms that often emerges as a result of trauma is hypervigilance. This can look like an exaggerated startle response—children
might be jumpy in response to very minor things, like jumping out of
their seats after hearing a noise. It might also look like constant monitoring of the mood states of others or a tendency for the child to take
responsibility for emotions they observe in others. After one experiences a trauma, key regions of the brain become overactive. They remain constantly on high alert in order to better detect threats and send
signals to the rest of the body to protect itself. After trauma, the brain
can misinterpret ordinary, non-threatening cues as a potential source
for extreme stress—like certain facial expressions or vocal tones, for
example. As a result, the child may be highly sensitive and defensive
and appear aggressive toward people with certain mannerisms or physical attributes. Essentially, hypervigilance is the result of chronic overactivation of the threat detection system in our brain, which can cause
us to misinterpret objectively nonthreatening cues as potential sources
of immediate danger.

Nina Richtman, a single mom living in Iowa, adopted her sons after
a period of time fostering them when they were two and three years
old. She shared that when she first got the call about the adoption, she
was advised that the boys were "hyper"—but as she developed a relationship with them, she noticed it was more than that:

> When I met them, I learned that hyper was the least of the challenges. It
> wasn't really that they always needed to be busy. It was like they were

constantly checking their environment. They couldn't focus because they were so preoccupied with "What is happening in my environment?"

One of the early struggles that I had was that my kids kept getting disenrolled from daycares. The daycares were giving me lists [of behaviors]: they're using swear words, they're fighting with other kids, they're biting other kids—some of which I saw at home and some of which I didn't. So, it was hard for me, being a new parent, to navigate: How much of this is typical kid behavior and how much of it is more? As multiple disenrollments happened over the course of a year, I started to think, "This is a little more than just your typical toddler going through transition."

My two kids present a little bit differently, but I think the root of it is the same for both of them. It's always about adults, and "Is my environment safe? I'm going to test it . . . to see if you will set limits that are focused on safety." My kids, if they're really excited, they need you to help them calm down. If they're really mad or really sad, they can't get themselves back to a regulated state. I think a lot of it is rooted again in the neglect and the trauma they experienced before they came to live with me.

Aggression

You've probably heard of the "fight, flight, freeze" response: When we detect a threat, our bodies release hormones that prompt us to either stand our ground and fight back, flee to a safer environment, or become literally frozen in place, as if paralyzed. Some kids who have been exposed to trauma can respond to triggers in their environment by entering a "fighter" state and may become verbally or physically aggressive toward others. Nina's description of her boys' inability to "get themselves to a regulated state" refers to what mental health professionals call emotional dysregulation, meaning a lack of ability to work through and process feelings internally so that they don't overwhelm one's ability to think clearly, inhibit destructive or self-destructive behavior, or move on to experience other feelings and gain perspective.

This response—and it is important to remember that it is not a conscious choice—is certainly a challenge, since it may make it difficult for them to tolerate various social settings and stressors without becoming aggressive. The controlled environment of school classrooms, and interactions with authority figures, may be especially difficult for them to navigate. They may even lash out at the people who they are the closest to. Even though friends and family may be safe people for them, there is still a possibility that they may exhibit aggressive behavior when triggered.

Holly Miles is a psychiatric nurse and mother in her early forties from Missouri who serves as the president of the Board of Directors for NAMI Missouri. She shared with us her experiences with her adopted son, who experienced trauma at a young age with his biological family:

> About four months after the adoption, we started getting into the behaviors, and that's when we started dealing with anger. I don't remember exactly when that was along the way, but the anger just kept escalating. It was running away, punching holes in walls. I hate you. You guys are not my parents. And I already have a mom and dad. And it's the most hurtful stuff in the world. But in the early years, probably within about ten minutes of him exploding like that, he would come and apologize. He would say, "I'm really sorry, I shouldn't have said those things."
>
> Now it's just a big old giant middle finger at the age of sixteen. With the behaviors and anger, he's realizing the impact that it has on me, that it has on Dad, that it has on his grandparents. And so, he gets feedback that he wants. So, it's, "Ooh, this gets my attention." And so, if he's not getting the attention that he's wanting from the situation, all I have to do is blow up or punch this wall or take off out of the house and run around the block and, by golly, I'm going to get the attention that I want or act out in another way that's inappropriate.
>
> The way we deal with the aggression is just letting him know that while what you did was wrong, it's not a reflection of who you are as a

person. We know deep down you are a good kid, you are the first one to go out and help people, but some really bad things happened to you. And it's those things that happened to you that are triggering you to have that response and that urge to want to do those things. It's not you and your soul and your heart that's wanting to do those things. It's this response to the things that were done to you. It's kind of this cycle that's making you then want to do these things to other people.

And that's where him going to therapy, it's been so hard. Because his favorite statement is: It's in the past, let's leave it in the past. I'm like: No, that's not how this works. You need to talk about this stuff or else it's going to come out when you're twenty and thirty years old in a very bad way. So, you have to talk to your therapist about this, process the trauma, or we're going to end up in a bad way. So, we're just reinforcing to him, we love you regardless of what actions you have taken. We still love you. You are still our son.

Jodi Bullinger is a Dutch-American former college athlete in her late forties who has dedicated her life's work to public education, student advocacy, adolescent mental health, and building culturally inclusive and responsive educational spaces. She has been a high school coach and psychology teacher and is currently a ninth grade dean of students. Jodi, based in Ann Arbor, Michigan, shared her perspective on children who exhibit anger and aggression in school settings, and how school personnel can respond:

Sometimes rage is the language of trauma. When you see behaviors, I think our traditional model is to think that a student is being rude or they're in need of some sort of discipline or what have you, when really we need to take a step back and we need to understand that when we're seeing certain things happen and angry outbursts of sorts can be trauma, it can be depression, it can be anxiety. And until we determine what is at the root of what we're seeing and we begin to provide supports for that student that are consistent with what's actually going on, we're never going to really put that young person in or help them get to a place where they can maximize their potential and live the life that they want.

And at the end of the day, that is our goal. Our goal is to provide the young people that come through the school system with the skills to be able to live the life that they want and be contributors to the world around them in a positive and meaningful way. And so there's a bigger picture with that. Sometimes the initial reaction that we might have is not going to be the therapeutic one if we look at the school system and the models of response to behaviors that we all probably grew up with.

Mood-Related Symptoms

The exhaustion of being in a constant state of fight or flight, moments of aggression, and intrusive memories related to traumatic experiences can often have an impact on a child's overall mood. It is not uncommon to see children who present as irritable, sad, or moody without any clear reason. Or they may appear overly anxious, secondary to their ongoing hypervigilance. This can be challenging because again, the child may be having difficulty articulating their emotional state to others and instead may communicate their distress through their adverse mood and behaviors.

Dominique Freeman, a NAMI employee whom we met earlier, shared with us some of her primary emotional memories from childhood, how she connected them to instability in her household, and how being asked about her home environment, instead of blamed, helped her heal:

> There are two big emotions that I remember from when I was a child. One of them was sadness. I can remember crying often, and I couldn't figure out why. Now it makes sense because my primary caretaker struggled with an addiction, and so it was chaotic often in the home.
>
> And then I remember relief. I think about how relieved I felt just to have been asked, "What's going on at home?" And it was that specific question that someone asked me because I had never been asked that. It was always

like, "What's wrong with you? You never act like this." It was always pointing at me. I think when someone asked me, "What's going on at home?" it just felt like I could talk about it. It wasn't me this time. It was what was happening around me. So I think that would be helpful.

Sometimes I think we question the behavior. What's going on presently in front of us? But sometimes I think it's environmental. What's happening around you? What does your day-to-day look like? Something happened to you, and you showed up this way, and so let's get to that, rather than, "What are you doing?"

Now, there's the affirmation that I tell myself often, which is "I am safe." I tell that to my younger self: You are not bad. And your emotions are your emotions, and they're okay to have. And it's okay to talk about it. That's what I wanted to hear when I was younger. It's okay. You have emotions. They're big sometimes. Sometimes they're small. But either way, you are worthy for feeling them and you deserve love and support.

Physical Symptoms

Having your mind constantly in overdrive detecting potential threats and potential sources of danger can be exhausting physically as well as emotionally. It can be very difficult for children who have experienced trauma to settle down from the constant influxes of stress hormones coursing through their bodies. They often have difficulty falling and staying asleep, and sleep is essential to their overall growth, development, and emotional regulation. Intrusive thoughts and memories related to the trauma that may resurface during the stillness that comes with bedtime, or nightmares and anxieties about having nightmares, can also interfere with sleep or make children fearful of falling asleep.

Because children are still learning how to make sense of their emotional experiences, they may not have the language to articulate all of their thoughts and feelings. As a result, their distress often manifests through physical symptoms. Many children complain of muscle aches, stomachaches, and other sources of physical pain following a trauma. These symptoms can be triggered by what are referred to as "flashbacks"—the experience of physically reliving moments of their trauma and its associated physical and emotional sensations.

Repression, Attention, and Dissociation

Children who have experienced trauma have many things weighing heavily on their minds. In addition to constantly detecting threats, having difficulty sleeping, and experiencing intrusive thoughts, memories, or physical sensations, they may also have lost the ability to recall certain details related to the traumatic event. The brain does this as a way to protect itself from the emotionally overwhelming flood of feeling the trauma triggered. The intensity of the event causes the brain to shut down its operating system and then reboot, as though the event didn't happen. The reality is that the traumatic event lives on in memory, but it may not be fully accessible to the child. They may experience a feeling of being detached from their own body, as if they are watching their body move through the world from outside of it, or watching themselves in a movie. This is referred to as dissociation.

We can't tell from the outside whether a child is having these types of experiences. What we may observe is that the child is having difficulties being fully alert and present. They may appear as though they are wandering off (literally or mentally) or daydreaming while you are talking to them, have difficulty concentrating, or not recall details from previous conversations. These behaviors may occur because the child is dissociating.

What Constitutes a Traumatic Experience?

For many years there was an assumption that if you were not a combat veteran having war flashbacks, or hadn't had a dramatic near-death experience, the symptoms you were experiencing could not be the result of trauma. But research in the past few decades has changed our understanding of what causes trauma and how trauma manifests. The definition of trauma that we are working from in this book is that it is an event or incident that an individual perceives or experiences as shocking or intrusive in nature and that poses a threat to their sense of self. In other words, what is or isn't traumatic to a given individual is not something that an "expert" or outsider can determine. At the end of the day, if an individual experiences and perceives an event to be negative, intrusive, and uncontrollable, then it can be considered a traumatic event. To explore this more, we'll dive into some of the neurobiology behind a trauma response.

Our bodies are wired to protect us from harm and get us away from danger in the face of a perceived threat. Several different neurological processes and physiological responses make that happen. Within our brains, neural connections between specific regions allow us to detect a threat and then orchestrate our body's physical and emotional response to that threat. Our brains take in sensory information from our environment in the form of smell, sight, sound, and touch and quickly determine if this sensory information signals evidence of danger. The smell of smoke, the sight of a wild animal, or a behavioral cue from another individual, like a facial expression or body language, could be perceived as a threat. In response to a perceived threat, the body releases stress hormones, which trigger an automatic physiological response: our heart rate increases, our breathing speeds up, our palms get sweaty and our muscles become tense. We may run, fight, or freeze as part of our reaction to the perceived threat. Past experiences that we have had influence this automatic response. Parts of the brain communicate to other parts: "Yikes, this sensory information reminds me of that other really bad thing that happened to me before in a similar situation; we should do something about it now!"

This is why some people may perceive a stimulus or event as dangerous or stressful when others don't: perceptions are informed by previous experience. For example, many people would respond to the sight of a group of ambulances and police cars on the side of the road with curiosity or mild concern, but the sight could remind one person in particular of the emergency response team that arrived at their house following the death of a loved one and set their heart racing.

Kirsten Colston, a teacher in her late twenties from the Kansas City metro area who has been living with bipolar II disorder and PTSD since age sixteen, shared with us how a traumatic incident at the dentist shaped future experiences for her that may have seemed completely benign to others:

I remember feeling just a lot of panic in everyday situations where I didn't have complete control. And it wasn't even situations that had to do with the dentist. Like riding in a car where someone else was driving. I would feel a little panicky. Just anything that reminded me, I'm not in control at this moment. And I received no therapy during this time, no targeted treatment. And I think it's just because no one, even me, recognized this tiny incident that other people could go through and be fine, I wasn't able to do that.

So we went back to a different dentist and they said, "Oh, that'll never happen again. That's a fluke." But I told my parents, "I cannot do this. I am not doing this." And they respected that and listened to me, but I think they were just very confused and didn't see it as a bigger problem than it was. It wasn't me trying to avoid the dentist, per se. It was me scared for my life. If I let someone else give me anesthesia, I will die, and I don't want to die that way. That was truly my thought process. And now I know that's not logical, but I totally remember feeling that way and feeling like 100 percent confident that that was my reality.

The Impact of Trauma on the Future Self

Having had traumatic experiences doesn't necessarily mean a child will develop symptoms consistent with a diagnosis of PTSD, a condition in which an individual who has experienced trauma develops intrusive memories related to the event and engages in avoidant behavior to mitigate distressing memories or feelings about the event. However, ongoing exposure to trauma during childhood not only impacts a child's future relationships with others and their ability to regulate their mood and behaviors; it can also have a lasting mental health impact into adulthood.

One uniquely important aspect of childhood trauma is the point in development at which it occurs. A child's sense of self is still being developed, from both psychological and biological standpoints. Children are still learning what "normal" is, and therefore children who have experienced trauma may not perceive their experiences as traumatic. Those experiences are at the foundation of their understanding of the world, and they don't have anything different to compare them to. Especially when the trauma is chronic or inflicted by a primary caretaker, they can shape the child's understanding of themselves. The child may feel that there might be something inherently wrong with them that led to the traumatic incident(s), that they caused what happened to them, or that they were not worthy of being kept safe from circumstances or people that are frightening or harmful.

When the trauma involves a caregiver or occurs within the home, it can have long-term effects that interfere with the child's ability to form and maintain relationships with others and with their sense of self. This is referred to as complex trauma.

Complex trauma is a condition that describes the chronic, repetitive, and unrelenting nature of trauma that often happens at the hands of caregivers or other trusted adults who are a part of the child's life. Experiencing repetitive trauma by adults in the child's life who they may regularly encounter or are in a position to keep the child safe in a way normalizes the ongoing negative experience. Rather than it being a single traumatic event or what could be referred to as an acute trauma, in which the child experiences an event that could be considered an outlier in the overall scope of their life, complex trauma highlights the fact that this is their life—there is no one single event but rather a reflection of a lack of safety in their relationships with adults and a lack

of safety in their environment. Examples of situations that could contribute to complex trauma include chronic exposure to community violence, domestic violence, sexual abuse by adults who are close to the
child, physical abuse, and neglect. For children who have experienced
complex trauma, it can be incredibly challenging to feel safe in relationships with other people they may encounter, whether that be
friends, teachers, coaches, or other adults. It can also be hard for them
to read certain social cues that are unconsciously used to communicate
safety to others. For the child with complex PTSD, their behavioral
and emotional responses to certain social situations can be unpredictable and somewhat erratic since it can be hard for them to read these
cues. The same goes for the child's ability to regulate their behavior. The
adults in their lives who were supposed to model how to regulate behavior and be in control over their emotions might have also been the
ones who were abusing them. Given that fact, it can be hard over the
course of their childhood to pick up on healthy and adaptive emotional
coping skills that most kids naturally acquire from being in a safe
household environment.

Adverse Childhood Experiences

For many years, there was a limited understanding of the lasting impact
of childhood trauma. There was this idea that children are resilient and
that it's easier for them to recover from a traumatic incident than if
they were to have experienced that same incident as an adult. However,
what we have come to learn over the years is that for some individuals
the scars of trauma can endure for many years and not only have an
impact on one's mental health but also their physical health. Particularly
for children who have experienced complex trauma that has profoundly
altered their perspective of the world, that trauma can also alter their
physical well-being, even during adulthood.

In the mid-1980s, Dr. Vincent Felitti was the chief of the Department
of Preventive Medicine at Kaiser Permanente in San Diego, where he
was working in an obesity clinic. In face-to-face interviews with

numerous patients who had lost weight in the clinic but dropped out and soon regained the weight shortly thereafter, he learned that the majority of these patients had experienced some form of childhood trauma and now as adults were living with various chronic medical conditions as well as obesity.

This information led to a partnership between the health maintenance organization Kaiser Permanente and the Division of Violence Prevention at the Centers for Disease Control and Prevention (CDC), which resulted in the creation of the landmark Adverse Childhood Experience (ACE) study from 1995 to 1997. With more than seventeen thousand participants, the ACE study was one of the largest investigations ever conducted about the impact of childhood abuse and neglect on later-life health and well-being. The study's aim was to describe the long-term relationship of childhood experiences to important medical and public health problems. Participants—mostly middle-class, highly educated white adults with health insurance—completed a confidential survey containing questions about childhood maltreatment and family dysfunction, as well as items detailing their current health status and behaviors.

The study found that nearly two-thirds of participants reported having one or more adverse childhood experiences, and one in eight reported having four or more ACEs. The most commonly reported ACEs were physical abuse, substance use by a household member, and parental separation or divorce. As researchers followed participants over time, they discovered that the number of adverse childhood experiences that a person encountered during childhood had a clear relationship to numerous health, social, and behavioral problems throughout their lifespan, including substance use disorders.

So, what did this teach us? Prior to the ACE study, the general assumption in the field of psychiatry was that children were resilient: that they could withstand stressful events with fewer consequences than adults, and that negative experiences during childhood would not impact children in the long run. But we now understand that, while children are indeed resilient, that doesn't mean they are impervious. Exposure to traumatizing environments and circumstances can have lasting mental health impacts, too, even when that exposure does not fit the classical definition of a traumatic event.

Special Considerations: The Child Welfare System

Children who have been involved with the child welfare system are more likely to have experienced trauma at some point in time than children who haven't and more likely to experience more of it. Nearly half of children who have been involved in foster care have reported exposure to four or more types of traumatic events, which could include neglect, physical abuse, sexual abuse, or witnessing violence directed toward someone else. Children who have been exposed to trauma within the system have also been found to have higher rates of emotional and behavioral issues which require more extensive mental health supports. Children who have been involved in the foster care system have been separated from their primary caregiver and forced into living situations in which they have to place their trust in the hands of a stranger. This experience can make it difficult for them to form secure, stable attachments with adult figures. And unfortunately, given the frequent shuffling from one household to the other that occurs in the foster care system, those attachments to those adult figures may change every so often. Frequent moves from one school to the next can make it difficult to form meaningful relationships with peers as well. For these reasons, many children in the system lack the opportunity to form reliable attachments to people capable of providing support and guidance, or who might model various coping strategies for navigating life's challenges.

A child's exposure to trauma also creates physiological changes that affect these children before they reach a foster parent or eventually an adoptive parent. If you are caring for a child who has been in the child welfare system, it's important to be aware that you may experience a number of trauma-related reactions by your child over the course of your relationship. You need to understand that the behaviors and emotions your child may display are likely not a direct reflection of anything that you might have done wrong, but rather the child's way of communicating distress in that moment in a way that is familiar to them, and that is difficult for them to control in the moment. It is important to not take their behavior personally, but instead to be curious about what might be driving that behavior. The hope is that you will begin to learn what may trigger certain behavioral or emotional responses, which in turn will inform the way in which you support the child. It is of the utmost importance to demonstrate that you are committed to being a steady, constant force in their life.

Life Stressors and Trauma in Children

There are a number of events or circumstances that children are exposed to over the course of their childhood years that they can experience as traumatic, even though they don't fit the classical definition, and even though the adults in their lives don't perceive them as such. We do know that stressful life events experienced during childhood have been associated with low self-esteem, anxiety, depressed mood, and some behavioral problems. Problematic behaviors such as substance use or disordered eating can also develop during or following the stressful event. Some examples of experiences that may be perceived as traumatic include parental divorce, moving to a new place of residence, or changing schools.

There are also stressful events that are experienced collectively—for example, the Covid-19 pandemic, natural and environmental disasters, and war. Children may be affected by the sociopolitical climate, which is reflected in news reports and on social media as well as during dinner conversations. Children notice when adults are stressed and take notice of how the adults in their lives navigate that stress.

Although these events may not be classically defined as traumatic, they undoubtedly have a lasting impact on a child's sense of safety in the world, their sense of security, as well as their sense of their own identity. Children thrive on consistency and certainty. These stressful life events disrupt all that. As adults, it is important for us to recognize that children may exhibit fluctuations in their mood, anger, irritability, or anxiety following these events. They can become more "clingy," and have difficulty separating from you. They may also complain of various physical ailments. Again, we need to maintain awareness that our children are affected by events in the wider world and to be curious about what is driving changes in our kids' mood and behavior rather than minimizing the significance of these events to the child.

Generational Trauma

Trauma can have an impact that extends beyond the individual who first experiences it. It can create ripple effects throughout entire families and communities and into subsequent generations. As caregivers, it is important to also be cognizant of how the traumas that we might have endured during our childhood may impact our dynamics with our children, in our families, and with others we encounter in the outside world. In recent years, there has been a significant amount of research into the ways in which trauma can be transmitted to others. Additionally, there has been interesting research that indicates that parental traumatic experiences can have not just an emotional impact but also a physical impact on their children. Studies have demonstrated that the offspring of trauma survivors release increased levels of various stress hormones due to alterations in molecular pathways that then also alter the structure of the offspring's DNA and affect the expression of certain genes involved in emotional, physical, and behavioral responses to stress. This is not the fault of the caregiver who experienced the trauma, but it is important to know the wide-reaching effects that a traumatic event has not only on the person who experienced it directly but on future generations.

Traumatic experience changes the way we see ourselves in relation to the world, the lens through which we see the world, and the way we perceive different experiences. There are caregivers who, again through no fault of their own, may instill certain perspectives or worldviews on their children secondary to the trauma that they themselves have experienced.

Don is an Asian American agender person from Michigan. They live with bipolar disorder and ADHD, and they currently facilitate a local support group for people who are affected by mood disorders. Don is also a second-generation immigrant, and shared the challenges of relating their own struggles with mental health to their mother, who went through extreme hardship and trauma on her journey to the US.

My mom would often tell stories about how she came to this country with flip-flops on her feet, the clothes on her body, and not a word of English, and that's it. And she was able to find success in this country. She was able to go to high school, take care of her siblings, learn English, and then get a college degree. If she was able to do that, why couldn't I handle my trivial struggles of adolescence? So that was one of the difficult parts that I had with wanting to talk about how I felt. My parents were able to overcome so much adversity. There are these mountains; they were able to overcome so many things. How come I, being an American-born citizen, couldn't even just get through these supposedly invisible feelings? I put my parents on this pedestal as the standard. If they were able to overcome, well, specifically my mom, pirates, poverty, coming from a communist country, why couldn't I manage my depression and anxiety?

It can be a challenge for children to not compare their traumatic experiences with their caregiver's history of trauma. However, as caregivers, we need to ensure that we provide space for our children to express the pain they are experiencing from their traumas and own life experiences.

Responding to Trauma

As caregivers, we may want to minimize the potential impact of a traumatic event on our children. It is painful to acknowledge that we did not or could not protect our child from the events or circumstances that were traumatic, and to worry that the child may never be the same as before the trauma had occurred. We may think that minimizing it will somehow help minimize its impact; that if we "don't make a big deal about it," our child will get the message that they have the capacity to move on from what happened too. But while we may be well-intentioned, minimizing the impact of trauma actually denies our child an opportunity to process the negative experience with the support and guidance of an adult, and thus increases the potential for the child to experience long-term impacts on their overall mental and physical development.

Children look to the adults in their lives for validation. They turn to us to make meaning of the world around them and to provide them with feedback about their experiences when they don't understand what may be happening. When children turn to us and share certain traumatic experiences that may not automatically register as traumatic to the caregiver, we may immediately downplay the incident primarily out of our own discomfort at not knowing exactly how to respond to what the child is sharing. When we make comments such as "Yes, that was hard, but everything will be fine" or "Don't worry about it" or "I'm sure the other person didn't mean to do that to you," we are completely invalidating that child's experience. That invalidation from the caregiver can inflict further trauma—the support and care that they need to heal and process the event is gone. The wound remains open as the tools that are necessary for healing are nowhere to be found by the child.

Understanding the profound and wide-ranging impact that trauma can have on a child's sense of self and of the world, on their relationships, and on their capacity to regulate the intensity of their behavior and emotional responses in the face of stress is critical for understanding how to effectively support a child who has experienced trauma.

Trauma-Specific Therapies

Children's reactions to traumatic events vary, but there are several different therapeutic modalities that have been found to be particularly helpful to children who have experienced trauma. In part I, we discussed some of the most commonly used types of therapy, such as CBT and talk therapy, which remain valuable interventions for helping children (and caregivers!) understand their own emotions and work through emotional distress. Here is a brief overview of several types of therapy that more specifically target childhood trauma and that help families work through traumatic events together. Many of the therapeutic interventions shown to be effective in helping children typically involve caregivers; they teach skills and provide strategies to help caregivers communicate with and support their child most effectively.

Child-Parent Psychotherapy (CPP)

This is a specific intervention for children between the ages of zero and six who experience a traumatic event that results in a noticeable change in mood and behavior, as well as a disruption in the relationship with their primary caregiver. These therapy sessions include both the child and caregiver, and they focus on strengthening the relationship between the two. The goal is to strengthen the attachment between the child and their caregiver, enhancing and restoring the child's social, behavioral, and cognitive function.

Parent-Child Interaction Therapy (PCIT)

This therapy was developed for children between the ages of two and seven who have experienced trauma. During this therapy, which includes both the caregiver and the child, caregivers learn specific skills through didactic sessions, and then caregivers and children participate in live coaching sessions in which caregivers receive real-time feedback on their interactions with the child during play sessions. The goal is to strengthen the caregiver/child relationship with the aim of reducing negative behaviors from the child.

Play Therapy

Play therapy is typically used with children between the ages of three and twelve. These therapy sessions are typically led by the child, allowing them to engage with their therapist through fun and stimulating activities. Unresolved traumas that are difficult for the child to communicate may come to light during the play session through behaviors and play patterns. Once a good relationship is established with the therapist, the child has a safe environment to reenact certain traumatic experiences, allowing the therapist to gain some insight into the child's understanding of the experience and help the child process the event.

Trauma-Focused Cognitive Behavioral Therapy (TF-CBT)

TF-CBT is geared toward children and adolescents between the ages of three and twenty-one. It incorporates principles used in family therapy and provides strategies for how to effectively navigate intrusive thoughts to reduce negative behaviors and feelings related to those thoughts. This type of therapy incorporates caregivers, teaching them strategies for best supporting their child through the negative thoughts they experience.

Child and Family Traumatic Stress Intervention (CFTSI)

This type of therapeutic intervention was developed to be implemented within thirty to forty-five days after experiencing a trauma or a disclosure of a trauma to reduce related symptoms and to reduce the risk of developing PTSD and strengthen communication and family support. Geared toward children and adolescents between the ages of seven and eighteen, it is a brief course of therapy that typically includes five to eight sessions with just the child.

Cognitive Processing Therapy

Cognitive processing therapy is a specific type of cognitive behavioral therapy (CBT) that targets symptoms of PTSD and is generally delivered over twelve sessions. It involves having the participant write out an "impact statement," in which they articulate their understanding of why the traumatic event occurred and its impact on their beliefs about themselves, others, and the world. Its aim is to guide participants to challenge and modify unhelpful beliefs related to trauma, which can help alleviate PTSD symptoms and improve overall functioning and quality of life.

Eye Movement Desensitization and Reprocessing (EMDR)

EMDR is an evidence-based form of psychotherapy that provides people who have experienced trauma with the ability to transform the meaning behind a traumatic event. Events that were experienced and remembered as painful, disturbing, or horrific are instead transformed into less distressing memories, which reflects the person's ability to cope, adapt, and overcome. The theory behind EMDR is that traumatic experiences can produce a kind of mental and emotional shock, such that our brain does not process those experiences into memory the way it does with other experiences in our lives. EMDR is a method that stimulates the brain to process those unprocessed traumatic experiences so that we can "absorb" them emotionally. It does that through bilateral stimulation intended to create electrical activity between the right and left hemispheres of the brain. During an EMDR session, the therapist asks the individual to imagine a particular scene or element from the traumatic incident. While that individual has that scene in their mind, they are then instructed to use their eyes to follow the therapist's hand that is moving rapidly back and forth across the individual's line of vision, or to listen to a sound that is played in one ear and then the other. Throughout the process, the therapist assesses the person's level of distress related to negative thoughts and sensations that are associated with the scene from the traumatic event. Over time, as memories are processed, the distress related to the reimagined scene decreases. This form of therapy relies on the individual's own ability to emotionally process the traumatic event rather than to rely on the therapist's interpretation for healing and growth. While the theory behind EMDR is just that, and not scientifically proven, the therapy has had very significant positive results, particularly for people whose experience of trauma is of a discrete event or set of events.

Prolonged Exposure Therapy (PE)

This type of therapy helps patients gradually approach trauma-related memories, feelings, and situations to learn that they are not dangerous and do not need to be avoided. It does this by having the participant recount the traumatic event in extensive detail in an environment in which they feel safe, allowing the participant to "rewire" the learned associations in the brain and overcome the physiological fear response.

• • •

Ultimately, most therapists will use elements from many different types of therapies and therapeutic models to best meet the needs of the participant. If you have questions or are interested in pursuing a specific type of therapy, you can start by asking your child's current health care provider.

For more information on the many types of trauma-focused therapy intended primarily for children, adolescents, and their families that may be available to you, the National Child Traumatic Stress Network (NCTSN) is a great resource. Created under the Children's Health Act in 2000, NCTSN is a network of frontline providers, family members, researchers, and national partners that seeks to raise the standard of care and increase access to services for children and families who experience or witness traumatic events. Their website provides a wealth of information about trauma and trauma-informed care, for families and caregivers as well as for health and education professionals.

Medication Management

Although therapy has been proven to be effective for a number of children who have experienced trauma, some children may benefit from medication that can help ease or reduce trauma-related symptoms. Sometimes, reducing symptoms helps children become better able to engage in and get more out of other therapeutic interventions. Most medications available to treat trauma help to mitigate some of the physiological responses related to trauma exposure. Medications can also help improve sleep, focus, and concentration, and reduce aggression, irritability, the frequency of nightmares, and the intensity of the body's flight/flight/freeze response. Clonidine and guanfacine are medications that specifically target physiological responses to a perceived negative threat—both flight/fight/freeze and hypervigilance. Clonidine helps reduce heart rate and breathing rate and makes people feel less tense and more at ease. This can be helpful for some to take every day to dampen that fight-or-flight response or as needed if they happen to experience a reemergence of trauma symptoms. Guanfacine can help kids be more attentive, be less hyperactive and reactive, and exercise more impulse control. It is often used to treat symptoms of attention-deficit/hyperactivity disorder, but unlike many medications that target ADD, it is not a stimulant. For children who experience nightmares following a traumatic event, a medicine called Prazosin may help to reduce their occurrence. Given that the medication can be sedating, it can help kids who may be experiencing insomnia and make it easier for them to sleep. Some children may benefit from antidepressant medications to help to reduce the overall mood-related symptoms that they may experience daily. Although these medications are referred to as antidepressants, they are also incredibly effective in reducing symptoms of anxiety. They can dampen the heightened emotional response to a particular trigger and thus reduce the frequency and intensity of panic attacks and dissociative episodes, and ease other symptoms including insomnia and poor appetite.

Trauma-Informed Caregiving: The Basics

We cannot predict how children will respond to a traumatic event or adverse childhood experiences. The trauma symptoms discussed in this chapter—mood changes, hypervigilance, aggression, physical symptoms, and changes in the child's ability to focus—are some of the many ways in which children can experience distress related to the trauma. As adults, we should be curious about what is driving these behaviors rather than take them personally or jump to conclusions.

As caregivers, it is up to us to notice these changes in our children and to validate the event that may have precipitated those changes. It is not up to us as adults to label an event as traumatic since there are a number of events that may be considered insignificant by some but may have a profound impact on the way in which the child experiences and perceives the world. And it is important not to minimize the potential impact a traumatic event or circumstance may be having in the present moment, and that it may continue to have as the child becomes an adult. Keep in mind that making comments such as, "Oh, don't worry about it," or "That wasn't that big of a deal" are invalidating and can create further harm, whereas talking about the trauma provides an opportunity for our child to develop the language for communicating their distress rather than internalizing it, and fosters healing and growth.

There are effective evidence-based treatments for children and families who have experienced trauma. Don't delay in getting the help and support your child—and you—may need.

EIGHT

Navigating Anxiety and OCD

F ear is a natural, instinctual response to perceived danger that all animals, including humans, experience. It is an intense emotional and physiological response that has played an important role in our survival, both as a species and as individuals. Fear's milder cousins, worry and anxiety, can also serve important functions, motivating us to do the things that we need to do. A bit of anxiety just before a job interview, performance, or even first date can help our energy levels stay high and our focus stay sharp. Your worries about your child's well-being, for example, may have inspired you to pick up this book.

In small amounts, anxiety is a good thing. But sometimes we experience fear that is disproportionate to the situation or thing that provoked it, in ways that tax our bodies and minds. Carrying the worries and fears that come along with being a human being and a citizen of the world can be exhausting, scary, and challenging. As caregivers, we have an automatic desire to want to protect our children from the discomfort of experiencing anxiety. However, for children to learn how to navigate this challenging world, they need to be exposed to situations that teach them they have the capacity to withstand the natural stresses of living.

In recent years, the level of fear and uncertainty around living in this world seems to have increased, in part because of our constant exposure to news and information. There is anxiety about climate change and impending natural disasters. There is anxiety regarding personal safety given ongoing reports in the media of people being harmed because of their religion, the color of their skin, or who it is that they love—or just because they were in the wrong place at the wrong time. There is anxiety arising from the political discord dividing our nation and from economic insecurity, anxiety about powerful new technologies, information overload, and the rapid pace of change. There is still plenty of anxiety surrounding the Covid-19 pandemic, which disrupted the sense of normalcy that we often took for granted prior to the virus. We are living through anxious times that even the healthiest adults among us sometimes have difficulty managing. And whether we're aware of it or not, our kids are bearing witness to how we cope.

Because anxiety is not always pathological, it can be hard for caregivers to determine when anxiety experienced by a child is reflective of an actual mental health disorder. It is understandable for our kids to be anxious as they navigate the challenges of life with a limited set of coping skills. Their world is changing, their bodies are changing, their relationships with others are changing, and all this is happening for the very first time. We cannot always assume that when kids are experiencing anxiety, it is a problem. We need to exercise discernment in how we think about anxiety experienced during the childhood and adolescent years.

In this chapter, we will discuss what anxiety actually is and how we can shift our attitude on anxiety in childhood and adolescence to "prepare, not protect." I'll then talk about the typical ways in which anxiety might manifest in children and suggest ways to help them mitigate their anxiety. Lastly, I'll discuss the typical signs and symptoms present when a child is developing an anxiety disorder that may require more targeted mental health intervention.

Anxiety vs. Stress

The terms *stress* and *anxiety* are often used interchangeably. But while the two do have a lot in common, there are a few important distinctions to keep in order. Children will experience both stress and anxiety throughout the course of their development—our goal as caregivers is to support them in learning to manage those emotions.

When we say "stress," we are referring to an emotional response to an external experience that causes a level of discomfort. There are several external factors and situations that can create stress for children. Academic pressure, social group dynamics, moving to a new home, or changing schools are all external events that may cause an emotional response. Stress can be motivating—for example, if your child knows they have daily practice for their sports team and a math test on Friday, they might write out a detailed agenda for their days ahead to help manage their time, or not linger so long in the locker room when practice is over before going home. Stress can, of course, become overwhelming and need to be addressed, but it's different from anxiety in a few key ways.

Like stress, anxiety is a typical human experience that is nearly impossible to avoid. It can be beneficial—in small amounts—in helping us gauge what situations will be safe and which ones we should be wary of or perhaps will need to prepare for in some way. If your child is competing at a swim meet, a bit of anxiety when they're on the starting block will help their body get ready to move more quickly: It increases their heart rate, helping blood get to the body's extremities, while decreasing blood supply to the digestive system. It sharpens mental focus so they're not thinking about that impending math test when the starting gun goes off. However, as caregivers, we want to look out for anxiety that becomes a persistent state of worry, even without the presence of an external event. If the state of anxiety persists throughout the course of a child's day, consistently interfering with the child's ability to engage with school, friends, sports, or other activities, this is one of the most important indicators that a child's anxiety might benefit from some additional professional support.

Prepare Over Protect

Knowing how to manage anxiety is an essential skill for navigating the inherent challenges of the world. And as Dr. Mona Potter, a child psychiatrist and expert in managing childhood anxiety, explained to me, it's good to help kids develop this skill incrementally rather than to completely shield and protect them from those opportunities:

> Jeff Bostin, MD, a brilliant mentor of mine, uses this phrase that I really like a lot: Prepare beyond protect. It's this idea of really allowing the child to explore the world and get to know the world. And oftentimes they can go further than we as parents think they can. What we want to do is show the brain that, actually, you can get through it; you can do it. So give them opportunities to do something that might feel a bit scary.
>
> If they fall, they're going to learn about what caused them to fall so that the next time they might make a different decision. These are opportunities to discover, opportunities to learn. And if we deprive them of that, then they're going to rely on their external world to guide them—they're going to get very anxious or overwhelmed when put in these situations.

Given that our natural instinct as caregivers is to ensure that our children trust us to always be there for them, it can be counterintuitive at first to let them struggle with difficult feelings. But as our children grow, it's our job to help them become able to care for themselves too. Dr. Potter explained:

> Basically, are they looking to their external environment to help them manage their emotions in order to do the things that they need to do in their daily life? It's kind of what's at the core of anxiety, right? It's fear of uncertainty. It's discomfort with not knowing what's going to happen.

All these possibilities can happen and I don't know and I don't have control and it feels awful.

Is the child able to notice what emotion is coming up, identify it, and then assess how it's impacting their decision-making? Is it like, "Oh, I feel this worry, but I'm still going to go about my day and do the things I do and I'm going to be able to engage in them?" Or is it, "I feel this worry, I really need to talk to somebody, or I need my mom to tell me it's going to be okay," or "I need to go give my mom a hug or I need somebody to do this with me," and so it's almost that they need something external to help them manage this.

Some kids may have a more anxious temperament than others, which might make them more sensitive to the stressors of the world. That sensitivity is a valuable quality, one that can be a great asset in life, if the child learns to manage, express, and direct the anxiety that accompanies it. Allowing children to have opportunities to experience some discomfort related to anxiety allows them to learn the skills necessary to withstand anxieties that may come up over the course of their lifetime. And it's better they start learning by managing the anxiety of child-size stresses, rather than the ones that come with adulthood.

Yes, it is hard for us to bear witness to our children's worries, fears, and anxieties—especially those we feel they should not have to deal with. But we would be doing them a disservice if we didn't allow them to jump into the deep end themselves to try to navigate the waters. That doesn't mean withdrawing our support. We can be there to help guide our children and prepare them with strategies they can use to tolerate distress. We can encourage them, comfort them, and express our encouragement and our confidence in their internal capacity to get through what they're going through. We can praise them for their accomplishment when they emerge on the other side, and discuss what they gained or how they grew from their experience. But completely protecting children from these opportunities does not really serve them over the long term; it only serves to mitigate our own anxiety.

From infancy, we are constantly scanning our environments to understand and make sense of different situations. One of the challenging things for our children is that while they are younger, they are experiencing situations for the first time ever. These new situations and experiences inevitably come with some fear and anxiety. The more opportunities that children have to encounter different situations, the better their understanding of the likely outcomes for any given scenario. As children learn by doing, even when anxiety is present, they start to learn that they are capable of accomplishing things.

Normal Anxiety in Child Development

Over the course of a child's development, the types of situations that may provoke anxiety evolve. This is part of the developmental process. Preschoolers are at a stage in which they are quite egocentric and can become anxious in response to situations they perceive as direct attacks on their sense of self. For example, they often have extreme difficulty sharing toys and might be prone to tantrums when encouraged to do so. Kids who are in preschool and kindergarten also tend to engage in what's referred to as magical thinking and worry about rather abstract things arising from what they imagine. For example, they may have significant worries in response to a rather benign comment from a caregiver such as "If you don't brush your teeth every day, then monsters will grow in your mouth." Although you might have made that comment jokingly to motivate the child to brush their teeth, that might be interpreted by the child literally. It can be difficult for them to distinguish what is reality and what is not—a skill referred to as reality testing.

Children who are in elementary school have had more experiences in the world and often have developed a better capacity to self-regulate and reality test. Much of the anxiety that children at this age experience centers around a fear of being rejected or not being accepted by their peers. They also have developed a basic sense of expectations that they have for themselves and can become more anxious when they feel as though they are not living up to those self-imposed expectations.

Both preschoolers and elementary school–aged children may also experience separation anxiety, becoming anxious or upset when separated from their primary caregiver (when they are dropped off at school, for example).

Maddie Stults is a college student from North Florida who uses she/they pronouns. She experiences depression and anxiety, and has been involved with NAMI in various ways for four years now. Maddie shared with me her memories of experiencing separation anxiety in particular in elementary school, and how it was amplified by an even deeper fear:

> My psychiatrist has told me that I've kind of always been anxious; it just presents differently throughout different years. When I was really young, my mom was going to night school for college and I had crazy separation anxiety. I think I was in elementary school, probably in third grade, super stressed out every time she would leave, really just waiting until she came back.
>
> It was also saying good night to my parents. I remember one of my friends at the time, her mom had passed away, unfortunately, which is really sad. And it was during the night, after she had said good night to her mom. And so after I heard that, I freaked out again. And so I would be really, really nervous saying good night to my parents because I would just catastrophize and stuff.

Yeska Aguilar, a thirty-five-year-old Hispanic woman from Miami, Florida, who currently works as a social worker, also described her early experiences of anxiety and how confusing it was for both her and her family to acknowledge and understand them:

> I grew up with anxiety, generalized and social anxiety, and, on top of that, witnessing traumatic things in the home. So when you're a child, it's like you know something feels off but you're not sure what it is. All

these things were happening in my body such as shallow breathing, chest tightness, shortness of breath, restlessness, and I'm like, "What is that? What is wrong with me? Am I broken or something?" Because as a kid you don't know. And then my parents, I'm not sure if they knew what was going on or if it was an elephant in the room. If we don't talk about it, it's not there, or maybe they thought it would eventually go away, or that I would grow out of it.

In teenagers, social anxiety and anxiety over the future is often predominant. A key milestone during adolescence is puberty, which is associated with a whole host of physical and emotional changes. During adolescence, there is a preoccupation with appearance as well as anxiety related to the changes that their bodies are going through. Fear of rejection by peers and academic failure can weigh heavily. They are starting to navigate romantic relationships and identity formation. The prospect of separating from family and living independently may feel alluring, terrifying, and sad in turn. All these things can be sources of anxiety.

The key thing to note is that children will experience anxiety as they grow, and this is a normative experience that shouldn't automatically be concerning. We want our kids to be exposed to situations that will challenge them. As caregivers, our job is to help our kids acknowledge and cope with their anxieties so they can continue to live their lives despite them, without offering to solve problems for them or take the anxiety away completely.

Mindfully Manage Your Own Anxiety

An important component of preparing over protecting is monitoring our own anxiety. As our children grow to adulthood they are learning every step of the way, taking in critical lessons from various social interactions and experiences including how the adults in their lives deal with challenges when they arise. What this means is that children will learn from you, their caregiver, how to manage their anxiety.

Dr. Potter shared with us how mindfulness techniques have helped her manage her own anxiety, which in turn helps her model that behavior for her kids:

We think our kids are not listening, but oftentimes they are, and they're watching how we deal with things. So what we do is very impactful for them. They're watching to see, when we're in a scary situation or when we're in a stressful situation, what are we as adults doing?

I have really bought into the concept of mindfulness, especially as a parent: being aware of the present moment in a nonjudgmental way, and just allowing yourself to be there and making deliberate decisions about how you will focus your attention and energy in that moment. As parents, we're pulled in so many different directions, and there are competing demands externally and internally. We have our own judgments of ourselves. It's very, very easy to get caught up in all of that.

And so just being able to practice that mindfulness of: How do I bring myself back? How do I acknowledge that my frenzy actually encourages my kid's frenzy, and then when my kid is now in this frenzy, that's going to make me worse, and it's a self-perpetuating cycle? I'm not saying at all that the parent should be this automaton that shows no emotion whatsoever; I don't think that's appropriate either. It's more about showing an ability to feel the emotion and then still be in charge of your decisions and actions.

It's providing a model, first of all. At times when you're feeling anxious, talk about what you do to get through it: "Ugh, I have to go meet a new person at work today, I've never met them before and I'm feeling really nervous about it. What am I going to do to prepare for it?" Or, as you're taking them to school on the first day, hold that anxiety with them: "I'm kind of nervous about meeting your new teacher. I wonder what she's going to be like." Give the child the opportunity to experience times of anxiety and get through it with you. Talk through the experience afterward: "Was it as bad as you thought it would be? Look at us—we got through it!"

This practice of demonstrating to your child that experiencing anxiety is normal and can be managed well is referred to as co-regulation. Returning to the distress radius model, co-regulation is one way of "locking in"—supporting your child through the experience of anxiety, modeling for them the ways in which you navigate your own anxieties. Communicating about anxiety in this way can be an opportunity to bond with your child and reinforce a trusting relationship between you.

Coping Mechanisms

Having conversations with your kids about the things that make them anxious or stressed also allows you to work with them to identify coping mechanisms—for managing, expressing, or redirecting their feelings. Coping mechanisms are exercises or activities that have the specific purpose of helping an individual manage difficult emotions, anxiety included. What follows are a few examples of simple grounding exercises to teach your kids. There are many activities beyond this list—physical and mental—that can help restore a feeling of calm. For example, your child might enjoy a handheld toy or craft, like a fidget spinner or a small knitting project, to occupy their hands when they're experiencing anxiety. They might like dancing to music videos in the living room or shooting hoops at the playground. I encourage you to explore with your child activities that are fun and engaging for them and also help alleviate some of their anxiety. The goal is to have your child assemble over time a toolbox of different strategies that they can use whenever they feel anxious. Here are some simple, everyday coping mechanisms:

Physical Activity

Teach your child how to notice signals that may be telling them that their body is getting worked up with anxiety. If they start to notice that their heart is beating fast, their breathing has become shallow, they have butterflies in their stomach, or if they feel like they have a number of thoughts running through their head at a rapid pace—all that could be a signal that they are anxious. Encouraging your child to go outside and take a walk, run up and down the stairs, or pick up a basketball and shoot some hoops when they feel anxious helps them reduce some of that restless energy coursing through their bodies, and provides them with a strategy to mitigate distress that also has many other benefits. Physical activity can be fun, it promotes physical health, and there are opportunities to socialize and connect with other people who enjoy the same activity. Both the movement itself and the social component are key ingredients for helping your child experience less anxiety. You can model this strategy for them whenever you're feeling anxious, which can really go a long way. The more that they see you utilize coping strategies, the greater the likelihood they will use them themselves.

Grounding Exercises

Anxiety can cause an influx of thoughts that can be overwhelming in the moment. Teaching your child a grounding exercise can provide them with a strategy for distracting their mind from distressing thoughts. One of the most widely used techniques is called the 5-4-3-2-1 Grounding Exercise. The idea is to have the child focus on using their senses to tap into and to be more fully present in their surrounding environment in order to distract themselves from their thoughts. You'll ask your child to do the following:

- Name five things you can see
- Name four things you can touch
- Name three things you can hear

- Name two things you can smell
- Name one thing you can taste

This exercise can be done anytime and anywhere and is quite effective in reducing anxiety. This can be helpful to people of all ages!

Breathing Exercises

- One of the physical changes that children can experience while they are experiencing acute anxiety is that their breathing becomes rapid and shallow. Rapid shallow breathing is a consequence of anxiety—but it also causes or perpetuates it. Feeling like you can't get enough air, just physiologically, makes you feel panicky. Learning how to slow down and breathe more deeply will help the body to gradually calm down by allowing more oxygen to circulate in the body and by soothing the sympathetic nervous system.
- Younger kids love playing bubbles and this can be a great activity to get your child to focus on their breath while at the same time have fun. You can have a bubble set available at home that you can grab whenever you notice that your child may be getting anxious. Asking the child to blow bubbles is a great way to distract them from all of their anxious thoughts and to focus on using their breath to have fun.
- Finger breathing is a great activity that can be tried in children of all ages. All you have to do is tell your child to spread out the fingers of one hand and slowly move the index finger of the other hand up and down each outstretched finger as you take a deep breath in and out. The idea is that going up and down each finger will help them regulate their breath. You can tell your child to do this as many times as needed to make them feel more calm.

All the strategies you teach and model for your child are ones they can use to help manage their anxiety over the course of their development. Some of them may even blossom into prime opportunities for children to discover activities that they may grow to love over the course of their lifetime. Whether that be a particular sport, dancing, music, art—whatever it is, these are all amazing channels to help manage anxiety.

When to Intervene

I have spent half of this chapter normalizing the experience of anxiety through childhood and adolescence. Ideally, though children will have ongoing worries, they will still be able to go to school, hang out with their friends, participate in their extracurricular activities, and enjoy the more pleasurable aspects of their lives. However, if you have noticed that your child's anxiety seems to be the primary focus of their life, and it is challenging for the child to engage in or prioritize other aspects of their lives because of the distress that has emerged from their anxiety, then you may want to seek additional support.

To evaluate whether a child has a diagnosable anxiety disorder, mental health practitioners typically look for a prolonged, enduring pattern of behavior in addition to functional impairment. We do not want to be too quick to label a child's response to their anxiety as problematic or suggestive of a disorder. Next, I provide some general information about a few of the known anxiety disorders that reflect more severe and persistent distress in a child's life. But if you think that one of these diagnoses seems to describe your child's experience, I caution against jumping to the conclusion that your child meets the criteria for a specific disorder. Instead, consider it helpful information you can use to generate a conversation with your child's primary care provider. It's also helpful to remember that managing anxiety is a skill, and a diagnosis of an anxiety disorder, especially early on in life, is by no means a lifelong prognosis. It's simply a way to better understand your child's experience, and identify more targeted supports for your child.

Generalized Anxiety Disorder

There are children who seem to worry about everything—no matter how big or small. Friends and family may be well aware of a child's propensity to worry and may conclude that being anxious is just a part of their personality. Children and adolescents who often express worries about a number of different things are often told by others that they are overthinking a situation or that they should simply just stop worrying about things. But for children and adolescents who are experiencing these constant worries and fears, it can be incredibly difficult to function.

Generalized anxiety disorder (GAD) is a condition in which kids have excessive fears and worries about a number of different events and activities that they find incredibly difficult to control. The anxiety that children who have GAD experience is often in response to situations or events that objectively are not dangerous or pose no immediate harm. However, the kid with GAD really has difficulty thinking about anything other than the thing that they are worried about and all the potential bad things that could happen. The anxiety they experience anticipating a given situation can make it such that the only solution they can identify is to avoid the situation altogether. And often the child or teen is paralyzed with anxiety about a number of different things, including school, relationships, housing, money, or health, just to name a few. It is difficult for their mind to shut off the worry since so many different thoughts fuel the anxiety. One of the key things about GAD is that even if there are objectively no real reasons to be concerned about whatever the person is worried about, they worry anyway. They can be a straight-A student and worry that they are going to fail all of their classes. They can be living with parents who are financially secure in a house they've owned for decades and still worry that something bad will happen and they will be out on the street. Other people can find it kind of ridiculous for them to have these concerns but for kids with GAD, it is not ridiculous; it literally occupies all of their thoughts.

In addition to the constant worry, kids with GAD can also experience a number of physical symptoms and behavioral changes resulting from their anxiety. They can have problems with their sleep, as it is hard for them to shut their minds off so that they can rest. Children who are experiencing sleep difficulty related to their anxiety also experience low energy. Kids are fatigued not only due to lack of sleep but also because the act of constantly engaging with worried thoughts generates a level of cognitive acrobatics that can cause a significant amount of emotional exhaustion. All the worried thoughts can also make it difficult for children with GAD to remain fully engaged in the present moment. They may appear more distracted and have difficulty concentrating—symptoms that can sometimes be confused with the problems of inattention arising from attention-deficit/hyperactivity disorder (ADHD). Children with GAD can become quite moody and irritable since it can be hard for them to find the language to articulate exactly what they are worried about, and they may use their actions and behaviors to communicate their distress. This could manifest in them getting into arguments with family members, friends, and teachers or even becoming more verbally and physically aggressive toward others. Other symptoms that are seen in GAD include muscle tension, restlessness, and feeling on edge. Children diagnosed with this condition typically have a history of at least six months of experiencing this level of anxiety on most days.

Panic Attacks and Panic Disorder

For some children, ongoing worry and fears about a number of activities can generate episodes of significant panic and a sense of feeling overwhelmed. Children who have GAD or other anxiety disorders can also experience panic attacks. A panic attack is defined as an "abrupt surge of intense fear or intense discomfort that reaches a peak within minutes and involves a number of symptoms that reflect an overactivation of the fight-or-flight response. Symptoms can include racing heart rate, fast breathing, shakiness, sweating, chest pain, nausea/vomiting, abdominal discomfort, lightheadedness, feelings of choking, and a feeling of losing control. These symptoms can be scary for the child experiencing them in response to a known trigger, but these same symptoms can sometimes be experienced out of the blue, and be all the more terrifying. Kids may avoid going certain places or engaging in certain behaviors because they are fearful of having another panic attack. When children experience ongoing fear of having future panic attacks and engage in avoidant behavior, the condition is known as panic disorder.

Separation Anxiety Disorder

Many caregivers have endured the experience of having a toddler throw a fit when it's time to drop them off at daycare: wailing, crying uncontrollably while grabbing your leg, begging you not to leave them there. Or you may have had the experience of dropping your eleven-year-old at their first sleep-away camp and having the counselor call you the following day saying that your child is homesick and begging to leave. It can be hard for children to separate from their caregivers and it can generate some worry for them since they are unable to rely on the safety of your presence. But when children experience what is considered to be excessive fear or anxiety from being apart from a primary caregiver, it is referred to as separation anxiety disorder. Children who have separation anxiety disorder experience a level of anxiety that is developmentally inappropriate and goes beyond what is typically seen when separation occurs in kids of a similar age.

There are many situations in which children may experience intense anxiety related to being apart from their caregiver. Typically, however, the child gets used to being apart over time and finally settles into a routine of not being close to their caregiver. For kids with separation anxiety disorder, the intense worries and fears about being apart from the adult caregiver can last for four weeks or more.

Being able to determine whether or not your child's difficulty with being apart from you is due to separation anxiety disorder can be a challenge since some symptoms related to the condition can be somewhat vague and may resemble symptoms arising from another condition. Children may complain about a variety of physical symptoms such as headaches, stomachaches, nausea, or vomiting whenever they are apart from the caregiver. In many cases, the child may complain of these physical symptoms and insist on staying home from school. As a caregiver, it's hard to send your child to school whenever they complain of feeling ill, and caregivers may want to bring the child to their primary care provider for evaluation. So, it isn't uncommon for children with separation anxiety disorder to miss multiple days of school. Refusing to go to school allows the child to avoid the thing that is driving their anxiety, and can reinforce this pattern of complaining about physical symptoms since they know that doing so will allow them to stay at home under the care and supervision of their caregiver. This ongoing pattern of not wanting to go to school can result in school refusal, a significant issue that can be really challenging to overcome.

Separation anxiety disorder typically develops in children during the preschool years up through elementary school. Anxiety related to being apart from their caregiver often arises after a life-threatening situation has occurred in the family, whether that be a serious illness or a recent accident. Children's separation anxiety can even include worries about being separated while at home, such that they refuse to or resist falling asleep. They may even have difficulty being in a separate room from the caregiver. They can worry excessively about the possibility that some major incident will occur that may lead to a separation from their caregiver such as illness, getting lost, an accident, or being kidnapped.

Treatment for separation anxiety disorder would include what is called exposure therapy, in which the child is engaged in opportunities to experience separation and to tolerate the distress related to the separation in small doses, such that over time they build up tools and the capacity to tolerate longer stretches of time away from their caregiver.

But caregivers also need to be included and supported in treatment since they have often been reinforcing some of the behaviors that the child uses to avoid separation. It can be hard for caregivers to change the way in which they respond to a child's distress over separation, but learning how to establish boundaries can be beneficial to both caregiver and child over time. Caregivers are encouraged to develop a new reward system for the child; for example, the child could receive a special prize at the end of the day if they are able to meet a specific goal relative to the amount of time they are able to tolerate being apart from the caregiver.

Social Anxiety Disorder

It is not uncommon for children growing up to experience awkward social encounters with strangers and peers. Kids may be anxious about attending birthday parties with kids they haven't met before or conversing with other kids' parents. They may have a difficult interaction with a peer that leaves them feeling humiliated or worry that they are going to do something to embarrass themselves in front of a group of people or that peers will exclude them or talk about them behind their backs. Most people reading this book will remember having anxieties like these in childhood.

However, there are some kids who have an ongoing, persistent worry or fear of a wide range of social situations, driven mainly by a worry that they are going to be negatively evaluated by others, be rejected by others, or do something to embarrass themselves. This ongoing worry makes it difficult for children to form and maintain relationships, which can then have an impact on their ability to develop the tools that are necessary to navigate the world independently as they grow older. As a result of this ongoing worry about social interactions, they start to engage in avoidant behavior, which can be disruptive to their overall functioning. This is where normal social anxiety blossoms into social anxiety disorder. Carrying this ongoing anxiety about being in social situations is particularly difficult as a child since a lot of what kids do takes place in social settings or is centered around social events, such as going to school, making a class presentation, ordering lunch and finding a place to sit in the cafeteria, or participating in sports or enrichment activities. A strong desire to be accepted by peers is developmentally appropriate for school-age kids. But kids with social anxiety disorder may avoid social interactions altogether. This avoidant behavior can result in a lack of friends, school refusal, and more negative health impacts arising from isolation.

Children who are socially anxious may exhibit behaviors that at first glance may be viewed as excessive and over the top but that reflect the child's difficulty in keeping their anxiety under the surface. These behaviors may include temper tantrums, tearfulness, appearing overly clingy to a caregiver or family member whenever they encounter a social situation, remaining completely mute in social situations, or not responding at all even when addressed directly. Although there are plenty of kids who become shy whenever they are in unfamiliar situations, social anxiety disorder is really about a level of anxiety that is out of proportion to the actual threat posed by the situation, and the avoidant behavior that the child engages in that interferes with their ability to function.

Obsessive-Compulsive Disorder (OCD)

Children who experience one of the anxiety disorders typically engage in avoidant behavior as a way to cope with the situation or thought that brings on the anxiety. The distress caused by the anxiety and the avoidant behavior both then make it a significant challenge for the child to be able to get through their daily activities. However, some children and adolescents engage in specific rituals or routines to help reduce anxiety related to sudden thoughts that are difficult to ignore.

Obsessive-compulsive disorder, or OCD, is a condition in which children can experience intrusive thoughts or images that they can't stop themselves from thinking or having, known as obsessions, that generate a significant amount of distress. Obsessional thinking leads the child to engage in compulsive behavior to help reduce the anxiety related to the obsessions. The obsessions that children with OCD experience can range over a variety of topics and can be incredibly challenging to ignore or suppress despite their best attempts. Some of the obsessional thoughts can occupy a lot of space in the child's mind; they may be thinking about them for hours on end.

Sarah Horne, a thirty-year-old woman and mother from New Hampshire who has experienced symptoms of OCD since childhood, shared with us her experience with obsessive thoughts and compulsive behavior starting very early in her childhood. Anxieties and intrusive thoughts that quickly escalated in intensity prompted her to repeat behaviors that didn't make sense to others—covering her face, refusing to sit for meals, or getting caught in cycles of action like touching a doorway or mirror. Sarah describes when her actions and emotional state finally prompted her parents to seek professional help:

> It became so difficult to even get out of bed in the morning, I just knew that all day I'd be living in fear and then just performing all these rituals to try to minimize that fear. My parents did notice that something was wrong. I remember just crying on the couch to my mom and she's like, "Okay, let's go get you some help," because she kept asking me, "Why is the light on every time you close the bathroom door?" or telling me "You're throwing away massive amounts of unused toilet paper." They started noticing little things that I was hiding and I finally just came out with everything. They took me to see a therapist, a child psychologist.

Over half the people living with OCD as adults first experience symptoms during their childhood and adolescent years, and during those years they can experience the greatest changes or fluctuations in the types of obsessions and compulsions that they have. There can be periods in which the OCD symptoms are at their peak and then other periods when the symptoms seem to have disappeared. This fluctuation can be quite frustrating since it can seem like things are getting better but then symptoms return and sometimes are more severe than they were before. Children are quite distressed by this condition given that they feel they have little control over the anxiety they experience related to the obsessional thoughts and find it hard to ignore the intrusive nature of these thoughts. Older children may recognize that perhaps some of their obsessions are not necessarily things that they should be worried about, yet still find it challenging not to be distressed by the thoughts. Younger children may not be able to recognize the intrusive thought as being about something of little concern in reality. Both children and adolescents may try their very best to ignore or suppress their thoughts, but it can be incredibly difficult. Additionally, some of the compulsive behavior they engage in to mitigate the obsessional thoughts and the anxiety related to them can be repetitive in nature, such that it becomes difficult for the child to navigate through the day without getting bogged down in certain rituals.

According to the Child Mind Institute, a nonprofit that provides evidence-based resources on youth mental health, the following are examples of obsessions and compulsive behavior found in children with OCD.

Obsessions
- Contamination: Kids with this obsession are sometimes called "germophobes." These are the kids who worry about other people sneezing and coughing, touching things that might be dirty, eating food after the expiration date, or getting sick. This is the most common obsession in children.
- Magical thinking: This is a kind of superstition, like "Step on a crack, break your mother's back." For example, kids might worry that their thoughts can cause someone to get hurt or get sick. A child might think, "Unless my stuffed animals are lined up in a certain way, mom will get in a car accident."
- Scrupulosity: This is when kids have obsessive worries about offending God or being blasphemous in some way.

- Aggressive obsessions: Kids may be plagued by a lot of different kinds of thoughts about bad things they could do. "What if I hurt someone? What if I stab someone? What if I kill someone?"
- The "just right" feeling: Some kids feel they need to keep doing something until they get the "right feeling," though they may not know why it feels right. So they might think: "I'll line these things up until it just kind of feels right, and then I'll stop."

Compulsions
- Cleaning compulsions, including excessive or ritualized washing and cleaning
- Checking compulsions, including checking locks, checking to make sure a mistake wasn't made, and checking to make sure things are safe
- Repeating rituals, including rereading, rewriting, and repeating actions like going in and out of a doorway
- Counting compulsions, including counting certain objects, numbers, and words
- Arranging compulsions, including ordering things so that they are symmetrical, even, or line up in a specific pattern
- Saving compulsions, including hoarding and difficulty throwing things away
- Superstitious behaviors, including touching things to prevent something bad from happening or avoiding certain things
- Rituals involving other persons, including asking a person the same question repeatedly, or asking a parent to perform a particular mealtime ritual

If you're concerned that your child may be engaging in repetitive behaviors or seems to be distressed by ongoing intrusive thoughts, it is important to discuss this with your child's primary care provider.

A specific form of therapy that can be helpful for children and adolescents who are struggling with symptoms of OCD is called exposure and response prevention. Over time, this form of therapy helps to reduce the distress that is associated with the child's obsessions. During therapy, the child identifies specific triggers and obsessions or fears that interfere with their functioning and works with the therapist to develop a "hierarchy" of them, from those that cause the least amount of distress to those that generate the most. The child is then engaged in a set of activities in which they are exposed first to the trigger that causes the least amount of distress, and over the course of therapy, they work up to exposures involving a trigger that results in significant distress. The idea is that over time, the exposure will help reduce the intensity of distress and in a way desensitize that person to that trigger. The response prevention part of this therapy involves the child learning different strategies or techniques they can use to discourage them from engaging in certain compulsions and to minimize the significance of a given trigger so that it is less distressing.

OCD and PANDAS

Although the exact cause of OCD symptoms is often unknown, there is an autoimmune disorder referred to as pediatric autoimmune neuropsychiatric disorder associated with group A streptococci (PANDAS), which can result in the abrupt onset of OCD-like symptoms that are secondary to exposure to a certain bacterial infection. OCD in the case of PANDAS can literally occur overnight and be associated with some neurological issues such as unusual movements and sensory changes. Your child's primary care provider can perform certain laboratory tests to detect if your child has evidence of the bacterial infection due to group A strep. Treatment with antibiotics is indicated for children with PANDAS in addition to the therapeutic interventions that are specifically used to treat OCD such as selective serotonin reuptake inhibitors and cognitive behavioral therapy.

Treatment of Anxiety Disorders

When anxiety disorders go untreated, the ongoing worries and fears about given situations can result in avoidant behavior. The process of constantly having your brain operating out of a state of fear can be exhausting. Treatment for anxiety can help children feel less distressed by fears that arise from uncertainty and address some of the physical experiences that make it hard to function with an anxiety disorder.

Cognitive Behavioral Therapy (CBT)

CBT is an evidenced-based form of psychotherapy that has been found to be effective in mitigating symptoms of anxiety. The premise of this form of therapy is to understand the connection between how we think, the types of thoughts that we have, and how that can impact the way in which we feel and behave. CBT teaches people how to recognize certain patterns in their thinking that make them susceptible to falling into certain traps. These "thinking traps" can create a pattern in which your thoughts can quickly result in negative behavior and emotions. CBT gives youth the skills that are necessary for them to change their thinking process so that they have a more positive mood and behavior. Youth are encouraged to practice certain skills that will help them avoid certain thinking traps through the use of homework that they engage in outside of the sessions. The idea is that by practicing these strategies over time, youth will naturally integrate them as coping strategies that they can use while navigating the various stressors of the world.

Medication

We have found that for most youth who are experiencing significant symptoms of anxiety, starting a medication in combination with therapy can be highly effective. For all anxiety disorders, the first line of medications are referred to as selective serotonin reuptake inhibitors, also known as SSRIs. Medications in this category include sertraline, escitalopram, fluoxetine, paroxetine, and fluvoxamine. Other medications include venlafaxine, duloxetine, clomipramine, and imipramine. These medications help with some of the physical symptoms that children with anxiety experience but also can help relieve the frequency and distress that they experience from their anxiety. Reach out to your child's primary care providers if you're concerned about your child's anxiety. They will ask a series of questions to determine whether or not there is an indication to start a medication.

Anxiety Disorders vs. the Ordinary Anxieties of Life

Anxiety disorders are the most common mental health condition in children. It's important to recognize when your child has a pattern of anxiety that may indicate that there is an anxiety disorder. Timely help and support will not only reduce some of their distress, but also ensure that the symptoms do not continue to interfere with their overall development and ability to fully engage in life. Children and adolescents who have anxiety disorders that go unnoticed can experience some significant consequences, including academic underperformance, difficulty acquiring important social skills, and the development of problematic behaviors that are used to mitigate some of their anxiety.

However, it is also important to recognize that anxiety is a fact of life and is not necessarily indicative of an anxiety disorder. Allowing children to fully experience the uncertainties of the world will better prepare them for the future that lies ahead. Yes, it can be hard to see your child distressed by an upcoming speech that they have to deliver in front of their class, and you may feel compelled to write the speech for them so that they can avoid any embarrassment. It can be a challenge to endure their anxiety about earning an average grade on an exam or that they may fail a class, and you may want to call up the teacher to mention that the grading rubric might have been unfair. There will be situations in which you feel an urge to intervene to protect your child from the burden of anxiety. However, these are the moments that, if we

get out of the way, enable our children to develop the capacity to tolerate uncertainty. They can learn to identify outlets for channeling their
anxiety and find coping strategies they can use to ride the wave of anxious feelings that will continue to come their way. The caregiver's job is
not to head off the wave, but to help them learn to surf.

NINE

Supporting the Child Experiencing Depression

C hildren are supposed to be happy, right? That's surely what we want for them. And that's certainly how childhood is portrayed in the media: a constant stream of images of smiling children playing with their peers, running and laughing, exploring the world with a sense of innocence. We know the world can be cruel, full of challenges, pain, heartache, and devastation, but these images reinforce our sense that it's our responsibility to shelter our children from all that, to preserve their innocence, and ensure that they are joyful and openhearted all the time.

Facing the reality that a child we love is often sad, depressed, or irritable can be tough. Sadness is a feeling that we all experience at various times throughout our lives, but witnessing our children grapple with the pain of that sadness can be deeply distressing. And there can be times when, despite our best efforts to guide or even pull a child out of that pain, nothing seems to give.

The narrative of the happy kid—the assumption that children live free from the significant pressures and challenges of the "adult world"—is a powerful one. Many adults find it difficult to believe that children as young as three can experience symptoms of significant sadness and depression. The reality is that children and adolescents are emotional human beings fully capable of experiencing sadness and low mood as intensely as adults do.

In this chapter, we will talk about depression and some of the factors that can contribute to it in children and adolescents. I will discuss how to distinguish depression from typical sadness and review the signs and symptoms of depression that may warrant seeking professional support.

Sadness vs. Depression

Anyone who has spent a considerable amount of time with kids knows that they can experience a wide range of big and intense emotions. Younger kids may burst into tears when you take their favorite toy away, appearing to be inconsolable about the minor inconvenience of no longer having access to it. Older teens may become irritable or shout a host of expletives your way when you threaten to take away their cell phone or car keys and may claim that you have totally ruined their life by doing so. These reactions can be intense and may persist for short periods, but for most children, the irritability and sad mood dissipate. Alternatively, a child may appear to be withdrawn, quiet, and disinterested in activities that they are usually into. As a caregiver, you may be scratching your head to understand whether a child's irritability, tears, or comments that "my life is over!"—or their apparent retreat from life, flatness of affect, or claims that nothing is wrong despite these changes—are or aren't signs that the child is struggling with depression.

Sadness is a normal human emotion that we ordinarily experience in response to a particular situation and that fades over time. When we are sad, we may have bad days or episodes of tearfulness, but we are still able to engage in our daily activities with minimal disruptions. We feel discouraged, or disappointed, or that we have lost something we valued, but we keep putting one foot in front of the other; we continue living our lives. And as we continue living forward, sooner or later sadness is in the rearview mirror.

How children and adolescents experience "ordinary sadness" can certainly look different depending on their age. You may see a young child who is visibly upset, tearful, socially withdrawn, or who may have difficulty tolerating even small frustrations. Older kids might be more irritable or angry and still struggle to find the right words to articulate their internal experience in the moment. Other kids may be quite stoic in nature, making it hard to tell when they are sad.

Depression is something different from ordinary sadness. It is characterized by low mood, irritability, lack of interest in usual activities, self-blame, guilt, hopelessness, and difficulty functioning during daily activities that persists for weeks, if not longer. Youth who are experiencing depression may withdraw socially and lose interest in hanging out with their friends, participating in extracurricular activities, or engaging with their family members. The negative thoughts depressed children have about themselves can make them feel as if they are a burden to other people or that they are not worthy of time and attention from others. Their self-loathing state may make them overly sensitive to what they perceive as a rejection or criticism by others.

These negative internal experiences can make it challenging for a young person with depression to function day to day. Changes in overall functioning in young people can manifest in changes in their appetite, leading to weight loss or weight gain, and they may have trouble falling or staying asleep at night. They may find it hard to focus and struggle to concentrate. Their energy level may be low, so they feel as though their movements and thinking have significantly slowed down. These challenges can make it more difficult for the child to get out of bed, to get dressed and ready for school, and to tolerate being in school for the full day. Young people may not be able to complete their schoolwork, and even lose motivation to learn, which can lead to a decline in academic performance. Marie, the mother from Massachusetts we met earlier, described what it was like when her daughter Jillian first experienced significant depression after starting school:

> Jillian did not thrive in daycare due to significant separation anxiety. I stopped working when she was two years old due to my husband's travel schedule and the demanding nature of my job. Because of this I spent a lot of time with Jillian in her younger years and she was such a sweet child. But her disposition could change so quickly and she could also become incredibly, incredibly difficult in a way that didn't seem to match her true nature. Just trying to brush her teeth or get her ready for bed could lead to an hour of screaming and crying. I didn't know exactly what it was. I would say that Jillian probably experienced depression for the first time in preschool, because we would get home, and she would put on her pajamas and then just want to be on the couch all day. Like many children, her depression also manifested itself as extreme irritability, and so at first I thought she was just difficult. I didn't understand that the irritability *was* depression.

One of the biggest challenges when it comes to depression in young people is that all of its signs and symptoms can be difficult to recognize. Many kids struggle with school, and not necessarily because of depression. Hearing a kid complain about feeling tired or having difficulties with sleep, or seeing a child "fall apart" and become distressed in response to criticism about a trivial thing, are not rare experiences in the life of a parent. Our children can display one or all these behaviors from day to day, or at some point in time. But if their mood and behavioral changes are present most of the day, nearly every day, and they're not functioning the way that they usually do, then that's a sign that depression could be present.

The same is true when it comes to older children and teenagers: All the moods and behaviors symptomatic of depression can also represent typical teenage behavior. If your teenager walks into the house, ignores you, and heads straight to their room, it may look very much like you are simply living with a teenager. However, if you've noticed these types of changes in addition to having concerns about their sleep, appetite, energy level, ability to concentrate, difficulty enjoying activities, feeling slowed down in their movements or restless, or changes in their overall functioning, then all those things together may signify that your teen is experiencing depression.

To distinguish a passing mood from symptoms of depression, apply the principles of the distress radius. What you're looking for is not just whether your child seems sad, but whether there is a pattern of change in how they are engaging in their usual activities and with the world around them. You may notice that a child who would typically come home from school and run to the couch to watch their favorite cartoon or play their favorite video game is instead coming home and going straight to bed without interacting with anyone in the home. A child who usually loves to talk about their friends might lose interest in attending social gatherings and in maintaining the relationships that were so important to them. Whereas they used to be able to get out of bed and get ready for school on their own, they are now difficult to rouse in the morning, refusing to get out of bed and missing multiple days of school. These are just a few examples of changes in a child's behavioral patterns; the point is that taking notice of changes in their social, academic, and overall functioning helps to shed light on whether the child is experiencing depression.

Kaila Miller, a mother of four from California who works for a behavioral health organization, shared with us how one of her children, Kenzie, experienced sudden and drastic mood and behavioral changes after the transition to middle school:

> Kenzie was born vivacious and spunky and all things colorful. She's just a bright human and she had a lot of confidence growing up. I noticed when we got into middle school that this vivacious, confident person was becoming really angry, lashing out at her siblings, pulling her hair

out of anger, hitting herself in the forehead out of anger. And she had only been in middle school for maybe two, three months.

And we were aware there was definitely some bullying that was happening. She was born with dyslexia, so that's complicated to deal with within the education system, just that alone. But I realized that she'd started to develop anxiety and then depression. And I was like, this is escalating to a point where I'm no longer an expert. I read all the books about dyslexia, but I wasn't prepared to be smacked with all of this as a parent, and then to have this elevated anger.

I work in mental health care. I know what the signs are of needing to turn to treatment. And I can see, as her parent; I can see them happening. She's not sleeping. She will not participate in family activities, and though she won't tell you that, she loves spending time with the family. And she was cut off in her room, wouldn't engage. I could see the signs. Lots of emotions, super quick to anger, shaking her fists in her brother's face, which is so just not like her.

Sometimes when children and teens are depressed, behavioral changes can be subtle, or we may misinterpret them as being responses to a particular stressor. Many children with depression may initially complain about their physical well-being. Children and teens at times communicate their distress via their bodies—whether that be through their behaviors or through their physical state. They may make comments about having headaches, stomachaches, fatigue, nausea, and muscle aches that don't appear to be symptoms of a known physical illness. Children can make these physical complaints, which medical providers often refer to as somatic complaints, when they are experiencing the internal manifestations of depression but struggling to articulate their emotional state. At times caregivers minimize or write off these somatic complaints, thinking their child is just inventing excuses to get out of a certain activity or to not go to school. And sometimes that's exactly what they are doing. But if you're noticing that there is a pattern, that a child is making these physical complaints and you've also noticed changes in their mood, relationships with friends, or academic performance, then it's important to approach your child to learn more about what might be driving their feelings and behaviors.

Another common but subtle mood-related change that we often see in youth who are experiencing depression is irritability. This often comes as a surprise to caregivers. When I tell them that their child is depressed, they'll say, "Well, I never thought that they were sad; they were just super moody and irritable for no apparent reason!" Young kids who appear cranky, disinterested, argumentative, stubborn, and disengaged could be experiencing depression. It's not that the child is trying to be difficult; it's just that their mood state, physical state, and thoughts about themselves make it difficult for them to tolerate other everyday discomforts and challenges.

Depressive Disorders and Diagnosis

Depression is a general name for a set of mental health conditions described in the *Diagnostic and Statistical Manual of Mental Disorders* (DSM) as well as in the International Statistical Classification of Diseases and Related Health Problems used by clinicians internationally. Clinicians diagnose depressive disorders in children and adolescents the same way they diagnose them in adults, applying specific criteria laid out in these guides.

When I'm evaluating symptoms of depression, I not only take into consideration the symptoms a child is experiencing and how these symptoms are interfering with their overall level of functioning, but also look closely at how long the child has been experiencing these symptoms.

Major Depressive Disorder
Children and adolescents who have symptoms of depression that persist for two consecutive weeks meet the criteria for what is referred to as a depressive episode and therefore would meet criteria for major

depressive disorder (MDD). Many people are surprised to learn that to be formally diagnosed with major depression, there need only be a change in mood over the course of two weeks; they assume that one would have to experience depressive symptoms for a much longer period. But for many kids—and, quite frankly, for adults as well—experiencing depressive symptoms for two weeks is significant. Though depression can manifest as irritability, such that your child seems easily annoyed by everything or is more argumentative with others, adolescents tend to experience a melancholic type of depression. They can experience a loss of pleasure in most activities, and become unresponsive to things they would have responded to positively in the past. The depressed mood can be more despondent, coming from a place of hopelessness. It can feel like being stuck in a deep hole that is getting deeper with each passing moment. As caregivers, we need to know that if we notice symptoms of depression in children, we should not delay in getting that child help. The symptoms do not need to go on for months and months on end. Two weeks is long enough.

All symptoms of depression are distressing for the child to experience and for caregivers to witness. But the most challenging symptom has to do with thoughts of suicide. Children and adolescents who have MDD may experience recurrent thoughts of death. The feelings of despair and hopelessness that come along with depression can convince them that their only option for getting out of the tremendous pain they are in is to end their life. What is especially alarming is that you may not know that your child is having such thoughts; you could know only if the child expresses them in conversation, in writing they share with you, or on social media you can access.

We cannot predict with absolute certainty who will or will not act on such thoughts. If your child is expressing suicidal thoughts you should immediately seek support. Call your child's pediatrician, access immediate mental health support either by calling 988—a nationally available phone number that will put you into immediate contact with a mental health professional over the phone—or take your child to the hospital emergency room for a mental health evaluation. When a child has either directly disclosed thoughts of suicide or you've been made aware by some outside means—coming across journal entries, notes, or social media posts, or hearing concerns expressed by your child's friends or others in their community—it is key to acknowledge that, however irrational it may sound to you, your child believes or is at least entertaining the belief that the pain of being alive is greater than the pain they imagine they would feel by ending their life. In chapter 10, I will delve more deeply into the issue of suicidality and how you can best communicate with and support a child at risk.

Disruptive Mood Dysregulation Disorder

When children and adolescents are episodically irritable, demonstrate poor appetite, low energy, poor sleep, poor concentration, lack of enjoyment, and/or slowed movements and thinking, and express feelings of guilt, their symptoms could be reflective of major depressive disorder. However, there is a subset of children who experience a more persistent irritable mood marked by distinct episodes of significant anger. This constellation of symptoms is reflective of a condition referred to as disruptive mood dysregulation disorder (DMDD). Children who meet the criteria for this condition typically are consistently irritable most days and have outbursts of anger about three times per week. The anger outbursts can be seemingly prompted by minor things and out of proportion to the situation at hand. Although it is typical for children and adolescents to get upset on occasion, a child with a disruptive mood dysregulation disorder has outbursts more intense than those you would typically expect from a child of this age. We'll talk more about these types of anger outbursts, what may be driving these reactions, and how to support your child when they occur in chapter 12, "Living with the Child Who Is Angry, Defiant, or Disruptive."

In order to meet the criteria for DMDD, the onset of the symptoms must have occurred between the ages of six and ten and the symptoms must have been present for at least twelve months and resulted in significant functional impairment. Also, to be diagnosed with DMDD, the child must not meet the diagnostic criteria for other mental health conditions such as autism, PTSD, depressive disorders, or any other mood disorder. Studies have found that as the child ages, the chronic irritability evolves over time such that the symptoms become less pronounced. Some children with DMDD may go on to develop major depressive disorder while others may eventually develop symptoms consistent with bipolar disorder.

When a child is constantly irritable and experiencing three episodes of aggressive behavior per week, it can be quite distressing not only for the child but for other people who care for the child. Treatment options for children who have DMDD include therapies such as cognitive behavioral therapy (CBT), which helps kids learn strategies to cope with their irritability and to reflect on their thoughts and behaviors. They learn how to better tolerate frustration and practice skills that diminish their susceptibility to being triggered by other people, mild inconveniences, or things not going their way. Parent management training can help you learn strategies for responding more effectively to your child during one of their outbursts.

There are also medications, such as antidepressants, which may be helpful in mitigating irritability and other mood symptoms that make it hard for the child to function interpersonally and fully engage in therapy. Children who have DMDD may also have other mental health conditions, such as ADHD. When that is the case, studies have found that children who take stimulant medication to treat ADHD can experience a reduction in their aggressive behavior.

Bipolar Disorder

When mental health providers assess for symptoms of depression, we typically ask about other mood-related changes that the child is currently experiencing or has experienced in the past to determine whether the child meets the criteria for major depressive disorder or for another mental health condition known as bipolar disorder. Similar to major depressive disorder, bipolar disorder is another episodic condition that is marked by distinct mood-related episodes that differ from the kid's baseline mood. However, in bipolar disorder, children and adolescents can have depressive episodes as well as episodes in which the child experiences mania, which is characterized by euphoria/elevated mood, irritability, decreased need for sleep, racing thoughts, distractibility, risk-taking and impulsive behavior, grandiosity (believing that they possess special skills and capabilities, inflated self-esteem), talking really fast, and increased goal-directed activity (spending many hours praying, working on an art project, researching a specific project, etc.). Over 50 percent of patients who have bipolar disorder present with depression as their initial mood episode.

As a caregiver, it can be a challenge to know what is going on with your child when they are experiencing fluctuations in their mood. It is common for children and adolescents to experience ups and downs, and to feel things intensely. However, in bipolar disorder, the low moments tend to be characterized by bouts of depression that interfere with the person's ability to function, and highs in which they are more energetic, euphoric, active, and inclined to risk-taking behavior. It can be a challenge to determine whether a child meets the criteria for mania; however, if you have concerns about extreme fluctuations in your child's mood that seem to be coming out of nowhere, you should talk to a mental health professional. The risk-taking behavior, grandiosity, and mood changes seen in bipolar disorder can make it a significant challenge for your child to function socially and academically, and to take care of their own physical health needs (sleep, hygiene, etc.). And the medication options recommended for treating someone who has bipolar disorder differ from those that are standard for depression.

When a child or an adolescent presents with a depressed mood and has met the criteria for a major depressive episode, the standard treatment recommendation is for therapy and an antidepressant to alleviate the child's symptoms. Unfortunately, if a child or adolescent receives an antidepressant to treat their depressive episode, the medication may trigger a manic episode, basically unmasking the fact that the youth actually has bipolar disorder. This can be frustrating for both the caregivers and the child if they were hopeful that the treatment would alleviate the child's depression. Instead, the medication has seemingly opened a new can of worms. The good news is that this new awareness will steer you to a diagnosis and treatments that will ultimately be more helpful. Prior to starting your child on antidepressant medication, your child's psychiatric prescriber should warn you of the potential risk for what is referred to as "manic activation." In addition to monitoring the child closely for suicidal ideation in the first few weeks after they start taking an antidepressant, the provider should also be monitoring closely to ensure that the child is not experiencing symptoms of mania.

Typically, treatment for bipolar disorder includes medications that help achieve mood stability, so that wide fluctuations in mood won't make it difficult for your child to function or regulate their emotions. These medications, referred to as mood stabilizers, don't impair a child's ability to experience the full range of emotions but do mitigate the intensity of the moods and the extreme fluctuations between them. Most primary care providers will recommend that your child see a child psychiatrist for management of bipolar disorder symptoms given that the side effects of these medications should be closely monitored. Examples of mood stabilizers include medications such as lithium, divalproex sodium, and lamotrigine, which can have significant side effects.

The side effects of lithium may involve the thyroid (hypothyroidism), kidney (renal impairment), GI system (nausea, diarrhea), acne, and psoriasis, as well as neurological issues including tremors, unsteady gait, and confusion. Your child's provider will regularly test the levels of lithium in your child's blood to make sure that they are not toxic, potentially putting them at risk for some of these adverse effects. It is important to note that information regarding the potential risk of using lithium while pregnant is discussed with all individuals who are female assigned at birth. Lithium can cause congenital cardiac malformations and spontaneous preterm labor while used during pregnancy. All these caveats notwithstanding, studies have found that, in addition to lithium's mood-stabilizing effects, it is known to reduce the risk of suicide as well as self-harm. It may be a life-saving medication for your child.

Divalproex sodium, is another mood stabilizer that is effective in reducing the frequency of mood episodes. Unfortunately, valproate is also associated with significant adverse effects that could make it difficult to tolerate for some. Adverse effects include tremors, alopecia, weight gain, liver problems, and low platelet count. It is important to note that using hormone-based contraceptives while on valproate can make the oral contraceptive less effective at preventing pregnancy. Other mood stabilizers that can also be used include lamotrigine, an anti-seizure medication commonly used in adolescents to treat bipolar disorder, particularly those who tend to experience more episodes of depression. Side effects associated with lamotrigine include sedation, nausea, and rash. There is the potential for developing a life-threatening rash called Stevens-Johnson syndrome that causes painful blisters on the skin and in mucosal areas. Prescribers of this medication recommend that people follow a standard dosing protocol in order to mitigate the risk of developing this rash, since typically this reaction happens when people increase the dose too quickly or start at a dose that's too high. For adolescents, it's important to know that using hormone-based contraceptives reduces the effectiveness of lamotrigine. Both your psychiatric and your medical prescriber should know about all the medications you are taking so that they can adjust the dosages accordingly.

Medications that are referred to as antipsychotics can also be used to help stabilize your child's mood. These medications include aripiprazole, quetiapine, risperidone, and olanzapine. Side effects associated with this class of medications include weight gain, diabetes, high cholesterol, and elevated risk for cardiovascular disease. For those who are prescribed antipsychotics, providers typically will perform periodic blood tests to monitor for the potential risk of developing some of these conditions.

Symptoms of bipolar disorder may not always be clear-cut in childhood or adolescence. Your child may be diagnosed with depression, be given medication for depression, and experience relief from depression for a long time without medication triggering an identifiable manic episode. Only years later, perhaps even in adulthood, will the symptoms of that other pole of bipolar disorder become evident. This is one reason why any young person who is taking antidepressants should be checking in regularly with their therapist and psychiatric prescriber.

Persistent Depressive Disorder

For some children and adolescents, depression occurs not so much in discrete and intense depressive episodes but through long periods of persistent if less severe symptoms. Persistent depressive disorder (PDD) is a mental health condition characterized by having a depressed and/or irritable mood for most of the day, nearly every day for—in the case of children and adolescents—at least one year. Kids who have PDD experience some of the same symptoms as major depressive disorder—appetite changes, sleep problems, low energy, poor concentration—as well as hopelessness and low self-esteem.

One particularly challenging thing about PDD is that kids with this condition may rarely experience life without symptoms for more than two months at a time. I have seen people who failed classes, lost friends, and were unable to attend tryouts for their favorite sport or sit for standardized exams due to persistent symptoms of depression. Time is of the essence when it comes to getting the child or adolescent into more intensive support through school and mental health professionals.

Premenstrual Dysphoric Disorder

Adolescents who are assigned female at birth may develop a specific depressive disorder that reflects mood-related changes in response to the timing of their menstrual cycle. This condition is referred to as premenstrual dysphoric disorder, also known as PMDD. Typically, in the days leading up to the onset of one's period or menses, people experience hormonal changes that can have an impact on their mood. These symptoms are usually mild and typically do not interfere with the person's ability to function. However, adolescents with PMDD may experience significant mood swings, sudden sadness, increased sensitivity to rejection, anger, irritability, self-critical thoughts, and hopelessness, as well as changes in their appetite, sleep, concentration, or energy level, during the week before the start of their period. These symptoms have a profound impact on their overall functioning and can be quite distressing, given that they happen for a week every month. Once again, caregivers can be uncertain as to whether their child's fluctuating mood and behaviors are or are not "typical teenage stuff." However, with PMDD, you would notice a consistent pattern of behavior change occurring monthly or before every period. If you notice this pattern, discuss what you notice with your child and with your child's pediatrician. There are treatment options, including antidepressants and oral contraceptives that suppress some of the hormonal changes fueling PMDD symptoms.

Prevalence and Causes of Depression

Depression among children and adolescents has become increasingly more common in recent years. Data collected from parent surveys administered between 2013 and 2019 found that the prevalence of depression in children increased with age. The prevalence of depression in children between the ages of three and five is lower (0.1 percent) than in children aged six to eleven (2.3 percent), which is again lower than that for adolescents ages twelve to seventeen (8.6 percent). Other surveys have found that almost 21 percent of adolescents between the ages of twelve and seventeen have experienced a major depressive episode, and a relatively high percentage of adolescents are experiencing persistent sadness or hopelessness. According to the National Youth Risk Behavior Survey from 2019, about 37 percent of high school students between the ages of fourteen and eighteen experienced persistent low mood.

Data has also found that there is a difference in the prevalence rates of depression between those identified as boys versus those identified as girls throughout the childhood and adolescent years. While some reports have found no significant differences in prevalence rates of depression in children under the age of twelve, others have suggested that depression in those years is more common among boys. However, during adolescent years, female teens are consistently shown to be twice as likely as males to develop depression. (It is important to note that the studies that have examined differences in rates of depression based on gender are limited by the fact that respondents were identified only as either male or female.)

The exact cause of depressive symptoms in any individual child can be difficult to pinpoint. But there are a number of risk factors that can contribute to the possible development of those symptoms, and when a child experiences depression there are usually several factors involved. There may be a genetic component to depression, but no single set of genes has been identified to be solely responsible. Still, depression can run in the family and increases the risk that a child in that family will develop depression at some point in their life.

Stressful environments and life events can have a significant impact on any child. However, for children who have a genetic predisposition for depression, being exposed to stressors and adversity can impact mood in such a significant way that it can lead to the development of depressive disorders such as MDD or PDD. So, in addition to the risk factor of family history, children who have experienced significant stressors at both home and school may be at increased risk for developing depression. Children who have experienced bullying, academic difficulties, or challenging relationships with their friends could potentially develop symptoms of depression.

Children who are growing up in chaotic home environments, experiencing ongoing trauma and abuse, and/or caregiver neglect are certainly at elevated risk for depression. Another factor that could contribute to depressive symptoms and that is unique to youth is the challenge of trying to make sense of the world, and understand their sense of identity in the world, all while experiencing intense emotions for the first time. These feelings could be related to issues of gender identity, sexual orientation, and acceptance by their friends and family. They could have to do with experiencing their first disappointment, whether that was related to their parents' divorce, the need to move and change schools, or experiencing their first rejection or a romantic breakup they perceive as impossible to recover from. We know that these stressful life events and changes in an adolescent's sense of identity can contribute to changes in their mood.

When to Reach Out for Help and Treatment

If you've noticed ongoing symptoms of depression in your child, don't let too much time pass before you intervene. Remember: Your child needs to be experiencing these symptoms for only two weeks in order to qualify for treatment, and it is possible to intervene early enough to prevent further impairment of your child's ability to function. Children and adolescents are learning and growing each and every day—in their home environments, within their relationships, as well as during school and other extracurricular activities. If a child is internally preoccupied with symptoms of depression, they are going to miss opportunities for growth.

Once you've noticed a pattern of change in your child's mood and behavior that is indicative of depression, the first and critically important thing to do is to have a conversation with your child, both to better understand their current emotional state and to let them know some of the changes you've noticed in their behavior. It isn't uncommon for a child or teen to minimize their symptoms, deny that there is a problem, or dismiss some of the concerns you raise about their behavior. They may roll their eyes, accuse you of being hyperanxious, or of overreacting. And maybe you are overreacting. But the reality is that when a young person feels depressed, they can feel unworthy of care and affection from others or believe that there is no way out of the deep despair that they're feeling. They may not want to burden others with their thoughts and depressed mood. For all these reasons, they may find it hard to open up to you. If you feel something is wrong, trust your gut.

During my residency training at McLean Hospital, I had a clinical supervisor who provided me with exceptional guidance on how best to support caregivers as well as patients who were having difficulty holding on to hope for the future. With this supervisor's teachings in mind, I tell caregivers: Be mindful while navigating these conversations of the importance of acknowledging that your child may find it hard to see a way out of the emotional hole that they are currently in and may not feel hopeful that treatment will make them better. If your child has lost a sense of hope for themselves and for their future, it is up to you to carry the hope for them and to carry it no matter what. Even if your child can't access hope for themselves, it is important for them to know that there is someone who still has hope for them. Tell your child that hope can come in the form of treatment, and that you want to work together to find the supports that will allow them to rediscover hope for themselves once again.

First Steps Toward Recovery

After discussing your concerns with your child, schedule an appointment to discuss them with your child's primary care provider. As we have come to recognize both that depression is a common mental health condition among children and how debilitating it can be, pediatricians and family medicine practitioners now routinely screen for it, and initial conversations about mental health concerns frequently take place first during primary care visits. It is important to know that symptoms of depression are considered to be primary care issues and do not always require discussion with a child psychiatrist. That's a good thing, because there are not enough child psychiatrists out there, and many of those who are accessible are not participating in the preferred provider networks of health insurance companies.

It is also important to discuss your concerns with your child's primary care provider because there may be underlying physical health issues contributing to the appearance of depressive symptoms. Some general medical conditions can present with depressive symptoms, including endocrine problems, which may include issues with the thyroid or parathyroid; electrolyte disturbances (low levels of potassium and sodium); various infectious diseases (HIV, pneumonia); anemia; low vitamin D levels; as well as neurological conditions such as post-traumatic brain injury syndromes, cerebral tumors, and stroke. Not only can your child's primary care provider screen for medical conditions, but they may also be able to connect your child with a therapist and recommend medication to help reduce some of your child's depressive symptoms.

Psychotherapy

Psychotherapy can be a useful treatment tool to provide support for a number of mental health conditions, including depression, and there are a number of different approaches that are effective. There is no one-size-fits-all model when it comes to providing therapy for children. There are children for whom connecting with their therapist may involve playing games, where play serves as an easy way to communicate their thoughts and feelings; or, if there are challenges within the family unit that may be impacting the child's mood, a therapist may suggest working together as a family in family therapy. It may not always be clear at the onset which therapy approach may be most beneficial for your child, but the most important factor in the effectiveness of therapy is not so much the approach itself but the therapist's ability to engage and connect with your child to foster a safe, trusting relationship. An effective therapist will provide a space for your child to explore their feelings, help them learn coping strategies for tolerating the day-to-day stressors that may be contributing to their depression, and instill hope that they can overcome their symptoms and feel better. For your child, a meaningful connection with a therapist, in a relationship in which they feel heard and understood, can motivate them to take the steps necessary to improve their overall mood state.

The therapy approaches that I'll describe here are just a sampling of those therapists frequently use in treating kids. Given the limited availability of child therapists throughout the country, it may be difficult to find a therapist who uses one of these approaches in particular. Therapists with a lot of clinical experience often take an eclectic approach, incorporating principles from multiple forms of therapy as they get to know your child. Nevertheless, asking the therapist on an initial visit which approach or approaches they tend to use and what they think would be most helpful to your child can provide insight into the way they work and into how they understand your child's struggles.

You may hope to find a therapist with certain personal characteristics—whether that be their race, gender identity, sexual orientation, age, spiritual or religious background—but it may be hard to find someone who meets all your desired criteria. It makes sense to prefer to have a therapist who shares some aspects of your child's identity and of your family culture, but again, given the small numbers of child therapists who are available, it may be a challenge to do so. Raise any concerns you have about a therapist's values, cultural sensitivity, or ability to relate to your child in an initial meeting. Many people feel reluctant to discuss reservations that have to do with matters of identity and values; they may believe that doing so is impolite or potentially offensive. But a good therapist will actually appreciate surfacing these issues; discussing them openly can be critically important in the process of forming a therapeutic alliance both with your child and with you.

Interpersonal Therapy

Young people who are experiencing symptoms of depression can have significant difficulty navigating the negative thoughts that they have about themselves. Those feelings can then manifest through their relationships with others, creating barriers and challenges that may be difficult to overcome. They may project those feelings onto others and defend against them, alienate others, or become increasingly isolated from others as feelings of unworthiness, guilt, or a belief that they're a burden to other people deepen. For some, ongoing difficulties within their existing relationships can lead to or worsen symptoms of depression. For others, symptoms of depression may be caused by a recent stressor such as the loss of a loved one, problems in relationships with friends or family, or a major life transition such as a parents' divorce or moving to a new community or school. The youth may feel as though they are to blame for these major stressors, which may make them feel even more depressed.

Interpersonal psychotherapy is a form of therapy that helps kids identify problems within their relationships with others. It aims to address any recent challenging event that is impacting their mood and help them build skills to improve their relationships. This is a short-term form of therapy that typically involves twelve to sixteen weekly sessions. Occasionally, toward the middle or end of the treatment period, a therapist will also engage caregivers in the sessions.

Problem-Solving Therapy

Young people can have a difficult time overcoming the problems and stressors they face since they are experiencing these challenges for the very first time. Given their limited life experience, they lack effective strategies for navigating these difficulties. When young people feel as though their capacity to navigate challenges in life is overwhelmed, they may start to experience negative thoughts about themselves and develop low self-esteem, which can result in some symptoms of depression. Others who are already experiencing depression for whatever reason may tend to ignore their problems or feel as though they do not have the motivation and energy to face those problems head-on.

Problem-solving therapy aims to help young people reduce the negative impact of stress on their overall emotional well-being and functioning through developing effective problem-solving skills. It teaches youth strategies for breaking down problems so that the problems feel more manageable to tackle. As they gain confidence in their ability to problem-solve and to address issues head-on, their mood symptoms may improve over time. As you can imagine, the techniques of problem-solving therapy can be beneficial for any young person, not just those who are experiencing depression.

Behavioral Activation

Youth who are experiencing a depressed mood may have significant difficulty finding the motivation and energy to get up and do what they need to do on a given day, whether that means simple tasks like getting out of bed and getting ready for school in the morning, or more complex activities like connecting socially with friends and family. Not functioning in multiple areas of one's life due to inaction, and having difficulty finding the motivation to do something, can worsen depression. Behavioral activation is based on the premise that symptoms of depression can result in avoidant behavior. The more a person avoids engaging in a certain behavior or performing important tasks that they need to do within a given day, the more daunting it may seem to finally do it. We adults can certainly relate to this. For example, imagine that you are feeling too unmotivated to wash the dishes after you eat. At first, this is not upsetting; you tell yourself you're just unusually tired today and that you'll do the dishes tomorrow when you have more energy. Then the next day comes, and you still don't feel like doing the dishes, and you add more dishes to the pile. Day by day, the dishes continue to pile up, and you become more upset. You ask yourself: Why have I let the pile get so high? What is wrong with me? Now the task feels overwhelming, and you may feel more depressed because you have allowed things to get to this point. Maybe you begin to feel hopeless about the situation and give up on yourself: You don't even want to think about tackling this growing pile of dishes.

Behavioral activation provides people with specific techniques to create routine and structure in their daily lives so that they are more engaged and less likely to withdraw and be avoidant. This approach posits that simply beginning to do the thing that you need to do, finding the activation energy to slowly get going, will make you feel better over time.

Antidepressant Medication Management

Therapy can be a helpful approach to reducing depressive symptoms, better understanding one's own feelings, and learning skills to navigate life's challenges. But for some children and adolescents, the severity of their depressive symptoms may make it difficult to fully engage in psychotherapy. Low energy, poor concentration, difficulty getting out of bed, poor sleep, feeling physically slowed down—all these symptoms can make it hard for someone to feel capable of being fully present and engaged in a long therapy session. A sense of hopelessness can make it seem futile to even try.

Medication is a reasonable option for young people whose symptoms of depression significantly interfere with their overall functioning. The medication can be targeted to help improve sleep, stimulate appetite, help with cognitive functioning, and improve the child's ability to show up for therapy and to absorb and retain some of the tools and strategies therapy has to offer. Many primary care providers feel comfortable starting children on commonly prescribed antidepressants. In some cases, a primary care provider may refer your child to a child psychiatrist or a psychiatric nurse practitioner for medication management, either because they don't feel comfortable or sufficiently knowledgeable to prescribe antidepressants to children or because there are complexities to or concerns about your child's case that require more expert counsel from a mental health provider.

Unlike most other medications, antidepressants typically must be taken for several weeks before symptoms begin to improve. Children often believe that once they start taking an antidepressant then their mood and symptoms will improve instantaneously, so be sure to caution your child that relief may take a little time. Typically, people experience symptom improvement over the course of four to six weeks.

The most common antidepressants prescribed are fluoxetine, which is prescribed for kids ages eight and up, and escitalopram for kids ages twelve and up, both of which are FDA approved for use by children. There are a number of other antidepressants that are currently available, which include sertraline, citalopram, bupropion, duloxetine, paroxetine, and venlafaxine. Unfortunately, it is hard for psychiatric prescribers to predict which medication will be most effective for a given individual. We don't yet have the scientific knowledge to make that possible. Prescribers may ask about a family history of antidepressant use to learn which medications may have been helpful in treating their depressive symptoms. Although it is hard to know which medication may be helpful for your child, there is some evidence to suggest that if one family member might have been responsive to one antidepressant it may also be helpful for someone else in the family.

If you've noticed that your child has been on an antidepressant for several weeks, the dose has remained the same, and you see no sign that symptoms are abating, it is important to have a conversation with your child's doctor to discuss the possibility of increasing the dose or switching to another medication. The first antidepressant prescribed for your child may not work, but do not lose hope; there are other medications to try. There may be some trial and error involved in finding an effective antidepressant for your child.

Antidepressants can have side effects. Common side effects include gastrointestinal upset including nausea, vomiting, and diarrhea; headaches; insomnia, and sedation; and for some, increased anxiety. For many children, these side effects are relatively mild and will abate as their body acclimates to the medication. Providers will often start a child on a very low dose of the medication to minimize those effects, and slowly increase the dose as the body adjusts.

One important, if rare, known side effect is the potential for an increase in thoughts of suicide. Research studies on the use of antidepressants in children and adolescents found that while there was not sufficient evidence to make a direct association between the use of antidepressants and suicidal thoughts, a small group of participants experienced a slight increase in suicidal thoughts. Given the slightly elevated risk found in study participants, in 2004 the FDA issued a "black box warning" about the risk of suicidality in children and adolescents under the age of twenty-five, which appears on the packaging for all antidepressants. The FDA issues such warnings for any drug known to pose a very serious adverse side effect, even if it's a rare one. Again, an increase in suicidal thoughts is a rare side effect. But it can be a hard one to wrap your mind around. If your child is already depressed and potentially suicidal, you may well be concerned that an antidepressant would make them worse. However, what we do know to be true is that the potential risk of untreated depression can be severe. There can be ongoing deterioration in the child's ability to function, worsening of negative thoughts about themselves, ongoing despair and hopelessness as well as thoughts of suicide. We do not know nor can we predict with absolute certainty that any given child will experience the rare side effect of suicidal thoughts after taking antidepressant medication, but we know with certainty that not treating depression can lead to those thoughts, and have many other negative consequences as well. Therefore, the potential known risks of untreated depression certainly outweigh the rare and infrequent risk of increased thoughts of suicide while on an antidepressant. Your child's prescriber should follow up within two weeks of initially prescribing an antidepressant to monitor for suicidal thoughts.

After your child has started taking an antidepressant, the psychiatric prescriber may ask for your observations during follow-up visits to assess how the child is responding to the medication. It can be helpful to prepare for the follow-up visit by reflecting on your child's overall functioning and changes that you have noticed in their depressive symptoms. The differences that you've observed in your child's mood and behavior can be of incredible value to the psychiatric prescriber since your child may not be able to perceive subtle changes in response to medication themselves. Some examples of questions that might come up during a medication follow-up visit include these: Have you noticed any changes in your child's ability to get out of bed and get to school, or in their academic performance? Do you still have concerns about their sleep, energy, and appetite? Is your child having trouble concentrating or making decisions? How are they faring in relationships with family members and friends? Be sure to tell the provider if the child has reported any side effects of the medication to you, or if you've noticed any negative changes in the child's mood or behavior since starting the medication.

It's important to have a conversation with your child's prescriber about the duration of treatment. Antidepressants should not be stopped abruptly since they can cause withdrawal side effects such as fatigue, headache, nausea, muscle aches, runny nose, irritability, tingling sensation (paresthesia), tremors, and vivid dreams. Medications are typically prescribed for up to twelve months following a major depressive episode. It isn't uncommon, however, for children to continue taking medication indefinitely in order to prevent future episodes of severe depression. Taking medication does not guarantee that your child will never experience a depressive episode again. But it does make it more likely that the frequency and severity of future episodes will be reduced.

Sometimes, a particular medication will be effective for a long time, but it is not uncommon for effectiveness to wane such that the prescriber will want to increase the dosage, change medications, or add another medication to supplement the first. If your child is regularly taking medication over time, your prescriber will want to check in at least every few months to reevaluate how they are feeling and to monitor medication effectiveness.

The Episodic Nature of Depression

For some, a depressive episode may happen once and then never again. However, more commonly, depression presents as an episodic condition, meaning it will recur periodically throughout someone's lifetime. It may not recur at regular intervals, though many individuals who experience episodes of depression find their symptoms are associated with certain times of year. Seasonal affective disorder (SAD), for example, is a type of depression that happens during certain seasons. Someone might have years between episodes, or they might have episodes a few times a year—it will depend on the individual.

This recurring nature of depression can sometimes make it feel as though you as a caregiver have failed in some way—and it can be heartbreaking to see a child we care about once again start to experience some of the symptoms that marked the beginning of a difficult period in their lives. However, I want to emphasize that you have not failed as a caregiver, and it is not your fault. It is simply that depressive episodes tend to recur, and this is just part of living with this condition. I want to encourage you as a caregiver for a young person with this condition to focus on what you can control: What supports do you have in place for your child if and when another episode begins?

If your child starts to experience the symptoms that marked the beginning of a previous depressive episode, do not ignore those signs. It is critical to learn to identify those indicators without catastrophizing—and have a plan in place for measures that can be taken early to ensure your child does not ignore symptoms until they become significantly more difficult to manage. Encourage your child to communicate if they or you notice changes in their mood, habits, or overall well-being, and tap support systems early (for example, let a trusted teacher or family member know that the child may need additional support).

Learning to recognize the specific signs and symptoms that indicate a depressive episode may be starting will be an important skill for your child. Remember that it's a learning process. Your child is learning how to identify and manage patterns in their own mental health—it's your goal as caregiver to equip your child to deal with these bumps along the road, and not to fix everything for them. You can help this process by keeping track of the things that helped the first time, letting your child know you are there to support them, and helping them figure out what it is they need as they navigate a depressive episode. What works may change over time—I encourage you to invite flexibility into thinking about recovery tools, especially medication. It's not uncommon to have to change treatment plans at some point in time, and checking in and communicating about the effectiveness of your child's medication is good practice.

If your child does experience recurring episodes of depression, reinforce these principles with each episode so that by adulthood, they know how to be proactive about their symptoms, and how to communicate their needs with their support system.

Self-Care for Caregivers

It is painful to acknowledge that despite your love for your child, the loving home you have created, the opportunities your child has had, and the support of family, friends, and community, your child can still experience depression. Some caregivers experience a lot of frustration, even anger, that they could not protect their child from stressors in the world that may be contributing to their depressive episode, including factors such as racism, food insecurity, or unstable housing. Please know that having a child who is experiencing depression does not mean that you have failed as a caregiver to provide them with a life full of meaning and purpose. Children and adolescents who are living with depression should not be blamed for the symptoms that they are experiencing, and neither should their caregivers. But if you experience periods of self-blame, frustration, anger, or sadness as you care for a child with depression, you are not alone. Research also shows that because humans are social beings, emotions are, in a sense, contagious. Living with someone with depression can affect how you feel too.

Through our local affiliates, the community at NAMI provides programming that will support you and your family members as you support your child with depression. NAMI Basics is a free six-week class for parents and caregivers of children up to age twenty-two living with mental health conditions, and there are ongoing support groups for families. NAMI also provides other educational resources about depression and information about treatment options and available community resources. In the resources section, we will provide more details about resources available through NAMI to better support you and your family as you navigate this journey in supporting your child.

Witnessing your child experiencing depression can feel like a roller coaster. Although there may be periods when you and your child both feel deeply discouraged, it is important to have hope that the darkness that you're seeing and experiencing will not last forever. You can lean into resources available through NAMI, but you can also find people to lean on within your community. I know that it can feel uncomfortable to tell a friend or someone in your family that you have a child who may be struggling with depression. You may worry that you will be judged, that you or your child will be the subject of gossip, or that you will be asked questions you can't answer, like "Well, what happened?" or "Why are they depressed?" I encourage you to not shy away from engaging in these conversations with people in your community. You might not ever know why your child is depressed, but you don't have to know why to help them recover. You need to support yourself as you do so. Talking to people you love and trust about your feelings and experiences, meeting others who have been where you are, learning about mental health, and discovering new resources will enable you to be more fully present and available for your child. And you will be modeling for your child the importance of self-care, the value of honesty and vulnerability, and the consoling truth that while the journey of life is not always smooth sailing, we don't have to navigate alone.

It can be hard to acknowledge that a child may be experiencing depression. But it is even harder for a child to figure out for themselves how to muster up the strength and energy to power through each day. You can help to carry the heavy burden sitting on the shoulders of a child struggling with depression. Be curious about and with your child, and communicate to them your desire to better understand their mood and what may be driving it. Explore the possibility of treatment in the spirit of providing your child the scaffolding they need in order to thrive and function. Although depression can be a chronic, lifelong condition, in which future episodes may occur, you are providing your child with the tools they will need to manage their condition independently in the future. With your support, they will learn to recognize signs that they may be struggling, learn to communicate those struggles to others, and know how to access the resources available to treat their depression.

TEN

Understanding Suicidal Behavior and Self-Harm

"Hey, I'm in pain. I need you to know I'm in pain." That's often what suicidal thoughts tell us, that the person is in pain. So . . . I do think opening that dialogue early, having it be a dialogue you're not afraid to revisit, and come back to, is important. I try to give people language around it.

—DOREEN MARSHALL,
former vice president, American Foundation for Suicide Prevention

. . .

Suicide and self-harm in children and adolescents are some of the most difficult topics for caregivers to think or talk about. We know that our children will experience pain and distress over the course of their lifetimes, and we hope they will learn to navigate the ups and downs of life with resilience and compassion for themselves and others. At the end of the day, we want our kids to be okay, and when a child comes to us with thoughts of suicide or self-harm, or we suspect they may be struggling with such thoughts, it can be incredibly overwhelming and upsetting. Panic or anxiety are not uncommon or unreasonable responses. It's important to know that you are not alone, your child is not alone, and there are resources available to help support you through these difficult experiences.

The 988 Suicide and Crisis Lifeline

In 2020, the nation took a significant step forward with the enactment of the National Suicide Hotline Designation Act, a bill NAMI advocated for that created a nationwide three-digit number (988) to assist people experiencing a mental health or suicidal crisis. The Federal Communications Commission (FCC) determined that this number would be available—by both phone and text—in July 2022, and is now available across the country.

This three-digit dialing code connects people to the 988 Suicide and Crisis Lifeline, where compassionate, accessible care and support are available for anyone experiencing mental health–related distress—whether that is thoughts of suicide, mental health or substance use crisis, or any other kind of emotional distress.

Every person nationwide can call or text 988 or online chat with 988lifeline.org to reach trained crisis counselors who can help in a mental health, substance use, or suicide crisis. You can also contact 988 if you are worried about a loved one who may need crisis support.

The goal of the 988 Suicide and Crisis Lifeline is to provide immediate crisis intervention and support. When someone contacts 988, a trained crisis counselor will answer, listen to the person, provide support, and share resources as needed. Crisis counselors are trained to help in a variety of crisis situations, and no one is required to disclose any personal information.

NAMI believes that every person in crisis, and their families, should receive a humane response that treats them with dignity and connects them to appropriate and timely care. You can reach the 988 Suicide and Crisis Lifeline by calling 988, texting 988, or chatting via Lifeline's website (988lifeline.org).

When kids are experiencing pain, it can be difficult to determine the full extent of that pain. We have tools we use to assess distress in our children. We look for patterns in emotions and behaviors and initiate conversations so that we might better understand what our child needs. We know that risk factors for youth suicide include having a mental health condition, stressors experienced at home, and a history of trauma, especially bullying. Stressors at home can include parental divorce, issues related to custody and legal problems, and substance use within the home.

But the current statistics on children's mental health, especially when it comes to rates of self-harm and suicide, are telling. We are too often missing the warning signs, too often failing to intercede in time to prevent catastrophe. Suicide is the second leading cause of death among ten- to fourteen-year-olds and the third leading cause of death for individuals between the ages of fifteen and twenty-four. Completed suicide and suicidal thoughts have been observed in children as young as five—in fact, suicide is the eighth leading cause of death among children aged five to eleven years old. And unfortunately, rates have been increasing over the past ten years.

The demographics of suicide in youth are also sobering. Studies have determined that the suicide rate among children between the ages of five and twelve is twice as high among Black children compared to white children. Rates of suicide in LGBTQ+ youth, especially transgender youth, are higher than that of the general population. Native American children and adolescents in rural areas have been identified as the group with the highest incidence of suicide.

There is a crisis in youth mental health, and something needs to change.

My goal in this chapter is to provide you with an increased understanding of suicide and self-harm, and guidance on how to start conversations with your child about both. We'll discuss how to respond if your child shares thoughts of suicide or self-harm with you, and how to respond if your child is engaging in self-harming behaviors. We'll also talk through when it's necessary to take your child to the emergency room, and what you can expect in that situation.

Recognizing and Differentiating Suicidal Thoughts

All thoughts of suicide are cause for serious concern. But it can be helpful to understand that there are different types of suicidal thoughts that may signify different things.

Suicidal ideation is a term that is used to encompass the range of thoughts, wishes, and preoccupations associated with ending one's life. Thoughts of suicide exist on a spectrum, ranging in severity from a preoccupation with death and dying to actively attempting to end one's own life. For example, one person may think a great deal about going to sleep and not waking up in the morning. This is referred to as *passive* suicidal ideation because it is not attached to an intent to act. Another person might be making a plan that includes details like where, when, and how they will end their life, which would be considered *active* suicidal ideation. All these people need the help of both a caregiver and a mental health professional, but the urgency of care might be different in each situation.

Doreen Marshall, former vice president of the American Foundation for Suicide Prevention, shared with us how she thinks about suicidal ideation:

One of the ways I think about suicidal thoughts—it's a bit of a crude analogy, so bear with me—is as your check engine light on your car. It comes on. You don't want to ignore it. It certainly means something, right? But a lot of people, they're going to drive around for a while with that light on, and not do anything about it. If it shuts off, it may mean that it was just something that doesn't need a lot of attention. But if you continue to have that light on, you're continuing to have these thoughts, and you're noticing other things along with that, it's an indicator; it's important to go talk to somebody to get this checked out, because it may mean your mental health is deteriorating, it may mean that you're in need of other interventions than what you're currently doing for your mental health. As a caregiver, you don't want to wait, because we don't know and often the person having the thoughts doesn't know what they mean.

So, it's a crude analogy, but just like you wouldn't want to drive around for thirty thousand miles with your check engine light on, this is not something you want to just ignore. If someone is having thoughts of suicide, it's their brain and body's way of letting them know something needs more attention, and opening that dialogue with them is really important from the beginning. It can happen for different reasons, but we want to be able to talk about it in a way that doesn't stigmatize it, doesn't make it seem like it's exceptionally rare, because we know it's not. Thoughts of suicide are not exceptionally rare, but also, it's something that there's treatment for.

Self-Injurious Behavior

Self-harm, which is also known as nonsuicidal self-injury, is a type of behavior in which people intentionally inflict physical harm onto themselves by cutting, burning, scratching, biting, or hitting themselves—any form of behavior that could pose injury. This form of behavior is typically seen in adolescents between the ages of twelve and fourteen, but it is not uncommon in other age groups, and can even continue into adulthood.

A key misunderstanding about self-injury is that it is always done with the intent to end one's life. But what we actually see in the research is that there are several different reasons individuals engage in self-harm. For many people, self-injury is actually an emotional regulation strategy, or a coping technique. On a physiological level, self-harm can literally "ease the pain": When an injury occurs to the body, the brain releases endogenous opioids (endorphins), creating a gently euphoric, numbing sensation. It might serve as a distraction from other negative emotions or a way of exerting control in one's life when other circumstances feel out of control. Sarah Horne, a mother from New Hampshire we met earlier, shared with us some of her reasons for engaging in self-harm as a teenager:

> It was something that I could control. And also, it releases endorphins. It was also something different to feel. I could feel overwhelmed by the OCD, obsessive, afraid, this mixture of feelings, and then it was like, "Okay, I can feel something different. I can just feel a little bit of pain. It's going to release something," and it became addictive for me. It's odd to say this to people who haven't experienced it, but it felt good and so I continued to do it. Even if it was just the smallest little bit, it was something that released a little bit of that. It was a pain that I could control, where all these other painful things were happening to me that I had no control over.

Another common misconception about self-harm is that it is a "cry for attention." Sometimes, caregivers express concern that by responding to the behavior, they are reinforcing it. Research finds that using self-harm as a way to communicate distress is less frequently reported than doing it for other reasons, but even if it is a way of asking for attention, it also communicates severe distress. "Asking for attention" by means of self-harm signifies that the child needs help. To ignore the child, or to respond in a way that invalidates the child's experience, will not make the problem disappear; it will likely make it worse.

Self-injury can serve a lot of functions for the kid who's engaging in it. In the short term, it can be an effective way for youth to regulate their emotions and to manage the discomfort from certain internal states. Adolescents have so much on their plates, between struggling with identity formation, forming and maintaining relationships with their peers, and trying to establish boundaries with caregivers while exploring their own independence. Adolescence is a period of time in which kids are experiencing these intense emotions while also still trying to identify the coping strategies or outlets that are most effective for managing their distress. Although self-harm is a highly effective coping strategy for many youth, it is ultimately a maladaptive one. We'll talk more in the next section about how to respond to self-harm in children, and ideally how to guide them toward more sustainable coping mechanisms.

Dr. Blaise Aguirre is an assistant professor of psychiatry at Harvard Medical School and founding director of 3EastContinuum at McLean Hospital, an array of programs for teens that target self-endangering behavior. An internationally recognized psychiatrist and author, he is also known for his extensive work in the treatment of mood and personality disorders in adolescents. He shared the following about self-harm as an effective coping mechanism for people in distress:

It's absolutely effective. And for many things that are effective, if you say, "I ride a horse to work, I've discovered a car, and a car's more effective." So, then you're going to switch to a more effective technology or technique. If something's effective in helping you in the moment, it's hard to convince people to give up that effective thing.

How to Talk to Your Kids About Suicide and Self-Harm

Reading the statistics on youth suicide and self-harm can certainly generate some level of concern as to whether or not your child may be at risk or has already engaged in those behaviors. Initiating conversations with your child about these topics will provide you with an opportunity to better understand your child, foster a greater sense of connection between you and your child, and place you in a better position to provide support to your child if needed. Despite these benefits of having such a conversation, people often feel uneasy about doing so. When you start a conversation about your child's safety as it relates to thoughts of suicide and self-harm, you cannot predict your child's response. It is hard to fully prepare yourself for the possibility that your child may have already contemplated suicide or have intentionally harmed themselves in the past. Adolescents who are engaged in the work of individuation, and on discovering or creating an identity distinct from their relationship to you, may react negatively to your "intrusion" into their private life. It is important to always keep in mind that knowing is always better than not knowing and that your adolescent child wants and needs you to be engaged regardless of their investment in looking like they don't.

Maleah Nore is a twenty-five-year-old Tlingit woman from southeast Alaska. She has lived with depression and PTSD for many years and now uses her lived experience to advocate for the needs and rights of Native people. Maleah shared with me that she attempted suicide for the first time at the age of five and now works in adolescent suicide prevention for the Northwest Portland Area Indian Health Board in Oregon. In our interview, she advised adults to pay close attention to the small cues children share, even for issues that may seem surface level.

> I think what would have been helpful is just for people to explore those invitations that I threw out, whether they were invitations about being abused or invitations about depression. People would ask, "How are you doing?" And I would always say, "I'm tired." And they would take that at face value. And I think taking the time to lay out, "These are the things that we are seeing, talk to us about it," to really push a little bit. I think that maybe I would've let someone in enough for them to be able to see that there actually was something wrong.

Should your child share some information regarding unsafe thoughts, you may experience a flood of emotions that can cover the gamut—shock, terror, anger, sadness, and anxiety. It is important to keep in mind in that moment that you want to create as much space as possible for your child's emotional experience, rather than let your own emotions crowd theirs out. This is incredibly hard to do. Your feelings are valid and important, and you need to express, work through, and process them, but not with your child and not in this moment. If your emotional reactivity in the moment becomes a distraction such that your child becomes preoccupied with how you're managing the conversation, that shifts the attention away from the child's emotional experience to yours. Prior to starting the conversation about the child, mentally prepare yourself for the possibility of experiencing some intense emotions and remind yourself that you want to create an environment in which your child feels open to being honest and vulnerable. You want to know everything. Later it will be important to address your own emotional needs and to find support for yourself outside of your relationship with your child.

Kaila Miller, the mother of four from California we met earlier, described how difficult it was to control her reaction when her eleven-year-old daughter told her she had been having thoughts of suicide:

> It was really hard to see my baby who I gave life to, say she didn't want to be here anymore. All I wanted to do was pull that out of her and take it and have it be mine. I didn't want her to feel those feelings. I immediately tried to wrap her in as much love as I could. I took a deep breath, tried to stay calm because I was shaking. I could feel this physically, I'm going to throw up, gut punch. I just held her, and I just told her that I loved her. And I was like, "If you're serious about this, we need to get you help." And she was like, "I am serious that I feel this way and I do need help."

Having your child or a child you care for express these things can be one of the scariest moments of your life. However unlikely you think it may be that your child could get to this place, it is so important not only to be ready if it happens, but to be sure to create a space where your child knows they can come to express these ideas safely.

Dr. Marshall shared some common reasons kids don't open up to those around them, and the importance of modeling by taking care of our own mental health as caregivers:

We did see results of one study where they were asking teens why they didn't talk to their parents. They were saying things like they believed the response wouldn't be helpful, or they believed their parent was too burdened to hear it, which I think is another important piece. We can also model how we take care of our mental health. We can model stress management. We can model going to therapy ourselves, and being open about that experience, that some things are going on with my brain that I need support, or medication, or help with. I think the more we can do that, the more we invite a conversation.

A big question for caregivers has to do with timing: When should you start to have these conversations with your child about what can be referred to as mental health safety? By the time we're caring for children, we have absorbed decades of messages around the importance of physical safety that we in turn have instilled in our children: Look both ways before crossing the street. Don't talk to strangers. Make sure to put on your seat belt. Smoking is hazardous to your health. Stay away from drugs! The list goes on and on. But we have not heard many messages about mental health safety nor gotten much guidance around either how or when to have these conversations with our children.

I strongly believe that it is important to start talking to your child about their mental health from the moment they are old enough to start talking about their emotions and the emotions of others, which can be around preschool age. From that point forward, it is important to talk with them about moments in which they are feeling sad, angry, or scared, and to have them explore what those emotional states feel like, both as sensations in their bodies (feeling shaky, sweaty, butterflies in the stomach) and as thoughts going through their mind. As children move through elementary school, it's important to continue having these conversations and to continue asking children to reflect on their own emotions, especially negative ones. Don't shy away from asking questions or having conversations about self-harm and suicidal thoughts. That doesn't mean that you have to ask a second grader if they want to harm themselves every day. But it is important to know that children that young are capable of talking about mental health safety and to keep the channel open for continuing conversations as they grow.

Dr. Marshall summarized it as this: You talk to them about suicide the way you talk to them about sex, as an ongoing conversation that develops over time with you following their lead:

You really want to tune into the developmental age of your child. Some eleven-year-olds are incredibly mature, and some will need a very basic explanation. I think this is part of what you have to gauge with your own communication.

With particularly young children, we try not to use metaphors, or euphemisms, things like, "they went to sleep and didn't wake up." We try to avoid all of that, because we know developmentally their understanding is really at a concrete level. If you tell them they went to sleep and never woke up, then they think sleep equals people not waking up.

And so we try to anchor it in things that they know, and one of the things young kids know is that things stop working, or things don't work properly sometimes. And so I would say to a young child, your parent had a thing happening with their brain, their brain wasn't working properly, and their brain made them think they didn't want to live anymore, so then they did something to make their body stop working. Something really kind of basic for them. And then not over-focusing on that, but just saying, "I can talk to you more about it if you'd like. I just wanted you to know that's what happened here. I'm here to support you. I'm here to answer questions as they come up."

Some parents worry that talking about self-harm and suicide with a child will actually plant the idea that self-harm and suicide are options for them. But research shows that asking about suicide does *not* increase someone's risk of engaging in suicidal behavior. That makes it unlikely that, if a child has not had such thoughts before, you are generating them. However, having the conversation may reveal that a child is at risk. As Doreen Marshall puts it:

> If you are not at risk, it's absolutely 100 percent okay. If you don't smoke cigarettes, I can talk about cigarettes all day. You're not going to smoke a cigarette. Now if you're at risk, then talking about it may activate thoughts. So, the thing is this: If people are suicidal and you talk about it, they're suicidal. If you don't talk about it, they're still suicidal. So better to know it, and know that it is a symptom of suffering.

There is no one set script to use to conduct these conversations, but there are some guiding principles to keep in mind:

Initiate the conversation with a general, open-ended question. Jumping into a conversation with your child by asking a question with a yes-or-no answer limits how much perspective you can gain into how your child is thinking and feeling. Open-ended questions like "How have you been doing lately?" or "What sorts of things have been on your mind lately?" can generate a wider range of responses from your child that offer you a deeper understanding of how they are navigating their emotions. Of course, you want to modify the language in accordance with your child's age. With younger children, you want to make sure your questions are easy to understand and to answer given that young children are only beginning to develop insight into their own internal experiences. Try to ask these questions by weaving them into other conversations you have with your child. Doreen Marshall explained how she might do this in a conversation with a preteen or teen:

I might say something like: I was reading something today, or I saw this movie, there's lots of stuff in the media about mental health right now, and it talked about how in the teen years, lots of teens struggle with their mental health. Some of them even have thoughts of suicide, or not wanting to live. Do you know anyone who has talked to you about those thoughts? Have you ever found yourself experiencing that? I think just starting with, making it kind of, and I heard about this, I noticed this, and this is something that I'm wondering about for you and your friends.

Normalize the experience of having unsafe thoughts. Many caregivers may feel that it's kind of random for them to just start asking their kids these questions when they haven't before, and that's okay. You can be open and honest about why you felt the need to start now:

The reason I wanted to talk to you about how you've been doing is because I know that there are a lot of kids who are having a hard time, and I was curious if that has been a part of your experience. How have you been dealing with things? Have you had thoughts that life is so hard that you just want to end it?

Or

Sometimes when kids are having a hard time, they may feel hopeless, trapped, and may even think about hurting themselves. Has that been the case for you?

Be curious about how your child's friends are coping with negative emotions. It can also be helpful to understand the types of conversations that your kids are having with their peers about how they are managing negative thoughts. Learning that your child has friends who are expressing thoughts of suicide or urges to engage in self-injurious behavior gives you a heads-up that these types of thoughts have come across your child's mind, even if it's just in the context of listening to their friend. Knowing that they can talk to you about a friend's struggles gives them the signal that it may be safe to talk to you about their own struggles. Some adolescents may even bring up an issue that a friend is going through, or pose questions as though they are asking for a friend, when in reality they are acquiring knowledge to support themselves. If your child is discussing issues related to their friend, don't minimize the issue, invalidate it, or move on. Use it as an opportunity to learn more about how your child and peers are discussing mental health challenges and coping tools, even the maladaptive ones, that they may be using. If your child does bring up significant concerns regarding the mental health of one of their friends, have a conversation together about what the best way to handle the situation would be. Adolescents often feel responsible for the health and well-being of their friends, but that can be a tremendous burden to carry. Remind your child that they are not the adult in the situation and should not shoulder the burden of determining what to do when a friend is experiencing a significant mental health concern. Remind your child that as an adult it is your responsibility to support them in how to navigate challenging situations. Inform your child that getting their friend connected to help is the next best step. Encourage them to talk to a teacher or counselor at school about some of the concerns that they have about their friend. Alternatively, particularly if they feel comfortable with you doing so, you can call the friend's family and inform them of the concerns.

Plant the seed and water it over time. Your kid may not want to engage in a conversation with you about having thoughts of self-harm or suicide. They may not know whether or not they can trust you to handle the information since they may worry about upsetting you, or that sharing their thoughts will lead to consequences outside of their control, or that you'll just "flip out." If you broach the conversation and they don't bite, there's no need to push the issue. Just let your child know that if they ever want to talk, that you're interested in and ready for a conversation. Continue to ask them open-ended questions about their mental health in a way that reminds them that you want to create conditions that will allow them to feel more comfortable to truly open up to you. You can also let them know that if they're not comfortable talking to you, there are other people to talk to. "Whether it's other guardians, other family members, coaches, people at their school, school counselors," Doreen advises, "make sure they know that there's a team of people around them to help their mental health."

Provide your child with a sneak preview of the steps that you would take if they were to express thoughts about harming themselves. You can let them know that you would call their primary care provider to learn about specific mental health supports that could be put in place. For adolescents, you can let them know that there is a special hotline to call, 988, that can connect them to a mental health counselor who can talk to them about some of the distressing thoughts that they have while offering community-based resources. Also, most youth are not aware of the fact that there are mental health supports based within their school, whether it's a psychologist, social worker, or licensed mental health clinician. You can share that information with them, and let them know that those resources are available if they feel they need them.

• • •

However your conversation with your child goes or doesn't go, having invited your child to have it is a victory. You are in the process of opening the channel of communication and creating an alliance with your child. As Doreen Marshall reminds us:

You can get it wrong, and go back, so if it's a conversation that's met with awkwardness, you can always go back a few days later, and say, we were trying to talk about something the other day, and I didn't know what I was asking, but now I've thought about it a little bit, and I want to talk more. You have to not be afraid to try . . .

The bigger piece is to always reassure your child that there's nothing we can't handle together. That even if they were feeling that way, and even if they were ever having thoughts of suicide, that this is something you can help them with. It's just as much of a health issue as if they had a sprained ankle, or a stomachache, and that you'd want to know, and that it's not something they'll ever get in trouble for.

Talking about suicide and self-harm is not a simple matter. But we do not want our fear of knowing the truth about our child to interfere with our need to obtain the truth. Cultivating an awareness of the risks and danger signs, and being prepared with an understanding of what steps to take if your child discloses information about suicidal ideation or unsafe behavior will make you feel more confident in navigating the conversation.

If Your Child Has Suicidal Thoughts or Has Engaged in Self-Harm

If you've engaged in a conversation about self-harm and suicide, and gotten an answer that disturbs you, do not let that stop you from continuing the conversation. First, breathe in and breathe out. Ground yourself.

Becoming aware of the fact that your child has had thoughts of suicide and/or self-harm can be a shock to the system. We already have an automatic response to medical emergencies; if your child spikes a high fever or breaks their arm, you know exactly who to call and where to bring them for help. But when caregivers find themselves confronting a mental health emergency because a child or teen has expressed thoughts about harming themselves, they can at first find themselves in a state of near paralysis, not knowing what to do or who to call. However, the only way in which you are going to be able to navigate through this situation is by trying to focus on your breath and being fully present so that you're in a mental and physical state that would best empower you to take the most appropriate next steps.

For guidance about what caregivers should and should not do when they learn that their child has engaged in self-harm, I spoke again to child and adolescent psychiatrist Blaise Aguirre. If your child has disclosed to you that they have engaged in self-harm, he advises to first be encouraged that your child felt the need to and felt able to share this with you. There may be multiple questions running through your mind: *How could they do such a thing? Why did they do this again when we already talked about this before? Why didn't they talk to me before they did it?* The urge to engage in an investigative quest by asking them lots of questions can be quite strong. But it is important to override that impulse in order to respond effectively and to understand what your child may need at that moment in terms of support.

As we discussed earlier, the function of self-injurious behavior can vary from person to person. What we do know is that there is a reason your child has disclosed to you what has been happening. The fact that they engaged in self-harm indicates that they were distressed or experiencing some form of suffering. Now they are trying to connect with you in the midst of that suffering. It is important not to become angry or to become overwhelmed by your own fear or grief but *to just be* in the moment with your child. As Dr. Aguirre advises, self-harm is "mostly a function of trying to feel better or feel different," and to be upset with your child about the behavior does not address the reason for the behavior. "It would be as if your child had asthma and then you're upset that they have asthma, that they're wheezing," he said. "Their actions are a manifestation of the suffering that they're going through. So, recognize that it is a manifestation of something that's happening to them." Dr. Aguirre thinks that "what tends to happen is that people say things like 'Cutting is bad.' Now to the child that says, 'You don't understand that this is helping me.' So, they feel judged."

We certainly do not want to make our children feel judged or guilty for engaging in the behavior. We want to communicate to them that we are there, see that they are distressed, and want to support them in navigating these difficult emotions.

How you respond to your child disclosing this information depends on your child's personal history. If this is a new behavior for your child, then it is clear that something in their life, externally or internally, has taken a new turn that they are struggling to deal with. Try to explore with your child their thoughts and feelings leading up to the self-injury in a way that conveys that you are seeking to understand and support them, rather than giving them the impression you are judging them. Asking open-ended questions about their feelings and experiences, rather than questions that convey your opinion or anxiety about their actions, or that convey that their behavior is somehow injurious or insulting to you, is the best way to proceed. "How could you do this to me?" is not the kind of open-ended question that will yield useful information about how to help them. You want to respond, not react, in the way most likely to help your child. Here are some tips about how to approach the conversation, and some language that you can use to better understand the motives behind your child's self-injurious behavior and gain some clarity regarding best next steps.

Breathe

A gentle reminder: Before starting a conversation with your child about their self-harm, remember to breathe. Slowing things down and focusing on your breath will also help to slow down your thoughts. You'll probably have a million thoughts and questions swirling in your head and taking up a lot of mental space and emotional energy. Focusing on your breath enables you to create more space to truly listen and lock in to the conversation with your child. The sense of overwhelm, fear, and anger are all natural and understandable emotions, but they can potentially cloud your ability to truly hear what your child is telling you.

Acknowledge and Validate

What you now know is that your child is distressed. The self-harm was an attempt to deal with that distress in a particular moment. It is important to keep in mind that your child most likely did their absolute best at that time to manage that distress. Granted, their chosen behavior was less than ideal, but it was nevertheless the best strategy available to them at the time for coping with the distress. A good first response to your child when they tell you they have engaged in self-harming behavior would be something like: *Thanks for sharing this information with me. I'm so sorry that you found yourself in a position in which that was the best option you had for dealing with the emotional pain that you've been experiencing.*

Remember to prioritize your child's emotional experience in this situation—by acknowledging our child's distress and validating it (even if we feel frustrated or impatient ourselves), we are signaling that we are a good option for continued conversation.

Assess Safety

As the caregiver, you need to ensure that your child is not in any immediate physical danger. Having an opportunity to see where and how your child harmed themself can help you determine whether they require immediate medical attention. Ask: *Given that I just want to make sure that you're okay, could you tell me where you hurt yourself and what you used?* It is important to note that if this is the very first time that your child has engaged in this behavior, or if they have harmed themself in the past but have now significantly deviated from their typical behavior, then calling your child's primary care provider to discuss next steps is appropriate. Caregivers who aren't health care professionals may not have the basic medical knowledge to determine if a self-inflicted wound requires immediate medical intervention, which is why having the information about the location of the injury and the method the child used to inflict it would be helpful to share with your child's primary care provider.

If Your Child Discloses Urges to Self-Harm

In the moment that your child is sharing the information that they have thought about hurting themselves, but have not yet done so, again, take a deep breath. Think: Here is an important opportunity to connect with my child and to provide them with tools that they can use to navigate this moment. The fact that your child approached you before engaging in self-harming behavior needs to be fully recognized and appreciated. Thank your child for coming to you before they acted, so that together you can explore what they need in the midst of their distress.

As a caregiver, you have to balance what it is that your child wants in that moment with what it is that *you* know that your child *needs* in that moment. Communication is key in providing clarity around both of these things while ensuring that your child feels heard. Striking this balance is important because you do not want your child to feel as though they are being punished for being honest, but rather to understand and accept the fact that they need help and support. Recognize when you feel a strong sense of urgency to jump into problem-solving mode. Sometimes when we automatically jump into problem-solving mode, we can actually create more distance between ourselves and our child rather than creating more connection. Connection, not a quick fix, is the goal in this moment. You can start with something like: *It's clear that you're having a tough time right now. What do you think will be most helpful for you at this moment?*

Starting the conversation by asking your child to suggest some potential next steps can provide some insight into what your child might find helpful in managing their own distress. They may make suggestions such as calling their therapist, going for a walk, or engaging in one of their hobbies. If they are not able to offer any suggestions then you can step in: *I can imagine it's hard right now to think about what you need, but I have a few thoughts and suggestions.*

If Your Child Discloses Thoughts of Suicide

No caregiver wants to have this conversation. At the same time, it is an absolute blessing that you've created a dynamic between you and your child such that they felt comfortable to approach you with this information before acting on such thoughts. If your child has shared this information with you, thank them for providing you with an opportunity to step in to support them. Tell them how glad you are that they decided to share the burden of carrying such intense, scary thoughts. Your child needs to know that they matter to you, at a time when they believe that their life no longer matters. Don't take for granted that they know this, and don't take it personally that they can't see at this moment the million ways in which you have expressed how much you love them in the past. Convey your love, support, and appreciation for the amazing human being that they are immediately after they disclose the fact that they have had thoughts of suicide.

After you have communicated to your child that you love them and know that their life has purpose and meaning and are thinking about what to say next, Dr. Aguirre provided a helpful framework for assessing the most appropriate response to your child, in light of your child's mental health and any previous history of expressing thoughts of suicide. There are three things to consider: (1) Always take it seriously; (2) if this is their way of communicating distress, then there is an opportunity to teach better communication; and (3) if expressing thoughts of suicide is a chronic problem, assess whether or not there is a change in what the child is saying or in how they are saying it. Another point that Dr. Aguirre makes is the importance of considering whether your child has a genuine desire to die or is saying that they are suicidal as a way of communicating distress that they don't know how to process or endure:

> Number one, I always take a kid's statement that they want to kill themselves seriously. Kids don't want to be in hospitals or emergency rooms,

by and large. So, if the statement is true, they have to be seen by a mental health professional. If the statement has a communication function, which is like, "Oh, this person broke up with me. I'm going to kill myself," meaning "I'm feeling very sad, can someone just soothe me?" then what I do is to tell the kid we need more precision and language. Rather than saying, "I'm going to kill myself," you might say, "I have this thought, but what I really need is to be with someone."

If your child is expressing suicidal thoughts for the first time, then that represents a pretty significant change from their baseline: It is a clear signal of distress. Something is going on that is overwhelming their capacity to cope such that suicide is the only option that they are able to consider in the moment. They would benefit from meeting with a mental health professional for evaluation. You should consider calling your pediatrician for immediate guidance. If you're unable to connect with your pediatrician in short order, then you should bring the child to a hospital emergency room.

If a child or teen has recently experienced an acute stressor, such as a death or major crisis in the family, a major disappointment academically, not making a sports team, or a romantic letdown, and says that they have suicidal thoughts in that context, the mention of suicide may be a tool they are using to convey the significance of the distress and pain that they are carrying. The statement immediately captures your attention; the words are quickly processed by you and others as signifying the worst possible emotional state to be in, which is what the child might be feeling in the moment. However, as caregivers, it is important to teach our children that there are other ways in which they can more effectively communicate by using more precise language to describe their emotional experience.

For a child or adolescent, it can take a lot of effort to take a step back, reflect on your intense emotions in the moment, and find the right words to communicate to other people how you're feeling. Being able to do this is a skill. We as caregivers need to teach our kids that it is a skill, and show them how to do it; and ultimately, how to do it in such a way that doesn't feel so effortful. Having more facility with this skill will give them more confidence that they can communicate the full extent of their distress to their caregivers, without actually creating more distress for themselves and those around them.

Although we've been discussing some of the steps to take if your child discloses thoughts of suicide, the truth is that you can't predict how you will respond in the moment. You can attempt to prepare yourself, which you have already done by reading this chapter, but when you receive news like this from your child, your feelings have a life of their own.

It goes without saying that our natural instinct is to protect our children. For many caregivers, there is a lot of uncertainty as to what could potentially happen if other people know that your child is suicidal. You can worry about how others will respond if you do not seek out mental health support immediately after your child discloses thoughts of suicide. Or, if you bring your child for evaluation of their suicidal thoughts, that the person evaluating your child may think it's in the child's best interest if they are sent off to inpatient treatment. In the moment that your child is telling you that they want to end their life, you want them to be as close to you as possible. Exposing yourself to the possibility that there will be more distance between you and your child at an incredibly vulnerable time can feel like the complete opposite of what you want to do. This is what Kaila Miller, the mom from California whose eleven-year-old daughter told her she was having thoughts about suicide, experienced:

> There is nothing scarier than going through your mind and going, okay, if I take her to the ER, they're going to take her from me. If we go to outpatient therapy, she's going to tell them she has suicidal ideation. They're going to force me to take her to the ER. They're going to take her from me. So every path leads in my mind as a parent to my child being taken from me because I'm protecting myself. I'm protecting my

kid at this point. My brain just is in protection mode. There was a part of me that was like, maybe I didn't hear it. Maybe I didn't hear it right. Let's pretend it didn't happen because it's easier to pretend and be like, you don't mean it. It's easier to be like, this is not real.

And that's it. It is real. My message to parents: It is real. It is happening. And if they're telling you that, listen to them. This is not a time to be worried about them being taken from you or anything like that.

It is important to recognize the fear that you may experience in response to the uncertainty about how the mental health professionals will respond to your child. But as Kaila said, you have to remind yourself that you need to act since the distress that your child is experiencing is part of reality. You can't deny its existence despite how much you want to believe that it is not true.

Moving Forward in the Aftermath

These are major moments: Your child has experienced unsafe thoughts that you are now fully aware of. How do you move forward? Some logistical steps for moving forward include talking to your child's primary care provider about mental health resources that can teach your child other skills and strategies that they can use. Your child may need the help of a hospital emergency room, inpatient hospitalization, or outpatient programs and services. Mental health professionals can certainly provide concrete tools for how to navigate the aftermath of having a child who has expressed unsafe thoughts.

But things are forever changed after you and your child have gone through this experience. The dynamic between the two of you may feel different. Your anxiety level may be high as you constantly assess your child's safety, monitor their emotional state, and track their every move. It can feel like a lot to bear, and you may feel a deep desire to have everything go back to the way it was before. The experience can rock your confidence that your child will be okay doing things on their own, or that they can handle significant stressors, out of concern that it may be detrimental to their mental health. Children and adolescents still need your unconditional love and support, but at the same time, they also need to have opportunities to take steps forward in their own development, learn how to communicate their feelings and needs more effectively, and fully integrate the tools they learn in their emotional healing—including those supplied through therapy and medications.

You need time to integrate a new level of awareness about your child and their needs and come to terms with a new sense of vulnerability. Your child may instantly begin to heal after they communicate their distress to you, but the likelihood is that you are beginning a journey that will have its good days and its bumpy ones. That doesn't mean there is catastrophe ahead. Your child is still growing, and you are still learning how best to support them.

The mother and Family-to-Family class graduate from Santa Barbara County, California, whom we met in chapter 3, talked with me about her own journey with her daughter, who lives with borderline personality disorder:

There are times when the dysregulation happens so fast that she can't catch herself, and then we have emergencies. So yeah, you never know when that's going to happen. I knew she was depressed; she'd broken up with her boyfriend, and in that moment she was having a conversation that didn't go well, and she was looking around her room, and she's like, "I know I've got something in here." And she found the Tylenol and just started taking them while she was on the phone. So I was in the house, my husband was in the house. I mean, you feel like an idiot because you didn't know how bad it was. She didn't talk about having a plan. To me it seemed really impulsive, although now she says, "I'd been planning to kill myself for weeks."

But the old mom would've been questioning, judging, "Why did you do this? Now you're going to fail." There would've been a lot of judgment and a lot of like, "I don't understand, what did we do wrong?"

More criticism and more questioning her when she wasn't ready to talk about anything. I can't imagine how hard it would be to take all those pills and then be like, "Oh my gosh, I just tried to kill myself. I need to call the cops." I don't know how hard that would be, so I don't have any right to question her.

I felt horrible that she's feeling this sad when we're all living under the same roof, and she can't talk to us about how sad she is, or we weren't picking up on it. I mean, I knew that she was sad, I definitely knew that she was depressed, I knew that things were not great, but it's so hard not to say the wrong thing because you don't know what the wrong thing is.

Joseline Castaños is a Latina mother of two and has been an educator for decades. She told me she was blessed to find NAMI at a time when she needed it most to support her teenage daughter through severe mental illness, and now volunteers with NAMI to help other parents and youth. Joseline talked about her struggles with whether or not to trust her daughter Raquel, who had been cutting herself:

I think one of the things that happened over time is that Raquel and I got closer, but it was not easy to get there. There were a lot of issues with trust. Because I think at first, I went 100 miles the other way. The door came down from her room, all the meds got locked up. For two years. I walked around with the key to the doors where everything was on a bracelet. Every time I wanted a knife, I would get the knife out of the drawer and lock it back up. It became such a habit. We got a metal file cabinet, put it in the kitchen, and everything went in there, all the meds, everything, including her own meds that we would give her every day. I so wanted to trust her. And mistakenly, sometimes I thought, *Well, I need to trust her*. I don't have to check her. Lo and behold, she starts "cheeking" them and one day takes all those meds. So that becomes a whole other issue of trust and just this battle of a relationship where, "I want to trust you, Raquel. I want to be here for you, but I can't trust you because I want you to be safe." Because then starts the, "I need to check you to see if you're cutting." And her going, "Mom, that's degrading when already I feel self-conscious about my body."

If Your Child Attempts Suicide

If your child has attempted suicide, this is a true mental health emergency. You need to bring them to the emergency room for a mental health evaluation right away. Yes, you will be filled with a lot of big emotions right in that moment, but the most important thing in that moment is your child's safety and to respond with urgency.

Your child may not be fully forthcoming about all the events that led up to the suicide attempt or the methods that they might have used as part of the attempt. There are children and adolescents who ingest various substances such as prescription medication, alcohol, drugs, or household chemicals as part of their attempt. Bringing the child to the emergency room will ensure that a full medical workup takes place to rule out the possibility of such an ingestion and that your child receives proper medical intervention if that is the case.

Another function of having your child in the emergency room is for safety and containment. Although you may feel relieved that the suicide attempt was not completed, simply moving on and not getting the child immediate mental health supports is dangerous. Youth who have attempted suicide and were unsuccessful are likely to continue to have thoughts of suicide and may attempt it again sometime in the future. To mitigate that potential risk, bring the child to the emergency room, or call 911 where you will get guidance regarding next steps.

Upon arrival in the emergency room, a triage nurse will ask you what brought you to the hospital. Please know that it is okay to say that you have brought your child to the emergency room to be evaluated following a suicide attempt. A lot of people believe that the emergency room is only for medical emergencies, but a mental health emergency such as a suicide attempt *is* a medical emergency that warrants immediate intervention. Emergency room personnel are accustomed to asking questions about suicide or self-harm. Please be forthcoming in answering their questions about what happened to your child.

Some caregivers may lack trust in the medical system because of ongoing inequities and discrimination within that system. They may have concerns that emergency room staff will get the Department of Children and Families (DCF) or Child Protective Services (CPS) involved when a child attempts suicide. That should not be the case if there are no concerns regarding any form of abuse and neglect on your part.

Some caregivers may worry about the judgment of hospital staff if they learn that your child's suicide attempt occurred under your watch. They may have concerns that people will assume that they are a bad caregiver or that they did something wrong. Sometimes in the moment it may feel as though it is all about you and everything that you did and didn't do, but really in the midst of a mental health emergency, following a suicide attempt, everyone's priority in the emergency room is the safety of your child, and meeting your child's immediate needs.

While in the emergency room, your child will be closely supervised by staff. The majority of youth who present to the emergency room following a suicide attempt will have someone on staff, commonly referred to as a "sitter" literally sitting by their bed to make sure that they do not engage in any unsafe behaviors, including running away. You and your child may feel like this level of monitoring, which differs significantly from what you'd experience going to the emergency room for a medical issue, is somewhat invasive. Children may be asked to change into hospital pajamas and to remove footwear with laces. Additionally, they may not have access to the belongings that they came to the hospital with, including their cell phone. All these measures are put in place to ensure the child's safety.

The third function of the emergency room is to determine the appropriate level of mental health care that your child should receive in light of the events that brought them there. After your child has been medically evaluated by a member of the emergency medicine team, a mental health clinician will meet with you and your child to ask specific questions regarding their behavioral and mood state prior to their arrival. They will also ask for more specific details about the events that led you to the ER. It can at times feel as though you are repeating the same story to everyone while you're in the emergency room, but everyone who is asking you these questions is asking them through a very specific lens. The emergency room physician, physician assistant, or nurse practitioner is asking questions to evaluate for any underlying medical issues, which include ingestion of substances and drug use. They will assess your child's vital signs and may perform basic blood tests, which include checking electrolytes, complete blood cell count, and thyroid levels. This medical evaluation is to ensure that there are no underlying medical problems that may be contributing to your child's behavior and mood state.

The mental health clinician is specifically trained to assess for any acute mental health concerns. In the emergency room, clinicians will ask questions of both you and your child. They rely quite heavily on your report as the caregiver since you are the one with a firm understanding of your child's typical behavior. They will ask more detailed questions about your child's mental health history, have you describe how your child typically behaves, and ask you to reflect on any changes that you have noticed recently. They are using this information to determine if there is an underlying mental health condition as well as to determine the appropriate level of care your child should receive.

If your child is an adolescent, the mental health clinician will most likely ask to interview your child privately. This can be challenging for a caregiver since you won't know all the details of what your child disclosed to the clinician; however, allowing your child to have that individual time to fully tell their story to a mental health professional is crucial. There may be details that your child did not feel comfortable sharing with you, and those details may give the clinician further insight into your child's mental health.

It can also be challenging to be in the emergency room following a suicide attempt or any other mental health emergency if the wait feels too long or if you no longer think that your child needs evaluation, because you can't simply change your mind and take the child home. Once you're there for this reason, you cannot leave until the mental health clinician has determined the appropriate next step for your child. The main determination that the mental health clinician is making is whether or not your child is safe to go home, whether they can go home but should be referred to a partial hospitalization program (PHP) or an intensive outpatient program (IOP) for intensive therapy, or whether they need to be admitted to an inpatient psychiatric hospital. This is the main decision that you are waiting for while in the emergency room. This process can take many hours in most emergency rooms so be prepared to wait.

Please note that clinicians in the emergency room do not typically write prescriptions for psychiatric medications that can be started after you leave the ER, nor do they provide therapy or simply just "talk" to your child. At the end of the day, going to the ER is about ensuring your child's safety and connecting them with the appropriate level of care so that they can stay safe.

If the ER staff determine that your child should be admitted to a hospital, then your child will be waiting in the emergency room until an inpatient child psychiatric bed is available. Unfortunately, there is a widespread shortage of available pediatric inpatient psychiatric beds across the country. There is also a limited number of child psychiatrists and pediatric psychiatric prescribers to meet the growing need. Due to this fact as well as other issues surrounding financial challenges that have plagued the medical system, children can wait in the emergency room for many days just waiting to be transferred to a psychiatric hospital.

It is important to know that even while your child is waiting for transfer to an inpatient unit, they most likely will not be receiving significant mental health treatment such as individual therapy and medication management. You will just be waiting to receive word about which hospital your child will be transferred to for ongoing care. Once your child has made it to an inpatient psychiatric unit, that is where they will start individual and group therapy as well as medication management if indicated.

An inpatient psychiatric admission allows for mental health providers to perform an extensive evaluation in order to obtain diagnostic clarity as to what might have contributed to your child's suicide attempt or their particular mental health emergency. The goal of the admission is for safety, containment, and stabilization. Not all the issues that your child may be experiencing will be resolved during the inpatient stay. The hospital admission really serves as a starting point for determining the types of intervention that the child will benefit from. Most of the work of therapy will take place in an outpatient setting.

No caregiver wants to go through this experience of seeing their child in the midst of a mental health crisis. This is incredibly hard and painful. The pain can also endure way beyond the crisis itself. My hope is that, by hearing these stories of other caregivers, you know that others have been through the same experience and have been able to come out the other side. You, too, can get through this with your child. There are known supports and resources that are available to help you and your child manage the intense emotions that may lead to suicidal behavior and self-harm. Help is in sight.

Dialectical Behavioral Therapy

Coping with really intense and big emotions can be a challenge for anyone. For some, contemplating suicide and engaging in self-harm is a way to cope with distress when it seems as though there are no other effective options. That can certainly be the case for children and adolescents, who have just begun developing the skills required to navigate big emotions. Dialectical behavioral therapy, also known as DBT, is an evidence-based form of psychotherapy that effectively equips kids with a useful set of those skills. DBT was developed by psychologist Marsha Linehan, who struggled with suicidality herself as a young person. It has been found to significantly reduce suicidal behavior, deliberate self-harm, impulsivity, and anger. This treatment focuses on emotions and provides a structured approach for how to recognize, understand, label, and regulate their emotions while also acknowledging the person's emotional reactions and problematic behaviors that can arise in response to difficult situations.

The full DBT experience includes weekly individual therapy, group therapy with skills training, and individual coaching to provide real-time support during challenging moments. The four basic skills that DBT emphasizes are mindfulness, distress tolerance, interpersonal effectiveness, and emotion regulation. These skills are certainly beneficial for children and adolescents to develop as they learn how to cope with difficult moments and challenging situations while also maintaining positive relationships with others.

Dr. Linehan developed DBT initially to treat people with borderline personality disorder, a condition that reflects a pervasive pattern of difficulty regulating emotions. People with borderline personality disorder experience intense anger, significant mood reactivity in the face of distress, impulsivity, and unstable and intense interpersonal relationships, as well as chronic feelings of emptiness, unstable self-image, and a fear of abandonment. They may have recurrent suicidal behavior and may engage in self-harm as a way to cope with their distress. However, the skills provided through DBT can also be beneficial for people who are living with a number of different conditions including PTSD, anxiety, depression, eating disorders, and substance use disorders. DBT for Children (DBT-C) is available for children between the ages of six and twelve, and adolescents thirteen years and up can be enrolled in traditional DBT.

The meaning of the word *dialectical*, and the essential theory behind the therapy, is that there needs to be a balance between acceptance and acknowledgment of the need for change, both in the therapist's approach to the patient and in the patient's approach to living. Dr. Linehan found that therapeutic strategies that focused solely on the patient's need to change their thoughts and behaviors could make patients experiencing intense emotional distress feel invalidated, that they were being criticized for how they felt and who they were, and thus make them more likely to end the therapy than to engage in it. She sought to develop a treatment that would convey acceptance, and coach the patient to accept themselves, their thoughts and feelings, other people, and the world as it was. In that acceptance begins awareness of the need to change and willingness to work toward new ways of being and behaving. Acceptance and acknowledgment of the need for change can seem like polar opposites, but both can be true at the same time. For example: "There's no way of changing what happened in the past when you really disappointed me. And I want to interact with you now in a way that will sustain rather than destroy our relationship." During DBT sessions, as Dr. Alexander Chapman describes it, the therapist works on providing a balance of acceptance and validation (focusing on radical acceptance, tolerating distress, and mindfulness of current emotional and sensory experiences) with problem-solving/behavior-change strategies.

The four core skills of DBT can be helpful to us all. Here is a summary of what they are and why they matter:

Mindfulness: emphasizes the importance of being present in the moment and slowing things down. Being mindful allows one to focus inward and to reflect on one's own thoughts, emotions, and bodily sensations in that moment without judgment. Mindfulness creates some space between your automatic negative thoughts or uncomfortable feelings, and your reactions to them, allowing you to slow down and use skills to better tolerate the moment rather than react in an impulsive way. Through deep breathing and being mindful of your breath, or observing and focusing on objects in the surrounding environment, one becomes more grounded in the reality of the current moment, and less embroiled in one's own distressing thoughts.

Emotion regulation: This is an essential skill that helps people to recognize the emotions that they are experiencing in the moment and take actionable steps to keep negative emotions from inciting negative outcomes. Strategies that are used in emotion regulation include "opposite action," or balancing emotional urges. You may have noticed that when you are angry you want to lash out by yelling or throwing objects, however with "opposite action," you identify the feeling, and you do the complete opposite of that. So instead of lashing out, instead take a step back and remove yourself from the situation. This can be so hard to do in the moment! But practice, when the circumstances are less charged and the emotion less intense, can help.

Interpersonal effectiveness: Navigating relationships can be especially tricky when you're experiencing intense emotions or interacting with someone who can be challenging. This DBT skill focuses on being aware of boundaries within relationships, how to assert yourself in an effective manner such that you can maintain positive relationships, and how to be attentive and mindful while listening to others.

Distress tolerance: This is a core skill that focuses on how to navigate situations that may elicit intense emotional responses. These skills are invaluable for everyone given that we will all inevitably encounter difficult moments in life and need to identify ways in which we can cope. Distress tolerance skills focus on the use of distracting techniques, grounding yourself so that you can reconnect to the present moment rather than focusing on the past or future, identifying signals that you may be on the verge of an emotional crisis in the moment, and being able to weigh the pros and cons to not responding to a situation in an effective way.

The TIPP Technique

One effective strategy that is often used to enhance distress tolerance is using the TIPP technique. TIPP is an acronym that stands for temperature, intense exercise, paced breathing, and progressive muscle relaxation. The mind/body connection is strong, particularly when one is consumed with overwhelming emotions and feelings; there often is a physiological response within the body that further intensifies the overall experience of the given situation. These skills allow people to quickly alter their body's physiology so as to better tolerate the distress within that moment.

Temperature: There is data to support the fact that reducing yourself to cooler temperatures can actually work to lower your heart rate and blood pressure, both of which tend to be elevated when you are experiencing really intense emotions. One strategy that can be used to achieve this effect is to expose your face to cold water, whether that be by splashing your face with cold water, placing your face into a bowl of cold water, or applying a cold washcloth. Some people have found it helpful to wet washcloths with water, put them in the freezer, and then take them out when they need to calm down; ice packs work in a similar fashion. Some mental health clinicians may also refer to this strategy as "ice diving."

Intense exercise: Again, with the idea of changing your body's physiology so that it is easier to be calm and to regulate yourself, expending pent-up energy generated by the intensity of a given situation that causes feelings of overwhelm can provide a sense of release. Brief intense forms of exercise work well and can be easily performed during strong emotional moments. Examples include running up and down a set of stairs, stepping outside and taking a brisk walk, performing jumping jacks, or running in place.

Paced breathing: This is a practice that reminds people of the importance of paying attention to your breathing by slowing down the pace. Focusing on taking deep breaths in for five seconds and then exhaling for seven seconds, for even five minutes, is a way to slow the body down and ensure your brain gets enough oxygen. Being calmer and well-oxygenated will help you make better decisions and respond to an intense situation in a more regulated fashion.

Paired muscle relaxation is another strategy that builds off of paced breathing. During moments of stress and intense emotions, our muscles tend to tense up. Paired muscle relaxation involves noticing the areas of your body that are tense, starting from the top of your body and making your way downward, and engaging in deep breathing as a way to release that tension.

· · ·

DBT therapists are trained to reinforce all these skills in practice, as well as to encourage their clients to contact them via phone or text in real time if they are struggling to use their DBT skills during a time of crisis. This real-time coaching helps people recognize that they have the capacity to incorporate these skills into their daily practice and that they have what it takes to pull themselves out of a crisis.

· · ·

Now that you're at the end of this chapter about children who are experiencing thoughts of suicide and self-harm, I invite you to take a deep breath. Reflect on how you're feeling in your body, whether that be appreciating the tension in your muscles, noticing your posture while you're reading this line, or recognizing the strong emotions that this topic generates for you. The skills and strategies that we want our kids to incorporate into their daily practice as they navigate a world in which they will undoubtedly experience intense feelings are the same ones we need to practice. They all involve being mindful and attuned to our own bodies and emotional states.

It is not easy to be a caregiver to a child who is struggling to cope. You're not alone in feeling that way.

ELEVEN

Caring for Youth Experiencing Psychosis

G iven that many of us have experienced depression, anxiety, or trauma at some point in our lives, we can directly relate to what it might be like for a child to experience them. We have a basic understanding of the feelings and can recognize many of the behaviors the feelings may give rise to. Our ability to empathize allows us to connect with our children when they are experiencing these emotional states and to support them even during difficult times. But what do you do if your child is having an emotional or behavioral experience that you struggle to understand?

In my clinical work, I specialize in working with children and adolescents who are living with a category of mental health conditions known as psychotic disorders. These conditions can alter thought processes and behavioral patterns, and distort a person's perception of reality. I have met with youth who are distressed by hearing voices from an unknown entity that is providing a running commentary about their daily activities, making it hard for them to focus during school or during conversations with loved ones. I have sat in hospital rooms with teenagers who are distressed by ongoing visual hallucinations of ghost-like figures that become more prominent during stressful periods of their lives. And I have heard from caregivers who express concerns for their teenager who has experienced a gradual decline in overall functioning, such that the kid who was sociable, performed well in school, and was able to attend to their personal hygiene has become increasingly more isolative, less communicative, struggled with school, disregarded their physical appearance, and appeared preoccupied and disturbed by their internal thoughts.

For children living with psychotic disorders, it can be a challenge to communicate their experiences to the caregivers in their lives; while at the same time, caregivers often feel at a loss and unable to relate to these experiences. How do you support your child when the root of the distress that they are experiencing seems to contradict your understanding of reality? How do you respond to behaviors that can only be described as bizarre and highly unusual? How do you communicate with others about what is happening to your child when you are struggling to find the right words to describe the strange thoughts that are preoccupying your child's mind?

Although some of the symptoms of psychosis can be distressing, the support of loved ones and community is essential to your child's recovery. Experiencing psychotic symptoms in youth does not dictate who they are and who they will become. I have had the great fortune of working with youth and adults who are experiencing recovery from their symptoms and are simply thriving. What I've noticed is that individuals who are further along in their recovery from psychosis with an overall better prognosis tend to have the added benefit of ongoing support from their loved ones. Their caregivers, friends, and other members of their community demonstrate an understanding of how to support the individual in a nonjudgmental way—a way that focuses on maintaining connection rather than invalidating that person's experience. Caregivers who adapt their communication and connection with their child while they are on the journey of living with psychosis are better able to see the whole child, rather than just their symptoms.

In this chapter, I will describe what psychotic symptoms are, how they can present during childhood and adolescence, and how to talk to your child about their psychotic experiences in a supportive and validating manner. I'll explore how to navigate community spaces with a child who is living with psychosis. And I'll also discuss specific treatment options available to children and teens living with psychotic disorders.

What Is Psychosis?

Our brains have an amazing ability to take in information from the surrounding world, process and interpret different sensory experiences, and use that information to decide how to behave in various settings. There are certain patterns of beliefs, behaviors, and thought processes that both children and adults have that reflect a relatively sound understanding of reality and how we fit into it. However, for some of us, a disconnect occurs that compromises our ability to distinguish what is real from what is not, which then impacts our beliefs, behaviors, and thinking process. When we say *psychosis*, we are referring to a loss of touch with reality that disrupts thoughts and perceptions of sensory information. For a young person, experiencing psychosis can lead to disorganized behavior and thoughts that can make it difficult to function socially, occupationally, and academically, and that can affect their ability to care for themselves. While psychosis is often more difficult to navigate than more common experiences like depression or anxiety, recovery is absolutely possible.

Initially, the signs and symptoms of psychosis can be difficult to recognize in youth. In most cases, symptoms tend to present gradually, over time, and changes in thinking, perceptions, and behavior can be subtle. Examples include mild confusion and forgetfulness, not being as communicative, losing their train of thought mid-sentence, and making unusual comments that seem to be out of character. Usually, symptoms of psychosis will start to appear during the adolescent years, though in some cases symptoms develop in childhood. Many of the caregivers that I work with who have children living with psychosis share that they noticed a gradual shift in their child's behavior: their child became significantly more withdrawn socially, spending most or all of their time alone in their room. They could appear confused, become less emotionally responsive, and have trouble thinking logically. Their interest in attending to their personal hygiene—or their ability to do so—would decline. These early stages of psychosis are referred to clinically as the "prodromal period."

It's important to keep in mind that many of these behaviors are simply part and parcel of the tumultuous experience that is young adulthood. Developing psychosis is still quite rare. However, if your child is demonstrating many of the symptoms described previously and it is disruptive to their day-to-day functioning, it's worth voicing your concerns to a primary care physician or other trusted health care provider. Psychosis often manifests in two primary groups of symptoms: hallucinations and delusions. Delusions are fixed, false strong beliefs and thoughts that are unlikely to be true and that often defy cultural norms. These delusional beliefs can be both irrational and persistent. It is typically difficult, if not impossible, for a caregiver to effectively challenge the belief, or convince the person that it is untrue. Some examples of delusions include suspicions that something or someone is out to harm them, beliefs that they possess special powers or capabilities, or beliefs that external forces are controlling their thoughts and behaviors. Hallucinations are perceptual disturbances that cause a person to hear things that other people can't hear (auditory hallucinations) or see things that other people can't see (visual hallucinations). Other hallucinations can include sensations that may be unusual and for which there are no clear explanations, which can also be distressing to the individual.

One family we spoke to elected to share their experiences with psychosis with us anonymously. The daughter described the first time she was hospitalized with psychosis:

The day they sent me to the ER, I hadn't slept for about five days, and I was completely delusional. I had been up all night dancing, singing, and talking to "myself." My hallucinations were religious in nature; they were about having to save the world from damnation.

There were voices telling me what to do. Before I went to the ER they were generally good; they told me who was a friend and who was a foe, and I couldn't make eye contact with those who were on the wrong side. But they would get angry and mean at times as well. On the way to the ER, they told me "This is how it ends," and I was psychotic, so I believed them. Once I got there "they" handed me over to whatever was trying to destroy mankind and then "they" were the new voices in my head.

That's when it got terrifying. I felt even more delusional in the emergency room. When I think about it now, it doesn't feel like I actually lived it. It feels like I was somewhere else. The voices had never been as loud or angry or scary as when they were taking me to the ER. I thought I was going to die. I thought my heart was going to explode. My chest hurt immensely, and I was terrified. I was very focused on trying not to shake uncontrollably or breathe too fast or slow.

It should be noted that not all hallucinations are distressing, and many individuals who live with psychotic disorders learn to manage these symptoms, but oftentimes—especially during the diagnostic process, when symptoms have become disruptive and warrant treatment—they can be very difficult for the child and the caregiver alike.

What Causes Psychosis?

As with most mental health symptoms, there is no single cause for what leads to the development of psychotic symptoms, and there is a lot we still don't know. Researchers have determined that there are multiple genes and environmental factors that could be involved. However, it remains unclear as to why certain people are more susceptible. There appears to be a genetic link—families with a history of psychotic disorders are more vulnerable to having other family members go on to develop similar symptoms. In addition to genetics, in some cases, individuals who have had a traumatic experience could also be vulnerable to developing psychosis.

There are a number of mental health conditions associated with psychosis that we'll discuss in further detail: bipolar disorder, depression, schizophrenia, and schizoaffective disorder. These conditions are known to have strong genetic links, which is why understanding your family history of mental health conditions can be valuable.

There is also increasing evidence that early usage of substances such as marijuana, hallucinogens (psilocybin, LSD, etc.), and amphetamines may be linked to the development of psychotic disorders. As a psychiatrist working primarily with adolescents who are experiencing symptoms of psychosis, I often encounter teenagers who have developed psychotic symptoms related to drug use. Over the course of the childhood and adolescent years, the developing brain is more susceptible to harmful disruptions in key areas that are responsible for cognition, executive function, and mood regulation, and drug use can impact this development. Although experimentation with drugs is a very common part of adolescence, and the development of psychosis occurs in only a small percentage of adolescents, it is worth having a conversation with your child about the risks of using drugs while their brain is still developing.

Schizophrenia

A percentage of children and adolescents who experience symptoms of psychosis go on to develop a chronic mental health condition known as schizophrenia. Schizophrenia is characterized by significant impairments in how one thinks, behaves, and interprets reality. People with schizophrenia can experience delusional thinking and hallucinations as well as disorganized thoughts, behavior, and speech. They can also exhibit what are referred to as negative symptoms of psychosis such as decreased communicativeness and emotional expression (flat affect), loss of motivation, social withdrawal, and difficulty attending to their personal hygiene. All these symptoms result in significant functional impairment, which makes it difficult for the individual to maintain strong relationships with others, or to perform well either academically or at work. To meet the criteria for a formal diagnosis of schizophrenia, individuals would have to experience this constellation of symptoms for at least six months.

Although it is rare, the onset of schizophrenia during childhood, prior to the age of thirteen, does occur. The prevalence of childhood-onset schizophrenia is 0.04 percent in the United States and early onset schizophrenia, which is defined as the onset of symptoms prior to the age of eighteen, is experienced by 0.5 percent of the population. Additionally, studies have found that obstetric complications that resulted in decreased oxygen flow to the brain of the fetus have been associated with early onset schizophrenia. Researchers have also found that children who have experienced trauma are at increased risk for developing schizophrenia.

Psychosis and Mood-Related Episodes

There are children and adolescents who experience symptoms of psychosis during severe mood episodes, either when they are experiencing depression or while manic. Experiencing psychosis during a mood episode signals that the episode is severe. Major depressive disorder with psychotic features is characterized by periods of low mood, lack of interest in usual activity, sleep disturbances, poor energy, difficulty with concentration, changes in appetite, and feeling guilty or a burden to other people. In addition to these symptoms of depression, someone experiencing a severe depressive episode also may present with impoverished thoughts—meaning, they can't think productively or creatively—and social withdrawal as well as hallucinations and/or delusions. It is important to be aware that psychotic symptoms can accompany depressive episodes, given that children who do experience psychosis while depressed are at elevated risk for suicide. Additionally, about 50 percent of children who have depression with psychotic features will eventually go on to develop bipolar disorder.

Bipolar disorder with psychotic features is a condition that is also observed in children and often warrants more intensive support, such as hospitalization. When children with bipolar disorder experience symptoms of mania—which include distractibility, increased risk-taking activities, age-inappropriate sexual behavior, racing thoughts, irritability, euphoria, rapid speech, and a decreased need for sleep—they can also experience psychotic symptoms. Examples of psychotic symptoms include delusional thinking—for example, believing there's no need to go to school because they are going to become a millionaire by playing online poker every day; paranoid delusions such as believing that they are under surveillance or being followed; hallucinations either auditory or visual; or disordered (illogical) thinking and impaired comprehensibility.

In both major depressive disorder with psychotic features and bipolar disorder with psychotic features, the symptoms of psychosis are resolved once the mood episode has ended. Children are provided treatment that focuses on addressing the underlying mood episode since once the mood symptoms improve, the psychotic symptoms will go away. In the case of major depressive disorder with psychotic features, treatment would most likely include an antidepressant and an antipsychotic; for bipolar disorder with psychotic features, it would include a mood stabilizer and an antipsychotic as well.

There are children who experience distinct mood episodes of depression and mania accompanied by psychosis, whose psychotic symptoms persist even when they are no longer in a mood episode. The mental health condition associated with delusions and hallucinations that occur in the absence of mood symptoms is called schizoaffective disorder, and it poses a significant challenge to children given the severity of the symptoms.

The symptoms of psychosis can also be an indicator for other mood-related mental health issues, a signal that there is an underlying medical issue or side effects of substance use. All children who are presenting with psychotic symptoms should undergo a thorough medical evaluation. Laboratory testing should be performed, which would include checking electrolytes, kidney function, complete blood count, liver function, and thyroid hormone levels, as well as ruling out possible signs of infection including HIV, syphilis, and a urinary tract infection. Laboratory testing helps to rule out the possibility that the psychosis is due to delirium, which can happen when there are electrolyte disturbances, infection, or even issues with low blood sugar and low oxygen levels in the body (hypoxia). A medical provider may perform additional tests to determine the underlying cause of the psychosis particularly if there appears to be some additional medical concerns. These can include obtaining an MRI or CT scan if there seem to be significant neurological issues such as difficulty with language production, weakness in the extremities, short-term memory loss, or evidence of a head injury. A complete medical workup is warranted whenever anyone experiences the new onset of psychotic symptoms, so please do not delay in having your child evaluated by their PCP or another health care provider.

Communicating with a Child Experiencing Psychosis

If your child is living with psychosis, understanding how to communicate effectively with them is essential to maintaining an ongoing connection, and to their recovery. As I've said, symptoms of psychosis typically first appear during the adolescent years to young adulthood, which is also when your child's developmental focus is assuming their own individual identity. Their sense of autonomy is keenly important to them. Given that the symptoms of psychosis can result in significant functional impairment, bizarre and unusual behavior, disconnection from reality, and social withdrawal, navigating conversations around your child's symptoms can pose a significant challenge. Identifying an approach to communicating with your child that demonstrates your willingness to offer support and provide guidance in a nonjudgmental way is critical. It can be particularly helpful to have a framework for navigating conversations with your child about their symptoms.

Marc DeGregorio, a father and grandfather from North Haven, Connecticut, shared what he learned after caring for his daughter, who has experienced psychotic symptoms of schizophrenia since the age of fifteen. Marc's ability to reframe his expectations and be flexible as a parent and support figure helped him gain empathy for what his child was experiencing, and made it easier to navigate her care:

With these kinds of illnesses, the arc of evolution is so long, it could take twenty, twenty-five years before, all of a sudden, now you have to redefine this person and redefine yourself. Especially if the kid had some success along the way and then fell off the rails. We've had that happen in my experience. They've been the football player, cum laude, and now they're psychotic.

You have to retool yourself. You have to redefine yourself, sometimes all the time. Until I started doing NAMI and meeting many families, you start to feel that you got the short straw, or there's a cloud over you, or whatever crazy thinking. But there is no perfect family.

The analogy I use is, there's the island of perfectly sane, and then the island of the insane. And most society feels that they're on the perfectly sane side and they can't cross over, when it's really a spectrum. We're all on the same spectrum. We're just at different degrees. Some are ten degrees, like my kid is ten, but I might be a four. We're all part of the same human family.

Having concerns that your child is experiencing symptoms of psychosis can be scary, and you may feel unsure about what to say or do in response to their psychotic symptoms. I've met with caregivers who were initially in denial when it came to their child's psychotic symptoms and might have brushed them off. Some people feel afraid to engage with their child because they've noticed that the child has become more impulsive and are worried about how the child might respond.

However, as I've said, it is important to look for a pattern of change in their behavior and to take notice. The following material may not be relevant to you at this moment, but knowing how best to navigate an interaction with a child who is experiencing symptoms of psychosis might be helpful down the line.

How to Respond When Your Child Shares Their Psychotic Experiences with You

When a young person first begins experiencing psychotic symptoms, it isn't uncommon for them to keep these experiences to themselves. They may be trying to make sense of those experiences themselves and are fearful of how others may respond. They may worry that other people will judge them negatively for having such experiences, pull away from them, or not believe them. If your child approaches you about their psychotic experiences, know that this is an act of trust that provides an opportunity for you to demonstrate your support and validate their experience.

In order to maintain a level of comfort and nonjudgment between the two of you, you need to approach the conversation from a position in which you want to *understand* their experience rather than *deny* that they are having the experience in the first place. Youth who are experiencing psychotic symptoms may have auditory hallucinations that provide distressing commentary throughout the day or that make negative comments to them about people and their surrounding environment. They may have visual hallucinations that would be difficult for others to understand. These experiences may be difficult for you to empathize with, given that you may not be able to relate to them. But you can relate to experiencing something distressing. You can relate to having difficulty putting your internal experience into words. You can identify with the experience of not feeling like your usual self.

When you talk to your child about their experience, lean into your ability to relate to the emotions and feelings that the experience is bringing on, rather than to the actual experience itself. Leaning into the emotional aspect of your child's psychotic experiences conveys the message that you care about them, that you hear them and want to support them. Respond to the emotion first. Questions to ask include:

- What was that like for you?
- What did you make of that experience?
- Is this something that you've been thinking a lot about?

Responding with a question about what the experience was like for your child will open the door for them to share more. If you start from a place of denial and try to convince them that what they experience is not real or valid, you close the door to connection. Although you may feel inclined to quickly challenge their strong thoughts and beliefs in hopes of reducing their anxiety and distress related to the symptoms, saying "That doesn't make sense" or "I don't think what you're saying is happening is actually happening in reality" can make them feel judged or invalidated. We all have a desire to emotionally connect; it's no different for your child with psychotic symptoms. If they are approaching you with this info, it's because they want you to know so that they no longer feel alone in shouldering the burden of these experiences.

After your child has revealed their psychotic experiences to you they may seek out validation to ensure you understand where they are coming from. They may ask you if you believe the experiences that they have described are real or true. It is okay to respond by saying that you believe that the experiences they've described are real and true to them and how distressing and scary (or whatever language the child has used to describe the experiences) they are. In other words, you can respond to what you know to be true about your child's psychotic experience—whether that be the emotional experience of having such symptoms or how the symptoms are interfering with their ability to function. After your child has approached you with their experiences of psychosis, it is helpful to tell them you want to better understand how to support them while they are experiencing these symptoms and seek to identify ways in which you can do so. Ask for their thoughts on what you can do in the moment to reduce their distress.

Reality Testing

During future conversations, if your child asks you if an experience that they are having is consistent with reality, this is an appropriate moment to gently state the facts of reality as you understand them, as part of what we clinicians refer to as "reality testing." Reality testing is a process by which the person experiencing psychosis can check in with their social supports to determine if their internal experiences reflect what is actually happening in the real world. It is different from telling your child directly that what they are experiencing is not real, which can be invalidating and stifle connection, because they are asking the question, and you are responding. For example, a person who is distressed by visual and auditory hallucinations may ask their caregiver if they are also hearing or seeing the same thing. Although it may be distressing for your child to know that they are having experiences that other people are not having, it can ultimately be helpful for them to know that there is not an external entity or actual threat out in the real world that is contributing to their symptoms. Reality testing can be one of the tools in your communication toolbox. It provides an opportunity for your child to learn how to engage with their symptoms and connect with those around them, bridging the gap between their internal experience and the rest of the world.

Alleya Ray and her husband adopted their daughters through the foster care system. The girls are biological half sisters and have been in their care for fourteen years. The oldest experienced her first known psychosis at age four, and has struggled with psychotic symptoms (hallucinations and delusions) as well as impaired cognitive symptoms ever since. Alleya shared with us how she thinks about responding when her daughter is experiencing active hallucinations:

I think you always have to keep in mind that to her it is very real and just saying "Oh, there's nothing really there" is not helpful to her. It's your responsibility to make sure that this child is equipped to go out in the world independently in the future. So you have to help them get the coping skills to recognize that this is happening, to recognize what they need in this moment, and to get what they need. And so I've learned that it's best to ask open-ended questions, that it's best to ask her how it's making her feel, to empathize with her and tell her that I think I would be very scared too, if I heard a voice like that.

But then I also have to tell her that I think that this is part of her illness and her brain is playing tricks on her, but that doesn't make it any less scary or any less difficult. And then I'll ask her, "What do we need to do right now? Do you need me to lie with you and scratch your back? Do you need to color? Do you need music to drown out the voices? What do you need to feel safe and supported?" And it doesn't really matter what that answer is, as long as it is something that your family's willing to allow. You find a way to make it happen. And to remind them after the incident is over that you're proud of how they handled it, that you're proud that they came to you and trusted you enough to tell you. Recapping it with them is important too.

Gently questioning and reality testing can provide some insight into your child's current state of awareness about that impairment and the extent to which their psychotic experiences are interfering with their ability to function. An example question could be, "Do you think that experience got in the way of your ability to do things the rest of the day?" If you've noticed a pattern of functional decline such that they appear distracted, withdrawn, or are not taking care of their personal hygiene, engage in a conversation with them about these changes. It is important to acknowledge the fact that, depending on the severity of psychotic symptoms and the level of disorganization in your child's thinking and behavior, you may not be able to obtain a coherent response to these questions.

Follow-Up Questions to Better Understand Your Child's Psychotic Symptoms

Additional questions to ask in order to determine the level of distress the psychotic symptoms are causing and how much they influence the child's daily activities include the frequency in which they experience the symptoms and whether or not there are different factors that are more likely to trigger the symptoms. You might ask about where they are when they experience the most symptoms, or if there are certain places they avoid because they find their symptoms are more severe in those settings.

Particularly if your child is distressed by their psychotic symptoms, asking them for their thoughts as to how you can be helpful and support them in the moment can provide you with clear guidance on what it is that your child needs from you. Their response can also provide some insight as to what may trigger some of their psychotic symptoms and perhaps give you a better understanding of the nature of their symptoms. In some cases, due to the bizarre nature of their delusional thoughts and hallucinations, their recommendations for how you can support them may not be reasonable or actionable. If that happens, you can simply state that to the child and ask if there are other things that you can do instead. Conversely, if their psychotic symptoms have caused them to become withdrawn and uncommunicative, they may not know or be able to tell you what it is that they need from you. That can certainly be a challenge. However, it is still important to find ways to remain connected to your child even if they want to isolate themselves in their room all day—which is a very common occurrence for youth and young adults experiencing psychosis. Let them know that you'll be periodically checking in on them at certain intervals. That way, you will not feel as though you are intruding, and you won't catch them by surprise given that this plan was discussed ahead of time. I've met with plenty of caregivers who have no idea what their child is up to or how they are experiencing their psychotic symptoms because they just leave them in their room for hours, days, and weeks without any human contact, perhaps because they feel helpless about the situation and are not quite sure what to do or what to say. Maintaining a consistent level of interaction demonstrates to your child that you're still thinking about them and that you're still supporting them. It also enables you to monitor your child's mood and behavior.

Please note that if your child is experiencing psychotic symptoms for the first time and they are approaching you with this information, then reaching out for professional help is certainly warranted. If their symptoms seem to warrant more immediate support—if you are concerned for their safety, or their behavior is so disorganized that you worry that they may cause harm to themselves or to others—call 988 or bring your child to the nearest emergency room for evaluation. Command auditory hallucinations—voices telling them to engage in specific acts, especially to hurt themselves or others—also warrant immediate attention. Examples of this would include hearing voices from God instructing them to stab other people with a kitchen knife, or a voice commanding that they walk into traffic without looking. Do not delay: Your child needs to be evaluated now.

How to Approach Your Child About Concerning Behaviors Associated with Psychosis

If you have recognized that your child's behavior may be consistent with psychotic symptoms, or have heard from others, whether it be other family members, friends, or people at school, that they are concerned about unusual behaviors, then it is important to initiate a conversation with your child about these concerns. I know that this can be an incredibly difficult conversation to have. You may worry that your child will feel offended or shut down or even just flat-out deny the fact that there are any issues. When you approach your child, it can be helpful to focus on the changes in their behavior that you've noticed:

I was hoping to talk to you about some changes that I've noticed in you. Over the past couple of months, I've noticed that you have been

keeping to yourself, spending a lot of time in your room, and it seems
like it has been hard for you to keep up with showering. I just wonder
why you think these changes are happening.

Or

A few of your friends and teachers at school recently contacted me about
some behaviors that they've noticed from you in the past couple of
weeks. They mentioned that it appears as though you've been talking to
yourself, that you're having a conversation with someone who's not
there, and that you've been keeping to yourself. What do you make of
the fact that they expressed these concerns about you?

To ask your child directly what they think may be driving some of
their behavioral changes is a nonjudgmental approach that allows them
to describe what's going on with them in their own words, potentially
making it easier for them to feel comfortable sharing the full extent of
their psychotic experiences.

It is definitely possible that your child will deny that there are any
issues. They may not have a response to your inquiry about what may
be behind the behavioral change. If that's the case, then you can simply
state that you're concerned about them, especially if there is evidence
that their level of functioning has deteriorated—they're not going to
school, socializing with others, participating in extracurricular activities, attending to their hygiene, etc., and that you want to explore the
possibility of getting them support so that they function better.

How to Talk with Your Child About the Need for Mental Health Supports

Studies have found that early intervention for psychosis can help to reduce the severity of symptoms, mitigate the duration of the psychotic
episode, and improve the overall prognosis for the child. Yet I, too,
often see families first seeking mental health support for an adolescent

with psychosis during a state of crisis, which is a difficult time to engage in mental health support. Sometimes, kids experiencing severe symptoms of psychosis end up encountering police and other emergency response personnel in the community before they've sought or received any mental health support. It goes without saying that interactions between people experiencing psychosis and emergency response personnel do not always go well. The level of distress the individual with psychotic symptoms may be experiencing can cause them to become agitated, and their agitation can further intensify when they are approached by unfamiliar people dressed in uniforms. A mental health crisis can even be met with a more aggressive response, escalating a difficult situation into a traumatic experience for both you and your child.

To mitigate the potential for a crisis situation, it's important to be aware of the options for treatment available in your community and to voice those options to your child. If you do find yourself in a situation with your child where emergency response is necessary, be sure to stress when you call that the help you need is for a mental health emergency and that you are requesting responders trained in de-escalating mental health crises. In many regions of the country, there may not be first responders who have extensive training in managing a mental health crisis. Since we do not know the level of training of people who show up in response to a crisis, make sure you clearly announce to all personnel who arrive at the scene that your child is experiencing a mental health crisis. This information will hopefully alert personnel that your child may not be able to control their behaviors and actions due to the psychosis.

If your child has symptoms of psychosis, you want to get your child help as soon as possible. However, your child may not be on board with that plan. Here are some things that you can say to help them understand the utility of getting help.

Discuss together the benefits of getting help for their symptoms early. Your child may be in denial that they are even experiencing

psychosis. If so, then you can let them know that they are not functioning at their usual level and that you're concerned. If there is evidence of academic decline or difficulty maintaining employment, and
negative impact on their relationships with others or their engagement in activities they once cared about, point it out, and say that it
is important to identify strategies to ensure that the quality of their
life doesn't continue to erode. Let them know that talking to their
primary care provider or a mental health professional may help them
understand why there has been a change in their ability to function in
their usual way.

**Let them know that mental health supports will help you to better
understand their experiences and to learn strategies for how to cope
with the symptoms more effectively.** You can share that you're eager
to learn ways in which you could mitigate their distress and ensure that
their symptoms do not continue to interfere with their day-to-day
function. Share with your child that by developing a team of support
they will be able to acquire skills and knowledge from others about
how to remain better engaged in the present moment and to continue
to enjoy aspects of their life while living with psychosis.

**Identify community supports in addition to mental health sup-
ports.** One of the biggest supports that should be explored is the community of people who are living and thriving each and every day with
ongoing psychotic symptoms or individuals who experience psychosis
during mood episodes. Support groups or other spaces where your
child can be with others who share elements of their experience—
commonly referred to as peer support—are some of the most important forms of support for your child. The same is true for you, as a
caregiver. In the community of people living with psychosis, peer support is exceptionally strong. NAMI provides support groups for caregivers, particularly for those who are learning how to support their
child who is experiencing symptoms of psychosis. There may be a

NAMI support group within your community—check out NAMI.org for a list of available support groups in your area.

How to Talk to Others in Your Community About Psychosis

Young people who are experiencing psychosis may not always feel comfortable sharing with others the particulars of their symptoms, and may not always be in a position in which they can strongly advocate for themselves, especially outside of the peer support community. At the same time, as a caregiver, you may be unsure how to talk to others—including even those in your community of support—about some of the concerning symptoms that your child may be experiencing due to psychosis. Regardless, you need to find a way to remain connected to your community so that you can receive the support you need, to sustain your support for your child. You have to talk about, not hide, what you're going through. Unfortunately, while there is nothing to be ashamed about when your child is experiencing psychosis, many people experience it anyway. People are still afraid of psychosis, and all the stereotypes and myths surrounding it; no one wants to be the person whose kid "has it." Others don't know exactly what to say to be supportive.

Marc DeGregorio from Connecticut, whom we heard from earlier in this chapter, also shared with us how finding NAMI and its associated community was a huge step in recovery for his family:

We adopted three siblings back in the early '90s. We had no kids, and we thought we could offer a home to homeless, family-less kids. We had a lot of issues with readjustment, never having a family, multiple placements. It was a learning experience. At fifteen, my oldest had a psychotic break. She ended up in a hospital in Middletown for a long time, eighteen months. The social worker said, "Have you heard of NAMI?" We were totally clueless on all this.

I took the course Family-to-Family at that time. It was in New Haven, and it was very helpful for me. I got to understand more about what was happening. She had been diagnosed with schizophrenia. I hadn't heard that word, didn't know what that was. It was very educational, and after, I was able to go to the doctors and ask more informed questions.

Well, later in history, my daughter's been impaired and sick, and still now at forty, they're very impaired. I became a Family-to-Family teacher in 2012 after I retired, and I've been teaching ever since. I have not missed a semester in eleven years.

The first step to take when considering disclosing to others in your community about what is happening with your child is to ask your child what they would feel comfortable for you to share about their psychotic symptoms and with whom. Having this particular conversation may be a challenge for some people with psychosis who are experiencing difficulty in their ability to think and communicate clearly. But you can still communicate to them, whether it be verbally or in writing, that you would like to let other people know about their specific experiences so that the entire family can receive support from others. You want to have people cheering you and your child on from the sidelines as well as lifting you up if you happen to fall along the way. As you're having the discussion with them about what exactly to share and to whom, let them know that in order for you to be a better support for them, you need your own support as well.

Your child's experiences are their own and they certainly have a right to privacy, which needs to be respected. If they tell you that they do not want you to share information about their symptoms, treatment, or any other aspect of their recovery then please know that it is okay for them to say that. At the same time, it is also fair for you to share that you may talk to people about your own personal journey supporting them while noting that the focus of those conversations will be your own personal experience.

Once you've determined the level of detail that they feel comfortable with you sharing about their psychotic symptoms and with whom, initiate the conversation with people in your community about what you and your child have been going through. Be open and honest about the experience while also being receptive to their love and support. There is no need to do this alone. Allow yourself to be taken care of by others and receptive to the support that they are willing to offer. These conversations can also provide you with an opportunity to communicate with your social support network about how you may be preoccupied with taking care of your child and in turn not as available as before.

Tools to Aid in Recovery from Psychosis

There is specialized treatment for individuals experiencing their first episode of psychosis that, when accessed early on during the course of their condition, has been proven to reduce the severity and duration of psychotic symptoms. This treatment is often referred to as coordinated specialty care (CSC), reflecting the fact that clinicians from multiple disciplines come together to provide psychosis-specific care to the individual. These programs are also often referred to as First Episode Psychosis programs. They provide comprehensive therapeutic supports that allow young people to develop a set of skills that will get them on the path toward recovery. First Episode Psychosis programs typically have patients enrolled in individual therapy and group therapy and provide both medication management and support from peer specialists. These programs also provide support for family members, whether it be through their own groups or family therapy.

For some individuals who are experiencing psychotic symptoms, it can be a challenge to focus on activities of daily living and maintaining relationships when preoccupied with symptoms. The goal of all forms of treatment for psychosis is to reduce distress and increase functioning. Individual therapy that is often provided in these First Episode programs uses a form of cognitive behavioral therapy (CBT) that is specific to the experiences of those living with psychosis, called CBT for psychosis. This form of CBT focuses on improving overall functioning and distress related to living with psychotic symptoms. Group therapy with other individuals living with psychosis can help youth learn from each other about various tools and strategies that they are using to navigate the world while living with psychotic symptoms. Group therapy also helps enhance social skills and encourages individuals to connect with others, reducing the potential for ongoing social withdrawal.

For many families of young people who are living with psychosis, it can be a challenge to adapt the way in which you communicate with your child in light of their psychotic symptoms. Family therapy provides an opportunity for caregivers to receive psychoeducation about the symptoms of psychosis and how they may manifest in their child and offers strategies for communicating with and supporting their child.

As is the case for most mental health conditions, the experience and guidance of those with actual lived experience of the condition can be so powerful in one's treatment and recovery. Peer specialists in psychosis provide young people with an opportunity to see themselves in others while at the same time giving them a sense of hope that recovery is possible. A peer specialist can provide practical tools, hope, and inspiration while also serving as a strong advocate for the individual living with psychosis. They deeply understand what supports are actually most beneficial for living with psychotic symptoms. Peer specialists can also be helpful when exploring treatment options and navigating the ambivalence some individuals may have about therapy and medication management. Having their perspective can be helpful to convince youth with psychosis about the utility of engaging in treatment.

The majority of people who are living with psychotic symptoms can have challenges with functioning in a variety of different domains, which is where medications can be helpful. Medications that are often used include antipsychotics, which help to reduce the frequency and intensity of psychotic symptoms such as auditory and visual hallucinations.

Distressing thoughts related to paranoid delusions or other strong beliefs that are not based in reality can also be reduced while on antipsychotics. These medications can help individuals who are experiencing sleep difficulty, anxiety, and agitation and can provide more clarity in thinking since they are less preoccupied by psychotic symptoms. Unfortunately, antipsychotics are known to have some significant side effects such as weight gain, sedation, elevated blood glucose, and involuntary muscle contractions known as dystonia. Some people can experience tardive dyskinesia, which is repetitive involuntary movements. Please alert your child's prescriber if you notice signs of dystonia and tardive dyskinesia. However, antipsychotics can make it such that your child is no longer distressed by their psychotic experiences and result in a significant diminishment of symptoms and improvement in overall functioning.

It is important to keep in mind that children are still able to live their lives while living with psychosis. Having a child with psychotic symptoms does not mean that they are no longer your child or that you have lost them to their symptoms. Their trajectory may be different than what you might originally have had in mind for them. However, support, connection, and communication are still essential to the relationship that you will have with them. You can still parent and support your child on their path toward recovery.

Marc DeGregorio provided these closing words of advice to parents navigating their relationship with a child in psychosis:

If it's a good day for her, it's good enough for me. Respect your loved one for the weight they carry every day to try to get up in the morning, to try to make a life in whatever form it takes.

My daughter does meager things in the home. She'll get up at twelve o'clock in the afternoon. She goes to arts and crafts. If it's a good day and she said, "I had a good day today," it's good enough for me.

TWELVE

Living with the Child Who Is Angry, Defiant, or Disruptive

Anger is the bodyguard of fear.

—DR. LORI DESAUTELS,
psychologist from Indiana

. . .

T he journey of raising children and adolescents is often rife with tumultuous interactions and moments of intense emotion. It is typical for children to feel a wide range of emotions, including anger and frustration, and to demonstrate aggression, defiance, and oppositionality in response to a multitude of experiences across their development. Children are still learning how to tolerate disappointment, navigate disagreements with people, be flexible, and be able to adapt to situations that do not go according to plan—and with the appropriate supports and skills, and over time, they do. For some children, however, there may be underlying factors that limit their ability to tolerate certain situations and encounters without significant displays of anger.

You may have experienced a situation with your child in which they have intense episodes of anger that seem to come out of nowhere and leave you scratching your head, trying to make sense of what just happened. Sometimes intense emotion arises as a consequence of anger, frustration, fear, or not getting one's way. Some children experience these emotions so intensely that it can be hard for them to put into words how they feel and to communicate those feelings to others. They may not understand why they are experiencing that feeling or know what to do with the feeling, and they may not possess the maturity to recognize that the feeling will pass with time. Given these challenges, the child may express that feeling by acting on it—through behavior—in ways that have negative consequences for the child, and that can potentially damage the child's relationships with others.

Taking care of a child during infancy and the toddler years can certainly be challenging: making sure they are fed, receive medical care, and have safe shelter; the multiple diaper changes and daily baths; dressing and grooming them; helping them learn to walk, feed themselves, and use the potty . . . But at the same time, there was a certain simplicity to providing for a child's physical needs. Certainly, there was ongoing emotional care—responding to the child's attempts to engage with you so that their needs were met, forming that emotional attachment to teach them that they can trust you to care for them—but what is etched in our memories of the early childhood years are the sleepless nights and long days of doing the basic chores involved in caring for our child's physical well-being and keeping them out of harm's way.

As kids get older, the relentless need to provide for their physical care starts to diminish. They sleep through the night; they're able to get dressed on their own, and you no longer have to lift a slippery squirmy body safely out of the tub. Eventually, you're not just done with diapers—you don't even have to remind your child to use the toilet. Many caregivers experience a palpable sense of relief once caring for their child no longer involves literal "heavy lifting." That is, until they begin to realize that new and more complex challenges arise as their child matures into a more complex socioemotional being.

One of the most challenging aspects of raising kids is providing support and guidance on how to manage and regulate intense emotional states. There is no simple playbook for teaching your child how to tolerate disappointment and frustration, navigate interactions with other people in a wider world, and manage the anger they feel when reality does not conform to their wishes, or when someone else mistreats, misunderstands, or abandons them. We cannot protect our children from experiencing intense emotions, and anger is one of the most difficult emotions even for adults to process. Our children will express anger, whether or not we think that they have a justifiable reason to be angry.

It is also inevitable that we will experience our own anger and frustration about the intensity of our child's emotional responses and our own inability to control the ways they may express their feelings. Ensuring that our children develop the skills they need to manage their emotions isn't an easy job even when a child is relatively easygoing. We hurt when our kids hurt, we worry when they struggle, and being human involves enduring emotional discomfort. But there are kids who have a particularly difficult time developing the skills necessary to tolerate and process emotions in healthy ways, no matter how responsibly and sensitively we try to help them do so, for a whole host of reasons.

For some caregivers, raising a child who struggles to manage their emotions can provoke bouts of anger, shame, or frustration. The glaring eyes and judgments of others who bear witness to your child's dramatic or commandeering or socially inappropriate expressions of intense emotion—their screaming at you at the top of their lungs in the grocery store because you refused to get them a specific item, storming out of the holiday party cursing because you wouldn't let them borrow your car—are not necessarily a figment of your imagination. People who have not raised a child who struggles to regulate emotions may have many opinions about what you must be doing wrong such that your child is not well-regulated or "well-behaved." And however irritating and unjustified that is, and however much you tell yourself that other people just don't "get it" about your child's temperament, you may also, simultaneously, judge yourself. What kind of parent should you have been, to ensure that your kid wouldn't behave this way? The caregivers I interviewed for this book had many stories to tell involving intense displays of anger from their kids and their struggles knowing how to respond in the moment; the confusion that set in about why their child had responded to a situation with such intensity and their sense of dread and fear associated with not knowing whether or not it was going to happen again.

It can be hard to remember at times that our children's brains are constantly undergoing architectural changes. We also may forget that because the brain systems involved in processing emotions and seeking rewards develop earlier and more robustly than those involved in good decision-making and future planning, it can be totally normative and age-appropriate for our kids to struggle to control their temper in the heat of the moment. But how do you know when your child's intense display of anger falls within the realm of what is typical for a child or adolescent of similar age? When our children continue to struggle with things that seem very basic to us as adults, we may start to question our parenting choices around discipline and our ability to teach our children the importance of respect for others. We ask ourselves: Why is it so hard for my kid to *just act right*?

It is painful to see your child in distress and to witness other people's pain or discomfort in response to your child's behavior. We never want to look at our kids or think about our kids as being bad people, so when our kids behave badly despite our best efforts to teach them right from wrong, we can also feel deeply worried or distressed. The pain of feeling as though you're walking around on eggshells, combined with the intensity and unpredictability of your child's outbursts, can put you on edge, and keep you there.

With some kids, angry outbursts punctuate periods of relative calm or happen in response to easily identifiable stressors. But for others, those islands of calm happen for the most part only when the child is asleep. What do you do when the majority of your interactions with your child are tumultuous? If your attempts to talk them down are often futile? When their behavior diminishes the quality of life for their siblings, as well as for you? You may also grow fearful. What if your child becomes verbally and physically aggressive with someone other than you? Or in a place or at a time when you're not around to intercede? Unimaginable things can happen in the heat of the moment when a child is very angry. When your child's behavior has triggered intense emotions in you, it can be challenging to take a step back and reflect on what might be fueling their intense emotional responses. You simply want your questions to be answered and for the behaviors to stop.

In this chapter, I will explore some of the underlying reasons why some children and adolescents have difficulty controlling and regulating their emotions over the course of their development. I'll explore some of the basic tenets of emotion regulation in neurotypical children and teens, and discuss specific mental health conditions that could contribute to significant difficulties in anger management within children and adolescents. Then I'll suggest some helpful approaches and strategies caregivers can use while interacting with their child.

Emotional Dysregulation—
What It Is and Why It Happens

Anger is, of course, a normal human emotional response. However, when a child's consistent emotional response to a given stressful situation involves anger, irritability, and aggression, especially if that response seems to be out of proportion to the actual stressor, or when the child's ability to control their impulses in that situation seems to be limited even when you try to soothe or redirect them, this "normal" human response becomes problematic. Why do some kids have this heightened emotional response to anger while others have a more temperate response? Understanding the science behind how children regulate their emotions can make it easier to appreciate the inherent challenges our kids face while struggling to manage their anger.

There has been a growing interest in the research community in better understanding why certain kids are more prone to angry and aggressive responses than others. One interesting finding is that there appears to be an association between experiencing fear and experiencing frustration. For some kids, experiencing frustration is perceived and processed by the brain as a type of threat, which can activate the body's stress response system; this can elicit an aggressive response. There have been interesting studies exploring how being ostracized or treated unfairly constitutes frustrating experiences and therefore ultimately are perceived to be threatening. Key regions in the brain that regulate our emotions become responsive to experiences perceived to be threatening, which may lead to a propensity to display reactive aggression. Studies examining how kids interpret the faces and emotional expressions of others reveal that kids who are more prone to anger tend to interpret neutral, nonthreatening, rather ambiguous faces as threatening compared to other kids, which is referred to as hostile interpretation bias. Anger-prone kids also manifest a level of hyperreactivity to certain social cues, whether from social interactions or environments, that reflects differences from other kids in overall functioning within the region of the brain that helps with mood and impulse control. All this is to say that kids who tend to be more aggressive, angry, and impulsive have brains that are wired differently than those of other kids. Their angry responses are not willful or strategic; rather, the child is doing the best that they can given the neurological wiring and skills that they have.

Dysregulation and Mental Health Conditions

You have tried your best to reason with them. You have explained to them on countless occasions the consequences of their actions. Yet here they go again, crying, yelling, lashing out, "throwing a fit," refusing to listen, drawing negative attention to themselves, disrupting whatever situation they're in, making life difficult for whoever else is around them . . . and, of course, for you. And once again you are asking yourself: Why is this kid being so difficult right now? It can feel as though you're talking to a wall with no clear sense as to how you will navigate the situation.

We've talked a little bit about the neurobiological reasons why some kids have more difficulty being flexible with others and may lash out in a fit of rage when something does not go their way. There are also a number of mental health conditions that can make it difficult for a child to regulate themself. Recognizing these conditions, and engaging your child in treatment for them, can be helpful in reducing both their distress and your own.

ADHD

As I explained in chapter 6, "Neurodevelopmental Disorders," attention-deficit hyperactivity disorder, or ADHD, is a condition characterized by difficulties with being able to focus or pay attention, increased distractibility, and impulsivity. Children who have a diagnosis of ADHD can have significant challenges controlling their behavioral responses around peers and adults, especially in situations they find boring or when they are called upon to do tasks that they either consider to be mundane or that require a lot of focus. The child can also become frustrated by their own need for sustained attention. They may lash out as a result: yell, throw objects, bang their fists, or stamp their feet . . . The behavioral response could take any number of forms, and those forms may change as the child ages. Adolescents may become disruptive in other ways: storm out in a huff, slam doors, make rude remarks or gestures behind a teacher's back to "entertain" classmates, erupt in a verbal tirade about the stupidity or pointlessness of whatever it is they're supposed to do—or whoever is requiring them to do it. Whatever the behavior, the response is secondary to their difficulty tolerating sustained engagement in a certain activity or being able to sustain focused attention.

Children with ADHD also have difficulty managing their impulses. They may go from 0 to 100 and immediately act on thoughts/ideas that pop into their head without thinking through all the potential consequences. They may want to run off while you're walking with them in the mall or shout out inappropriate comments. This can be incredibly frustrating for caregivers. You want to teach your child how to maintain safety and how to conduct themselves in public, and their refusal to comply with your recommendations can result in some tense interactions. You may react to their behavior in a big way, understandably so, and they may react to you with some big emotions, escalating the tension in what is already a tense moment.

Additionally, children with ADHD have difficulty being redirected from or transitioning away from certain activities, especially ones they enjoy. You can tell them multiple times that they need to get off of their cell phone and start their homework. They say, "Okay, sure"; fifteen minutes later you check in on them again and they are still playing around on their phone. You may confront them, and they react by throwing a tantrum and getting into a power struggle with you. One possible reason they didn't comply with your request to get off the phone is that they became distracted by something and forgot they had promised to do so; then when confronted they might be upset that you've called attention to their lack of focus. Or they could have clearly remembered the time limit that you set around cell phone use and had difficulty honoring it, which would involve transitioning away from something they enjoyed to doing something—such as homework—that they may be struggling with. Either way, they may defend themselves with full-fledged defiance, and impulsively do or say something while you are confronting them that will make the interaction worse.

We do see that kids who receive treatment for their ADHD symptoms tend to experience fewer temper tantrums. They are less oppositional, defiant, and impulsive, which helps to decrease the intensity of the responses they may have when they are told to do something that they don't necessarily want to do. Treatment can include medication as well as parent management training.

Trauma

Children who have experienced trauma, particularly those who have experienced repeated or complex trauma, very often have difficulty regulating their emotions. As I explained in chapter 7, trauma reshapes the nervous system, such that a child may live with an elevated level of hypervigilance—a kind of fearful anticipation. When they are in a situation that is objectively more stressful, they are even more inclined to become overwhelmed by their feelings and to react instinctively to protect themselves from the perceived threat—even if in a maladaptive way. Even though the situation may not require a response that they would need to protect themselves, they are wired to respond in a way that they enter into that fight-or-flight state. The "fight" part of that response could resemble argumentative behavior and oppositionality. Let's use an example to illustrate how a child's trauma history and certain triggers could elicit a response that will be experienced as bouts of anger, rage, aggression, and oppositionality.

Imagine there is a teenager who may be getting somewhat rowdy during class, joking around with their friends. The teacher, in an attempt to maintain order in the classroom, instructs this teen to sit still and be quiet. However, this particular teen may shout some expletives back at the teacher, while telling him that he has no right to speak to her in that manner and refuse to comply with that teacher's request. However, to the teacher, this incident could be experienced as a student defying their authority and the student is perceived to be verbally aggressive and disrespectful, warranting some level of discipline by the school. But then there's the student's internal experience of this same encounter. It turns out that this student has a history of sexual abuse by a male perpetrator. This teacher happens to actually be a substitute and this is the first time that she has ever seen this teacher. Hearing the demands to be still and quiet elicits intrusive memories related to her trauma in which she was told repeatedly to remain still and quiet as she was being sexually abused. Upon hearing these words, the student's body then becomes tense and certain regions of the brain become activated such that she suddenly fights back by shouting no she will not do as he says.

It is understandable that one would argue that students should be respectful of teachers and others who are in a position of authority within the school. However, when we notice a pattern of behavior from children such as defiance and opposition, it's important to be curious about what is driving these behaviors, not automatically respond with reprimand and discipline. Children who may be experiencing angry and aggressive behavior in the context of their trauma history may benefit from some of the therapeutic interventions that were described in chapter 7.

Learning Disabilities

Experiencing significant challenges related to academic learning can be incredibly frustrating to children. Despite the child's best efforts to keep up with the rest of their peers whether it be in math, reading, or writing, they may experience ongoing difficulties demonstrating these academic skills. There are some children who may exhibit bouts of anger, frustration, and irritability primarily in the school setting because they are having difficulty tolerating the challenges related to their learning disability. It may be hard for them to convey their frustration to their teachers or find the words to articulate what the emotional experience is like for them to not be able to keep up with the rest of the class. Caregivers may receive phone calls or messages from school informing them that the child is exhibiting behaviors that may be described as oppositional, defiant, or argumentative. The child may refuse to do work in the classroom, or be angry at teachers for pointing out their errors.

This is not to suggest that all children who have a learning disability exhibit angry feelings and behaviors while in the school environment. However, when we notice that this type of behavior tends to be limited exclusively to the classroom setting, it is important to think about the impact academic demands may have on the child's mood and behavior, and whether the child is communicating that they are struggling with something directly related to deficits in their academic skills. Dr. Lori Desautels is a white woman from Indiana who works with educators and schools in understanding how trauma and adversity impact the developing nervous system, whose work focuses on understanding children's angry and disruptive behavior in the school setting and the role that physiological response to certain elements in the school environment may play in triggering it, mentioned that most kids would rather their peers think that they're intentionally misbehaving than that they're stupid.

The most appropriate intervention for children who may be exhibiting bouts of anger due to challenges related to their learning disability is to develop an Individualized Educational Plan (IEP) and implement appropriate academic supports for that child within the school environment. I described the IEP process in more detail in chapter 6, "Neurodevelopmental Disorders." Providing the child with an opportunity to learn using a tailored approach that better meets their individual needs is likely to reduce some of the frustration they experience in a mainstream classroom.

Autism Spectrum Disorder (ASD)

Some children who are living with ASD may experience challenges managing their anger and frustration due to the individual differences inherent to their condition. As described in chapter 6, kids who have ASD tend to be rigid, engage in repetitive behaviors, have a preoccupation with very specific activities, interests, or objects, and may experience difficulty tolerating certain sensory stimuli such as loud noises and wearing certain textures. They also have challenges related to social communication. Given the nature of the condition, it affects different children differently, but some children with ASD may exhibit anger and aggressive behavior toward themselves and others in direct response to some of the challenges of neurodiversity that also affect kids with learning disabilities. Angry feelings and dysregulated behaviors may also emerge due to frustration related to experiencing a sudden change in plans that diverges from a daily routine, such as having to go to a doctor's appointment on a school day or to music class when they usually have art class. Or they may become aggressive, throwing a temper tantrum or turning the house upside down if you interrupt an activity that they have been intensely engaged in for an extended period of time. Because children with ASD may experience difficulty communicating their distress to others, anger and disruptive behavior may emerge as a way to get the attention and support that they need.

As I explored in more depth in chapter 6, children with ASD who have behavioral issues may benefit from applied behavioral analysis, known as ABA, to help mitigate episodes of aggression and help with emotional regulation. Some may benefit from taking one of the medications approved by the FDA specifically for the treatment of aggressive behavior in kids with ASD, risperidone or aripiprazole.

Oppositional Defiant Disorder

There are some children who just seem driven to make life more difficult for you and for other adults in their lives. Many if not most interactions with them feel like a debate. They constantly want to argue, often insist that they are right, and may even refuse to just simply do as they are told. They question why they should have to follow certain rules or comply with certain expectations at school or in other activities and may be disrespectful to the people trying to enforce these rules. You may feel like you're constantly walking around on eggshells trying to avoid conflict with the child.

Many caregivers may think to themselves: "Well, most kids are oppositional at some point in time." However, there are some kids who have a persistent pattern of angry/irritable mood and argumentative behavior that goes beyond what one would typically expect of a child of their developmental stage. In the DSM-5, this condition is referred to as oppositional defiant disorder (ODD), a diagnosis given only to children. ODD typically emerges during preschool and elementary school and persists throughout the teenage years. Children with ODD tend to easily lose their temper and may blame other people for their mistakes and misbehavior. They can often be angry and resentful and can become easily annoyed. Kids with ODD may also be described as being vindictive.

It is to be expected that most children will be angry, resentful, and irritable, and blame others for their mistakes or shortcomings, at various points in time, as they grow up—especially given that kids are still learning how to navigate some of the strong emotions that may result in some of these disruptive behaviors. However, what sets ODD apart from typical child or adolescent behavior is the intensity of the symptoms and the extreme nature of their behavior. ODD is a persistent pattern of behavior that is present for at least six months, and that interferes with their child's functioning.

Caregivers of children who have ODD can find it challenging to reason with their kid and to enforce certain rules that are necessary to provide structure, order, and safety in a child's life. You may find yourself in a constant power struggle that can leave both you and your child frustrated. It can be hard not to regularly engage in arguments or to be pushed to do the opposite and give up arguing, surrender, and simply let the kid have their way just to keep the peace.

Treatment for ODD requires multiple and sustained efforts. The main focus of the treatment is the relationship between you and your child. Chances are the relationship may be strained if you are consistently getting into arguments with your child and effective communication has broken down. Therapeutic programs that prioritize providing tools and strategies for how caregivers can better support their kids are most helpful. Parent management training, parent interaction therapy, and the Positive Parenting Program are examples of behavioral training programs for caregivers that focus on concrete strategies such as how to implement reward systems, how to establish and maintain consequences, and how to solve problems. These behavioral approaches can be beneficial for caregivers of preschool- to school-aged children as well as adolescents. In addition to specific training and support for caregivers, there are specific therapies focused on understanding the unique social context of the individual child, such as family systems therapy.

Conduct Disorder

Another childhood condition that is known to be associated with aggressive and defiant behavior is conduct disorder. This is a condition that is characterized by a persistent pattern in which the child or adolescent frequently violates the basic rights of others, engages in rule-breaking behavior, is aggressive toward people and animals, and may destroy property. These children engage in these sorts of behaviors in multiple settings and may find themselves in frequent trouble at home, at school, and potentially with the criminal justice system. According to the DSM-5, some additional symptoms of conduct disorder can also include intimidating or bullying others, cruelty toward animals, forcing people into sexual activity, using a weapon to inflict bodily harm to others, lying to others and stealing, as well as skipping school, running away from home, and consistently breaking curfew. Kids who meet the criteria for this condition engage in behaviors in which they are seriously violating certain rules prior to the age of thirteen. In addition to these features, some kids may lack remorse or guilt about their behavior, may display shallow emotions, and have a lack of empathy such that they are unconcerned about the feelings of others.

For children and adolescents who have conduct disorder, multisystemic therapy (MST) is an approach that provides intensive supports, whether that be within the home or in the community. It provides real-time support to caregivers on how to navigate a challenging interaction with a kid who may be displaying aggressive behavior or disobedience, refuses to attend school, or has run away from home. Clinicians who are trained in MST aim to empower caregivers with tools to reinforce positive behaviors with the kid and to help support children who are exhibiting disruptive behavior. The focus of MST is to understand what in a life may be contributing to these behavioral issues—whether it be certain family dynamics, their surrounding environment, or other psychosocial factors.

Disruptive Mood Dysregulation Disorder (DMDD)

There are children who have anger episodes, temper tantrums, and irritable moods that seem to come out of the blue. There is no underlying neurodevelopmental disorder; it just seems as though the kid is "moody" all the time. Kids between the ages of six and eighteen who are moody, have frequent temper tantrums at least several times a week, and become upset easily may have a condition referred to as disruptive mood dysregulation disorder or DMDD. For these kids, it is as though their baseline mood is persistently irritable. It may feel as though the smallest thing could just set them off and result in an outburst that could resemble a toddler's tantrum or meltdown. According to the DSM-5, the temper outbursts occur about three times per week and are grossly out of proportion to the inciting situation. DMDD can manifest differently over the course of development. When kids are younger, their outbursts tend to be more physical: hitting or throwing things. As the kid ages and becomes a teenager they may become more verbally aggressive, or the irritability may transition into a more internalized emotional state such as depression.

Treatment for DMDD aims to provide kids with tools to help them regulate their emotions such that they do not escalate from 0 to 100 so quickly and can prevent themselves from total meltdown. Therapeutic interventions such as dialectical behavioral therapy (DBT) can help kids learn to be more mindful, recognize their emotional state, be more effective in their communication to others, and utilize coping strategies in the moment to tolerate difficult emotions.

Given that children who have DMDD present with significant mood-related symptoms, they could benefit from starting medication to reduce the intensity of the anger episodes and the irritability. Medications such as selective serotonin reuptake inhibitors (SSRIs) can help, and at times antipsychotics may be recommended to reduce aggressive episodes if they are severe.

Depression

While major depressive episodes are often characterized by periods of sadness and tearful episodes, emotional symptoms of depression may manifest in children and adolescents in the form of irritability and anger. I can recall countless interactions with parents who simply cannot understand why their child has progressively become more socially withdrawn, irritable, and argumentative, and may even express that anger by getting into physical fights with others, punching the wall, or destroying material objects. If these behavioral changes occur in the context of a period of at least two weeks in which they don't sleep well, have difficulty enjoying their usual activities, feel hopeless or like they are a burden to others, experience changes in appetite and energy level, have difficulty concentrating and making decisions, or tell you that their movements and thoughts feel as though they are in slowed motion or that they are having thoughts of suicide, then they meet criteria for a major depressive episode. This can be a challenge since the child may not communicate to you that they are depressed, and may not even know that they are. It could take some detective work on your end to understand what may be driving this change in their behavior. Children who are experiencing periods of anger and irritability due to depression can benefit from individual therapy, including cognitive behavioral therapy, and possibly from antidepressant medication.

Bipolar Disorder

Anger, irritability, and aggression can also be associated with another mood disorder referred to as bipolar disorder. This condition is characterized by episodes of significant mood fluctuations in which they may experience periods of mania as well as depression. According to the DSM-5, manic episodes are distinct periods in which someone experiences a persistently elevated, expansive, or irritable mood. Most caregivers of children diagnosed with bipolar disorder would describe them as moody, having both intense moods and sudden swings from one mood to another that aren't necessarily sparked by or related to anything happening in the world outside the child's brain. Some describe the aggression expressed by children who have bipolar disorder as being explosive and more severe than aggression related to other mental health conditions. The symptoms of bipolar disorder can be challenging to recognize in children most of the time and go unrecognized in youth since irritability, anger, and aggression can be attributed to other mental health conditions or are presumed to be related to psychosocial stressors. For these reasons, there are often significant delays between the onset of symptoms and when children finally receive treatment for bipolar disorder. Unfortunately, many young people who have bipolar disorder go untreated, which can result in worse long-term outcomes. It's important to know that this condition is highly heritable, such that children of parents who have bipolar polar disorder are ten to twenty times more likely to develop the condition than children of parents who do not have bipolar disorder, which can be due to a combination of genetics and environmental and other psychosocial factors. If you know that someone in your family was diagnosed with bipolar disorder or had symptoms of the condition though it was never diagnosed, you should share this information with your child's primary care provider and mental health providers.

During episodes of mania, people have decreased need for sleep, such that they feel well rested despite sleeping for only a few hours or not at all for several days in a row. People can also present as more distracted and/or more talkative than usual and can experience racing thoughts such that they seem to leap from topic to topic. Children in the manic phase of bipolar disorder may also experience what is referred to as increased goal-directed activity, which means that they suddenly start to spend an excessive amount of time engaged exclusively in a certain activity, sometimes one that is out of character for them, like cleaning their room or editing and organizing years' worth of cell phone photos or the trading card collection they haven't looked at since third grade. Or they may start taking on a variety of different goal-oriented tasks all at the same time, performing such activities in the middle of the night or at odd hours. Some kids may focus on generating creative content by way of writing, drawing, composing music, or working on digital video projects, again for extended periods of time that are out of character for the kid.

People may also exhibit some behavior during a manic episode that others find unusual or disturbing, such as having grandiose delusions. Delusions are defined as fixed, false beliefs that a person thinks are true despite evidence to the contrary. In children, grandiose delusions can take on the form of elevated self-esteem, such as that they possess special powers or capabilities that no one else is in possession of. They may believe that they have superpowers that will allow them to fly or that they are so smart that they have already found a cure for cancer despite never having taken a class in biology—beliefs that are uncharacteristic of them and aren't a product of the kind of "let's pretend" fantasy play-acting children may engage in at younger developmental ages. Manic symptoms can also include hypersexual behavior, which in young children can take on the form of being overly preoccupied with talking about nudity, drawing pictures of naked people, or inappropriate touching of certain body parts on other people. Adolescents may engage in excessive masturbation, sexual activity either online or in real life with inappropriate or multiple partners, or other behavior reflecting a marked change in their usual behavior as it relates to sexual activity.

Treatment for children who have bipolar disorder often involves the use of medications to help provide mood stability as well as to mitigate irritability and aggression. Medications approved for use in children that your provider may consider include lithium, atypical antipsychotics, or an anticonvulsant such as divalproex sodium may be considered. Psychotherapy is beneficial alongside medication to reduce the duration and severity of a mood episode.

Helping the Child Who Is Angry, Defiant, or Disruptive

It can be challenging in the heat of the moment to forget about the fact that our children are trying to figure out how to function with the tools that they have access to at that particular moment in time. As I've mentioned before, the more emotional regions of the brain develop faster than the regions involved in regulating those emotions—areas in the frontal cortex that aid in rational thinking and impulse control. Not only that, but those frontal regions develop at a pace that varies from person to person, which makes it difficult to set expectations for a child's emotional development simply based on their chronological age. Neurodiversity, genetics, exposures while in utero, trauma, and life experiences all factor into a child's social-emotional developmental process. It is hard to anticipate when a child who is struggling to manage their emotions will develop the skill set to manage emotions. Everyone is on their own trajectory. Child psychologist Dr. Mona Delahooke talks about the importance of recognizing that there are individual differences in play:

> I think that will really take pressure off of parents to think, instead of "Oh, I'm a bad parent," or "This is a bad child," to think, "Oh, they're early on in the process and, oh my goodness, this behavior represents a need for some more support in their development rather than correction."
>
> I get parents' tendency to want to correct kids' behavior, because parenting is such a huge responsibility and we want to raise respectful, good humans. I totally get that. But once we understand development, it's important to ask "Is this a stress response or a purposeful misbehavior?"
>
> The most challenging behaviors like running away, kicking, screaming, spitting, yelling, what we might consider tantrums, especially in our toddlers, in our young children, and our neurodivergent children, our children who've been exposed to trauma, those fight or flight

behaviors are an indicator of a stress response, not an indicator of a child choosing to misbehave. This, I think, is the most important and new idea for parents to incorporate, that if we pause and understand if this is an automatic, instinctual, non-intentional behavior, we really want to go to soothing that child instead of punishing or consequencing or even trying to use logic with them in that moment.

Co-Regulation

As caregivers, one of our roles is to help teach our kids the skills necessary to foster strong, positive development of the parts of the brain critical for emotional regulation. We do that by modeling how to communicate about feelings and how to respond to certain situations. Kids are constantly watching us, monitoring our behavior, and learning from it. Despite your best attempts to provide these skills and to display good modeling, however, a child might still really struggle to control their anger. Patience is key here, since you are not in charge of how or when exactly your child's brain develops. It is also important to work with your child to identify strategies for managing big emotions when the child is in a calm state.

Co-regulation is a process in which you provide the external support your child needs to regulate their nervous system and their internal state. Doing this provides kids with the blueprint for learning what it is that their body needs in order to calm itself down. When a child is very young, caregivers can often figure out fairly easily what to do to calm their child down. Embracing them, sitting them on your lap, rocking them in a chair, patting them gently on the back, smoothing their hair, speaking to them in a calm, soft voice . . . All these actions help a child go from a state of hyperarousal to a more steady state, in which they feel more in control of their own mood and behavior.

Especially when they are young, kids who have difficulty with emotional self-regulation often experience and express agitation in their bodies, which can become an obstacle to engaging in the co-regulation that would calm them. Psychologist Dr. Lori Desautels offered some suggestions about how to tune in to your child, to make your way there in the ways you and your child can manage:

> If a child is out of control in their body, we call this a behavioral bio-marker. What that is a fancy way of saying is if the child is moving all over the place in an uncontrolled way, that could be moving their mouth by screaming or yelling or literally thrashing and hitting, that is a great indicator to make sure you stop what you're doing and realize that the child needs soothing in their body, rather than you talking to them. A child in that fight-or-flight response, I call it the red pathway, is not going to be hearing you very well.
>
> An out-of-control child's nervous system isn't poised to decode language; it's poised to move. We want to allow the child to move, make sure they're safe, don't inhibit their movement, don't try to hold them from moving, but make sure they're safe, and try to use your body language first before your words. That might look like just having a compassionate look on your face and saying, "Oh. Oh goodness, I see this is hard. I see you. How can I help?"
>
> Now of course I used a few words there, but the main body language would be moving toward the child and according to their individual differences, using something to soothe their body. Usually that's sensory rather than thought-based. What sensory means, it could mean maybe they would like a hand on their shoulder or maybe they would like you to walk with them or sing a song to them, or just be quiet, every child is different, but the advice is to go for soothing over talking first.

This process of co-regulation should continue across the childhood and adolescent years, though the ways you engage in it may look different. As kids get older and want to assert their sense of independence and autonomy, they may not want a hug every time they are upset. You can still offer them the tool of co-regulation by engaging with them, talking to them in a calm way, helping them label their feelings, and validating their experience—letting them know that you know that what they are going through is difficult.

Some kids are difficult to engage, making it more challenging for us to find a way for co-regulation to happen. When we flounder for ways to truly connect with our child over time, we may become more distant, not quite sure if our kid really wants us there, in precisely those moments in which our children need us the most. We should always push back against that feeling. Our child needs us to be there, even when we are floundering, and even when it feels as though we are not wanted.

Responding, Not Reacting

Being in the presence of a child who is angry and impulsive will inevitably elicit some kind of response from you. It would be highly unusual if it didn't, since the child is trying—even if unconsciously—to communicate their distress to the people around them in order to get some kind of response or reaction. In fact, having no response can be harmful in its own way, so we need to respond.

Caregivers can feel overwhelmed in these moments. The intensity of the anger and rage their child is expressing can be shocking. I've heard from many parents who have witnessed incredibly distressing displays of anger, ranging from their child throwing and breaking objects, to teenagers getting into physical altercations with them that result in serious injury. Their stories about what it is like behind closed doors to bear witness to the behaviors and actions of a highly angry and aggressive child are ones that you do not often hear. These incidents can be terrifying for everyone involved—not only for the family but also for the child.

Although it can be hard to remember in the moment, the child who is being destructive and aggressive is externalizing their internal suffering. Nobody wants to be angry all the time. Nobody wants to be aggressive toward the people that they love. Nobody does. And when they are, we need to always keep in mind, even in the midst of intense rage, that this is the best that this child can do with the skills and the brain they currently possess.

As caregivers, we can keep this in mind and also acknowledge our own emotional response to it. We, too, can be angry. We can also experience profound sadness that our child is treating us and others this way. We can feel anxious that another anger episode will happen out of the blue. The caregivers I interviewed for this book experienced all those emotions. But they also experienced unconditional love for their child.

There is a lot of pressure placed on caregivers to respond appropriately, and we feel that pressure keenly. But at the end of the day, we are humans, too, and may have difficulty controlling our reactions in the heat of the moment. As developmental pediatrician Dr. Claudia Gold told me, it is important to be mindful of the fact that a dysregulated kid can result in a parent who is also dysregulated. Becoming dysregulated ourselves can further escalate the situation. We all have been there before; there is no shame in admitting that. In that moment of intense stress, both child and caregiver enter a physiological state of fight, flight, or freeze, which can govern our responses to each other's behavior. We're being reactive. Our instincts kick in to protect ourselves from the situation. The same thing is happening with our child.

As adults, we are able to transition more quickly than a child can from reliance on the region of the brain that governs our survival instincts to regions that are responsible for regulating our emotions and that facilitate rational thinking and reasoning, which allows us to temper our response. Kids really struggle to move through these regions of the brain as quickly as adults. That said, many caregivers also very often have difficulty with emotional regulation. It's a skill that many of us did not learn in childhood, and there may be other factors in our lives like trauma or our own neurodiversity that can make it challenging to emotionally regulate ourselves in the moment. That's why it's important for caregivers to develop their own emotional self-awareness and learn techniques for de-escalating conflicts and making our way closer to "co-regulation" even in the heat of the moment.

Greater recognition and awareness of some of our child's limitations in terms of a lack of skill and tools, their current brain development, and any neurological vulnerabilities that they may possess can potentially help temper our reactions and slow down our own urge to respond impulsively in the moment. Dr. Gold suggests that the first step in responding effectively to your dysregulated child is to acknowledge when you're emotionally dysregulated yourself. We should not expect ourselves to be able to be emotionally regulated and nonreactive all the time, but when our own awareness grows regarding our emotional state so does our ability to detach from it, and put some space in between our feelings and our behavior.

The Three *R*s: Regulate, Relate, and Reason

Child psychiatrist and trauma expert Dr. Bruce Perry developed a model that provides guidance on how to support someone who is having difficulty managing intense emotions. This model is referred to as the three *R*s: regulate, relate, and reason.

During these moments when our kid is acting up, we tend to use a lot of words to correct and modify the behavior. We ask lots of questions such as, "Why would you do that? Why would you ask that? Why are you so angry with me?" As Dr. Claudia Gold reminds us, when a child, or teen for that matter, is dysregulated, they are operating out of the oldest parts of the human brain, the ones that deal with the basic bodily processes and emotions necessary to survival: respiration, hunger, fight-or-flight. Any language-based intervention, such as the caregiver talking, reminding them to use skills, or asking them questions about motivation, is not helpful. In that particular moment in time, the child won't even really understand what the parent is saying, or be able to access higher-order brain functions. We need to exit our own state of hyperarousal and help the child emerge from their fight-flight-freeze state first.

Some examples of what we can do to enter into the first stage of the three *R*s, regulate, is to engage in activities such as deep breathing, walking away, giving the child space to move their body in a safe way, or suggesting that they engage in a preferred activity. I recognize that it can be hard in the moment when a child is aggressive to do these things. Some caregivers feel that they are somehow "letting the child off the hook" by not continuing to wrestle directly with the undesirable behavior, or that to guide them to a preferred activity is to reward their tantrum, or at least to enable it. But the reality is that first and foremost, you want to ensure that you, the child, and everyone else is safe. When the child is dysregulated, it is hard to regulate them through reasoning; their physiological state needs to change first.

Dr. Perry's second *R*, relate, addresses the need to reconnect and communicate with your child when they are in a much calmer state. Being present such that you make eye contact with the child, listen to their concerns in an empathic way, validate their feelings, and engage in active listening will communicate to the child that you still care, that you are there for them, and that you will help them get through this difficult moment. Adjusting your tone of voice while communicating to them in short sentences that are specific and concrete can be helpful, such as "I see that you're upset right now and I am here for you." The focus at this stage is around connection, which will help them to regulate emotionally such that they can get to the stage where their brain is able to process and engage in rational thinking.

The third *R* is reason. Once the child is in a fully regulated state, their brain is able to engage in higher-order thinking and is more capable of having a conversation that involves reflecting on their behavior and learning tools or strategies to better navigate the situation in the future. During this period, you can provide them with feedback on how they handled the situation, and give them concrete examples of when they could have used certain coping strategies during the incident. You can discuss ways in which they could better communicate their distress to other people, and create a plan together for handling the situation if it arises again.

. . .

Living with a child who is experiencing or acting out on angry feelings can be distressing. But not all displays—or even periods—of anger and aggression signify that a child has a mental health condition, or that you have a major problem on your hands. I will take the liberty of adding a fourth *R* to Dr. Perry's model: reframe. If possible, reframe an angry outburst as an opportunity to identify whether your child lacks any skills that may empower them to regulate themselves. I interviewed Dr. Ross Greene, a psychologist and originator of the Collaborative and Proactive Solutions model to help support children who are behaviorally challenging. As he put it, children are not intentionally trying to be difficult or angry. We can help support them by striving to understand what may be contributing to the problematic behavior and what tools, supports, and skills they need to manage their own feelings. Over time, as kids mature, as their brains develop, and as they acquire those skills, the fits of rage may diminish. They can learn to care for themselves and to deal with their feelings in a more regulated way.

Even when your child seems to be trying to drive you away, they need you to stay in the game. There are many good reasons to believe that things will get better.

THIRTEEN

Substance Use and Mental Health

As caregivers, we often have to put our faith in our children to navigate the world making sound choices. We have to trust that they have internalized some of the guidance we have given them over the years about how they can stay safe and well. Wear a seat belt, look both ways while crossing the street, don't talk to strangers, put your hands at ten and two on the steering wheel if you are pulled over by police—these are examples of consistent themes around safety that we make a point to educate our children about. One of the biggest themes, and one of the biggest challenges that comes up for caregivers, has to do with the consequences of drug use. Many caregivers understandably wish their child would abstain from any drug use, but also assume that the child will probably experiment with alcohol and drugs at some point, like most kids do in the United States, and that they don't have much control over that. We don't always have control over the situations in which our kids can find themselves where they have access to drugs. We don't always know where they are hanging out or with whom. We also may not always know the internal struggles our kids are dealing with that may influence their attitude toward drugs and affect how they experience altered states of consciousness.

The reality is that human beings have used alcohol and drugs to alter their consciousness for many thousands of years, and young people in our society experiment with drugs and alcohol as well. The factors motivating kids to use substances today include peer pressure, social environments, curiosity, and emotional distress. There are also genetic and biological factors that affect both someone's inclination to use mind-altering substances and their physiological response to those substances. We are often angry when we find out that our kid may be using drugs, especially when it interferes with their ability to do what we expect our kids to do: wake up, go to school, do homework, respect their family members, and stay safe. But it will not be helpful to a child if we allow our anger to overwhelm any desire to understand what underlying factors may have led to their drug use.

In this chapter, we'll explore factors that contribute to substance use in children and, more commonly, adolescents. I'll discuss how to talk to a child or adolescent about drugs and alcohol, how to distinguish experimentation from problematic drug use, and treatment options for kids who are experiencing challenges related to their substance use.

Why Do Kids Use Drugs?

Children are like little sponges, continuously soaking up information from their environment and through interactions with the people in their lives. In addition to being exposed to certain adult behaviors and activities within their actual environment, they also have incredible access to a vast virtual environment full of information about how people cope with distress, outlets people utilize to escape from their problems, and activities people engage in to have fun. Children growing up in this society cannot escape the pervasive presence of substance use, whether that be within their schools, homes, and communities, in the movies and on TV shows they watch, or through social media and the internet. It has become nearly impossible to shelter your child from knowing that people use alcohol and drugs and that many of them enjoy, even revel in, doing so.

Many kids and teens have adults in their lives who use substances. Kids can see the impact that alcohol or drugs have on the adults' behavior and mood and on their relationships. They may also bear witness to the ways that one person's substance use causes suffering for others. Sometimes, they are the ones who are directly and negatively affected. But even kids who become fully aware of the potential negative consequences of drug use may still be curious about what it feels like to drink or use drugs and find the idea of "getting high" or "getting wasted" appealing.

Many caregivers find it quite a challenge to understand what drives a kid to start using drugs in the first place. In the clinic, parents have said to me that they don't understand why their child is using drugs despite their awareness of the negative consequences of drug use in other families, the warnings they've heard in public service announcements and health education class in school, or what they've seen just by driving around and witnessing the impact that substance use has had on their community. What is important to understand as a caregiver is that despite your best efforts to educate your child about the potential consequences of drug use, they still may use. But why?

Many—in fact the majority—of kids who experiment with alcohol and drugs do so without experiencing dire consequences. They learn what drugs do, have positive and negative experiences, and move on. Other things in their lives—relationships, education, work, hobbies, and interests—become ever more important to them; adult responsibilities and personal ambitions require their full attention; they are motivated to be their best selves. They may still drink or use socially on occasion but can take it or leave it. However, there are kids who do experience serious and life-altering consequences for their drug use. Some experience consequences because they lack resources, opportunities, and time to outgrow or move beyond their drug use—kids who, for example, are more vulnerable to engagement with the criminal justice system. But other kids experience more serious consequences of substance use because they have a harder time staying away from the substances. Chronic substance use diminishes their engagement with all those other things in their lives, limits socioemotional development, and causes enduring harm.

People who have challenges staying away from substances even when using them interferes with their ability to function—meaning it gets in the way of their ability to maintain relationships, go to work or school, and take care of their daily responsibilities—have those challenges both because of the effects drugs have on the brain and because their biological "wiring" informs the intensity of the impact drug use has on their brain. Researchers have found that there are certain genetic vulnerabilities that make it more likely for some people to develop problematic drug use than other people. People who have a known family history of substance use disorder have an increased risk of developing a substance use disorder themselves. Substance use disorders can be heritable, meaning that certain genetic factors are passed from parent to the child, which makes them more vulnerable to developing problematic drug use. This is also one of the reasons why some people can use a drug without significant functional impairment and others are more prone to become addicted to that same drug in a way that negatively impacts their life. Understanding the role of biology when it comes to substance use can be helpful in understanding why it can be so hard to break the cycle of substance use within a family.

Alice Held, a queer woman in their midtwenties residing in Missoula, Montana, told me:

One aspect of addiction is that it's so much more far-reaching than just drugs and alcohol. And really drugs and alcohol are the person coping with this much larger issue that's going on in our brain. Even if the kid stopped doing drugs and alcohol, there's a high likelihood that

there's still behaviors or symptoms that will need to be treated within
this person . . . If someone abstains from drugs and alcohol, it's not
going to immediately solve the problem.

In addition to the genetic vulnerabilities that can influence whether
or not kids go on to develop problematic drug use, the environment
in which kids find themselves can significantly impact their exposure
to drugs. Children who live with parents who are drinking or using
drugs are more likely to go on to develop substance use disorders
themselves because they are exposed to the drugs and witness the effects of the drugs. Witnessing the effects drugs have on people within
their home and community may lead them to wonder what effect
drugs may have on them. Also, exposure to drugs in the home can
increase access to drugs that kids would not otherwise be able to acquire easily.

Preadolescents and adolescents are at a stage of brain development
that actually predisposes them to engage in impulsive, reward-seeking
behavior. The average age at which kids in the United States first use a
mind-altering substance is around the age of thirteen, but studies have
suggested that for drugs such as cannabis, cigarettes, and alcohol, age of
first use can be much younger. But in addition to the neurodevelopmental challenges that drive kids this age toward substance use, there
are a number of psychosocial factors that can increase the risk that
youth of this age will develop a substance use disorder, including having poor or underdeveloped social skills—whether they manifest either
in aggressive behavior or in becoming passive or withdrawn—and poor
social problem-solving skills, a lack of self-esteem, or academic struggles. A decrease in social support as a result of a move into a new school
or a new community can be a risk factor. It's worth noting that all these
risk factors are fairly common. Teens are often experiencing feelings
and encountering social situations they've never handled before, including those related to sexuality; it seems self-evident that they would
not yet be skilled in handling them.

Of course, kids whose peers are using substances are more likely to use too. It is natural for children to be curious about substance use especially if their friends are talking about it, and it isn't uncommon for adolescents to experiment with drugs when peers offer them, or if they find themselves in social settings in which drugs are available. Peer pressure and a strong desire to want to be like their peers and to be accepted by their peers also factor into whether or not kids use drugs. About 21 percent of eighth graders have tried an illicit drug at least once and by twelfth grade over 46 percent of teens have tried an illicit drug. About 13 percent of twelve- to seventeen-year-olds report using marijuana within the last year. Nearly 63 percent of twelfth graders used marijuana via vaping within the past year and 62 percent of twelfth graders have misused alcohol. Substance use does increase as kids get older such that marijuana and alcohol use was three times as high in twelfth graders as it was among eighth graders.

There are of course many reasons to be concerned about the prevalence of drug use among teens and preteens. But the prevalence also indicates that experimentation is fairly normal, if not inevitable. Whatever you feel about drug use generally, the more important issue for you as a caregiver is whether your teen's drug use, in particular, is either problematic or symptomatic of a much larger mental health issue.

When you suspect that your child may be using substances or find out that they are actually using, it is natural to fixate on what they are using, when they are using, where they are getting it from, and why they disobeyed you by using. But it would be more beneficial for your child and for you to consider asking some other questions, like: What is the drug use doing for them? What feeling or experience does it offer them that they feel is lacking when they're not using?

Kids are doing the best that they can with the tools that they have. A teen may want to experiment with drugs because there are underlying mental health challenges that make the struggles of their day-to-day life difficult to tolerate. They may use drugs to blunt or soothe mental health symptoms including anxiety, depression, irritability, and intrusive memories related to traumas they experienced in the past, because they lack other strategies that may be more adaptive and sustainable. It is hard for young people to endure emotional distress, particularly when they lack the tools and strategies to help them cope. Seeking out drugs provides some kids with an option for dealing with the distress. Drugs may also be a means of coping with physical issues such as low energy, poor sleep, and physical pain.

For some young people, the emotional distress and pain related to their internal experiences, or the distress arising from physical pain or disability, may be so severe that it is hard for them to fully consider other consequences of their drug use. They just want the pain to go away, they no longer want to struggle, and drugs provide a temporary solution. Once someone is able to identify a strategy that helps to relieve some distress, it is hard to give that up.

This is also the case when it comes to other activities that function in a similar way to drugs, whether that be excessive or restrictive eating, binging and purging, excessive exercise, compulsive shopping, sex, gambling, or even engaging in self-harm behaviors such as cutting—whatever activity it may be that they are engaging in repetitively as a way to cope. For most young people who are engaged in these sorts of excessive, repetitive activities, including using drugs, there is something underneath that is continuously fueling the drive to engage in them, despite their potential for harm.

Being aware of a child's substance use is just the tip of the iceberg. It is important to uncover what is lying underneath, and why the iceberg exists in the first place. The problematic use of drugs and alcohol is very often a sign that the user is coping with a much larger issue with origins in their brain. Even if a kid who is using drugs and alcohol stopped using them, there's a high likelihood that they will still need treatment for other mental health symptoms.

Identifying what is actually driving these behaviors is often a challenge. How do you do that when your kid denies that they are using drugs, denies that they have a problem, or maybe does not even want to talk to you? Ongoing mental health symptoms may interfere with your child's ability to communicate their concerns to you—or to others—in order to get the help that they need. To connect with a young person about drugs, drug use, and the mental health concerns that may contribute to drug use, requires patience, courage, emotional self-control, and an open mind. Next I also suggest some approaches and strategies for initiating and conducting conversations that other parents and caregivers have found to be useful.

How to Talk to Kids About Substance Use

Even when you have no real concern that your child has begun using alcohol or drugs, it can be difficult to know exactly when to initiate conversations regarding substance use. For many of us, the conversation around substance use has a place on that list of uncomfortable conversations caregivers dread having, like the ones dealing with sex. Yes, it can be uncomfortable initiating conversations about things that we're afraid of, sad about, or may not have a lot of expertise in, but one way to view it that may help you overcome your reluctance to broach the topic with your child is through the lens of safety. There are a number of safety-related issues that we have to discuss with our kids and the truth of the matter is that both sex and drugs are on the list. Reframing your thinking about why you are having the conversation may make it easier to have. Think of it as an opportunity to learn more about the world in which your child lives and what sorts of things are on your child's mind. You'll also gain insights as to what it is their peer group may be up to and whether or not substance use is something that is being explored.

When should you begin talking with your child about drug use? The thing to keep in mind is that this is not a "one and done" conversation that you can just cross off that uncomfortable conversation list. Speaking openly about substance use is something you want to do on an ongoing basis. Because substance use is so pervasive in our society, kids are exposed to images and conversations about it fairly often, whether through television shows, social media, at school, or even by observing friends, family, and other people in their community. That's why it's important for the conversation also to be occurring at home, and for you to be participating in it and thus normalizing it.

How to Start the Conversation

The best way to approach conversations about drug use with children and adolescents will differ depending on their age, your relationship, and the context. The following are some examples of how you might engage at various stages. Some of these strategies are from Drugfree.org, which provides a number of helpful resources for talking to kids about drugs (https://drugfree.org/article/prevention-tips-for-every-age/).

Elementary School–Aged Children (Ages Six to Ten)

One way to bring up the topic of substance use is when you witness something together that depicts or relates to it. This may be a little challenging since you may not be able to plan the conversation ahead of time, but the idea is that as you and your child are exploring and navigating the world together, take advantage of those real-time scenarios to explore their understanding of a situation.

For example, if you are watching a movie together in which teenagers are smoking marijuana, you can ask, "How do you feel about those kids smoking? I ask because I think it's better for kids to not smoke so that they can stay safe and healthy. What do you think about that?"

This is a casual conversation that gives you some insight as to whether or not your child already understands what the teenagers depicted in the movie are doing, and has formed some thoughts and opinions around substance use. Opening the door like this could also lead to questions about the factors that have contributed to their perspective on substance use. You can use the conversation as an opportunity to share your thoughts about substance use and your stance on drug use by kids in particular, but not in the form of a sermon or lecture. Remember: You want to draw them out, learn what they know and don't know, and explore their feelings about the things they see in the world.

Middle School/Early Teen Years (Eleven to Thirteen Years Old)

If your child is in middle school, it is highly likely that they have already been exposed to substance use or at least had conversations about it with their peers. At this age, kids put heavy emphasis on the thoughts and opinions of their friends. They may respect and value their friends' opinions more than yours. They have also already seen plenty of representations of substance use through various forms of media, school, and probably elsewhere. It is possible that your bringing up the topic of substance use can really feel out of the blue and random, which may be off-putting for your preteen. But given that kids of this age are quite busy spending time with their friends or tied up in various school activities or may like spending more time alone in their room, it can be hard to find a moment in which you can casually bring up the subject in a way that relates to the moment at hand. Use moments in which you know that you'll have their full attention. For a lot of caregivers, car rides are a perfect moment to talk about sensitive topics. Your kid is a captive audience and really the only place that they can escape to avoid the conversation is looking out the window or at their phone. Ask about how their friends are doing. You can mention that you know at this age there are kids who start to become curious about substance use and explore whether or not that has been the case for their friends. Kids of this age may feel more comfortable talking about the experiences of their peers as a proxy for themselves. This could begin to give you a sense as to whether or not your child has close proximity to drugs. Let them know that if they have questions or find themselves in a situation in which they feel unsafe, to know that they can reach out to you, no questions asked.

Teenagers (Fourteen Years Old and Older)

During this stage, teenagers may already have their own well-formed thoughts and opinions regarding substance use and may hold beliefs that contrast with yours. As part of their desire to gain an increasing amount of independence, establishing some separation from some of the family values and beliefs may factor into their views on drug use. It is also challenging to talk to teenagers because it can feel as though they are living their own separate lives, and that you don't fully know how they navigate the world. They are able to drive, work, participate in various extracurriculars, and find their own way of arranging transport to different activities. For these reasons, it is important to be intentional about creating opportunities to connect with your teen to talk to them about their views on drug use. You may be experiencing things together in real time that would naturally bring up a conversation around drug use, in ways that would not happen with elementary school–age kids or preteens.

An important focus of these conversations is how they can stay safe if they find themselves in a situation in which they or their friends become intoxicated and they're unsure how they're going to make it home. These are scenarios in which you would want your teen to call you so that they don't find themselves in an unsafe situation. However, teens may hesitate to reach out since they don't want to be scolded and reprimanded for being in a setting with drugs. That ongoing fear could make the difference between deciding to pick up the phone and reach out or trying to take matters into their own hands. Let your kid know that if they find themselves in that situation, you'll help them out with no questions asked in the moment. If you know that your teen is heading out to a party or is planning to hang out with their friends, let them know that you want them to enjoy themselves, but that it's important that they make safe choices when they're out when it comes to alcohol and drugs.

How to Talk to Kids if You're Concerned That They're Using

There is a good chance that your child will at some point try alcohol, marijuana, or other drugs. This can be incredibly worrisome since they made a decision that could have put them in an unsafe situation and that defied your efforts to discourage them from using. If you have concerns that they are using, bring them up. When you do, try to remain calm, even if your internal experience is the complete opposite. You can let your child know that you're disappointed, angry, sad, or anxious about the fact that they are using. The main goal of the conversation is simply to understand your child's experience. The only way that you'll be able to understand the experience is if there is space for them to share it with you. Set an intention that your teen should do the majority of the talking. Ask open-ended questions in a neutral tone of voice. Try to understand what function their drug use serves for them. Are they using because everyone else is using and they think it's no big deal? Do drugs help them sleep or make them feel less anxious?

Understanding what is driving them to use can give you an opening to talk to them in a way that may resonate with them. Simply just saying drugs are bad and to stay away from them is not enough. The issue of what drove them to use will remain. Focusing on the underlying factor that led to their use can be a thing that you all can agree on when there is a clear difference of opinion when it comes to using drugs. It's important to also acknowledge the fact that kids use drugs because they simply like getting high or being in an altered state. It's a fun experience; it's something that they enjoy doing with their friends, or it's a tool that helps them escape the realities of their world. However, one can still be curious as to why drug use is the main activity they're engaging in for fun or for escape given that there are known consequences for ongoing use.

It's hard not to overreact once you find out that your kid is using substances. Yes, it is reasonable to worry about the consequences of ongoing use and it is important to share those concerns with your child. However, it is also helpful to be mindful of whether or not their drug use is interfering with particular aspects of their life. With the distress radius framework in mind, it is helpful to think about whether the substance use is interfering with their relationships; whether it is affecting their academic performance or their ability to take care of themselves day to day, and whether it is having a negative impact on their physical health. Your kid may minimize their use, as well as the impact of their use on them. But it is important to share that their use over time could potentially result in functional impairment in key areas of their life. They may not care what you have to say about drugs or are not future-oriented enough in their thinking to worry about the consequences of their drug use. At the end of the day, you still need to voice your concerns. And at some level, they hear you, and know your concerns come from love.

Your kid may think that using drugs is not problematic, and you think it is, but you can both agree that being anxious every day is really hard. You can agree that saying no to something when everyone around you is doing it is hard. You can agree that life can be stressful and that many people use alcohol and other substances to relax without necessarily becoming addicted. You can also probably find agreement that people develop substance use disorders that hijack their lives, and that those people probably thought at some point that they weren't doing anything harmful. Finding some common ground with your child will demonstrate that you hear them and can validate their experience but also encourage them to consider their own motivations for using and potential consequences. If they are using drugs to self-medicate emotional distress, an honest and forthright conversation opens up the possibility of you working together to find a more sustainable, less risky way to deal with that distress.

It isn't uncommon for kids to deny that they have a problem with drug use and deny that their using has had a negative impact on their functioning. Teens who are using drugs sometimes overestimate their ability to control their urge to use drugs. They may say to you, I can stop using drugs at any time, I'm not addicted, it's no big deal. Adults who use substances do and say these same things. Denial is both a symptom of a substance use disorder and a strategy for ensuring that the person can continue to use. But a teen's understanding of themselves and the knowledge it will require to support themselves and thrive as adults is even more limited than that of most adults. Alice Held, whose mother struggled with substance use disorder during Alice's childhood and who is now in recovery herself, described the role of the "I can stop anytime fallacy" in her own lived experience:

Let's go to an alternate reality where that's true: I can stop when I want to stop. Why don't I want to stop right now when the truancy officer is telling me I'm going to get kicked out of school? When my parents have doctors telling them that I should go to an eight-month, ten-month rehab facility? When the only friends that I have left are the ones that do as much drugs as me—and they don't even want to hang out with me!

I can't have meaningful relationships with anybody in my life—with mentors, with friends, with my family. I can't make authentic connections. So why is it that my whole life is up in flames, and I still don't want to stop? Maybe that's the problem. Even if I could stop when I wanted to, when am I going to want to stop? Is it going to be after I do something really harmful to my body and I'm really hurt? Because that doesn't sound like a healthy relationship with drugs and alcohol.

So that's really the conclusion that I came to after I was sober: "Wow, it's so crazy that I didn't want to stop even when every door in my life was being closed in my face."

It's hard when teens can't see the potential consequences of their drug use for themselves even when the writing is on the walls, but as Alice learned, that blindness is an aspect of substance use disorder.

Treatment Options

You can only have so many conversations with your kid about their drug use. These interactions can become frustrating. You're constantly at odds with your kid, there is ongoing conflict and denial, and you may feel stuck. Continuing to try to talk them out of using, especially if their functioning is deteriorating and you have significant concerns about their physical and mental well-being, will not do anyone any good. While mental health issues may be an underlying factor in drug use, there may come a time when the drug use itself becomes a distinct mental health disorder that your child needs treatment for.

According to the most recent edition of the *Diagnostic and Statistical Manual* (DSM-5), a substance use disorder is diagnosed when a person has a problematic pattern of drug use that causes significant functional impairment or distress for at least twelve months, along with several of these other symptoms: They continue to use despite experiencing negative consequences, have difficulty cutting down their use, experience strong cravings for the drug, spend a large amount of time seeking out the drug, have had problems in relationships attributable to drug use, have given up activities that they previously enjoyed just to use drugs, have experienced symptoms of withdrawal, and/or have to use an increasing amount of the drug over time to achieve the desired effect.

Seeking treatment options for your teen should always be an option for you. Many caregivers are not aware of the fact that treatment options are available for kids who have problems with using drugs. I'll touch upon some of the options that you could explore for your kid whose drug use has become problematic. If you have health insurance, including Medicaid, it will cover at least some of the cost of treatment for substance use. Good treatment should also simultaneously address any underlying and co-occurring mental health disorders.

One important thing to know is that the cultures of mental health treatment, and of substance use disorder or addiction treatment, don't always jive seamlessly. There can be culture clashes around issues like medication-assisted treatment, the use of some psychiatric medications including benzodiazepines and stimulants, and different views of the role in counseling of people with lived experience and without master's, medical, or doctoral degrees. In recent years these cultures have had more of a meeting of the minds, but differences remain. You should look for mental health professionals or facilities run by mental health professionals with significant experience treating young people with substance use disorders. Your primary care provider is again a good source for referrals, your insurance policy's preferred provider network will include substance use treatment-focused providers and facilities, and you can also visit the website (www.samhsa.gov/find-help/national-helpline) or call the Helpline of the Substance Abuse and Mental Health Services Administration (SAMSHA) for information about local treatment options.

Treatment for Substance Use Disorders

As previously mentioned, your child's primary care provider could be useful in helping you to determine whether your child's drug use is concerning and warrants treatment. They may refer you to a mental health professional who can provide further support on resources that are available for your teen. Talking to a medical provider or a mental health specialist first can be helpful to better guide you toward what type of treatment would be beneficial for your child and what you might expect over the course of their treatment. The type of substance your child is using, and any co-occurring conditions they may have that are further complicated by their drug use, will be important factors in determining the kind of care they need.

Given the nature of the drug that a kid may be using, receiving treatment in a structured setting may provide the best chance of success for recovery. For example, if a kid using an opiate such as a prescription pain medication or opiates they are obtaining from the street such as heroin or fentanyl, physically it is quite a challenge to simply stop the drug and engage in an outpatient therapy program without additional supports to reduce drug cravings as well as manage the symptoms of withdrawal. However, there may be other kids who are misusing cannabis to cope with their anxiety and are failing out of school. For them, an outpatient treatment program that provides them with tools other than marijuana to manage their anxiety may be more appropriate.

Types of Facilities and Levels of Care

Identifying an appropriate facility for your child to receive specialized treatment for their substance use disorder can be challenging just given the limited number of providers in the country who work specifically with teens. Many locations only provide services to people eighteen and older, which poses a significant access issue for caregivers trying to get the help that their child needs. The names for the types of facilities may vary from state to state, but here is a general overview of the types of facilities by the terms most often used to describe them. Note that, with the exception of detox facilities, treatment programs for youth at every level of care will consider caregiver engagement to be an integral part of the treatment. Clinicians will provide "psychoeducation" about addiction, recovery, and handling relapses, as well as strategies for supporting your child's recovery and navigating challenges regarding communication, autonomy, and trust.

Detox

This type of facility primarily focuses on providing continuous medical support to people as they taper off and discontinue using a substance they have become physically dependent on. Staff at these facilities provide medications to help relieve symptoms of withdrawal and monitor vital signs to ensure that a patient does not experience any life-threatening consequences from discontinuing the substance. These programs are short-term, and many do not provide ongoing therapeutic support; they are where people go to safely stop using a drug before they transition to another type of therapeutic program that will address the psychological aspects of their substance use.

Inpatient Hospitalization

Kids who are experiencing significant mental health symptoms in addition to substance use, such as thoughts of suicide, self-injurious behavior, or psychosis, may need to be admitted to what is referred to as a "dual diagnosis unit" of an inpatient psychiatric hospital. These types of facilities are equipped to both manage the physical symptoms of withdrawal by providing medications that are typically offered in a detox facility and to provide treatment for an acute mental health concern. Typically, the focus is on managing the withdrawal symptoms and stabilizing mental health symptoms enough so that the kid is able to engage in a longer-term, usually residential, program.

Residential Programs

The facilities are sometimes referred to as "rehab" and typically provide treatment for twenty-eight days or more to individuals who have been diagnosed with substance use disorder and have recently stopped using drugs. People who have gone through detox at a facility, who have detoxed on their own, or who do not require a medically supervised detox can enroll in a residential program where they will receive intensive therapeutic supports while living in a structured environment with other people who are in recovery from their substance use. These programs provide individual and group therapy and focus on providing kids with information, tools, and skills they will need to live without using drugs, including how to tolerate distress, cope with urges to use, cultivate peer support, and address underlying mental health issues that may have led to or that have been caused by their substance use.

Partial Hospitalization Program (PHP)

Teens who are typically referred to a PHP are not at imminent risk of experiencing significant symptoms of withdrawal and do not require close medical monitoring given the type of substance they were misusing and the duration of their use. Kids are still able to live at home but spend the day in treatment. This level of care is particularly helpful for kids who may also have mental health symptoms, and therapeutic supports can be provided to address those concerns. Sometimes kids are transitioned from a residential program to a PHP for ongoing support as part of their treatment plan.

Intensive Outpatient Program (IOP)

This level of care allows teens to live at home while attending a treatment program for several hours, several days a week. Most of the programming available in an IOP is provided during the late afternoon and evening hours so that kids can still attend school while remaining engaged in treatment. IOP can serve as a step down or a transition from a PHP or can be used to increase the level of support for a teen previously engaged in outpatient treatment.

Outpatient

In some parts of the country, there are outpatient clinics staffed by mental health professionals, substance use disorder specialists, and certified peer specialists who provide ongoing recovery support as well as medication management if warranted. Kids may be engaged in weekly individual therapy or group therapy sessions with a peer specialist who has lived experience being in recovery from substance use. These facilities may also offer individual support, group workshops, and recovery education for family members.

Therapeutic Interventions

Many substance use treatment programs are built on what is called the "Minnesota model," an approach to treatment pioneered by the Hazelden Foundation in Minnesota (now the Hazelden Betty Ford Foundation) starting in 1949. This model borrows 12-step ideas and the concept of a therapeutic peer community and weds it with structured professional treatment. This approach—centered on treating the whole person: body, mind, and spirit—was at the time a radically innovative and humane alternative to the way alcoholics had been "treated" before then—with disdain and punitive confinement in jails and psychiatric institutions. And it leveraged the power of connection and community, which we now know to be critical to mental health recovery.

There are now many critics of this approach to treatment. They argue that it is not sufficiently evidence-based and that 12-step concepts actually inculcate religious ideas and patriarchal values, and are based on a rigid and false "our way or the highway" assertion that complete abstinence is a necessary precondition for recovery. Some devoted members of 12-step fellowships are also critical of this model, saying that "using" the 12 steps in professionally run, hierarchal, sometimes for-profit facilities actually violates 12-step principles and alienates many people who might have benefitted, had they come to the program voluntarily, for support rather than treatment.

Nevertheless, many kids do benefit from what they learn about themselves through these facilities and the form of treatment known as 12-step facilitation, and some recent data provides evidence that 12-step-oriented programs can work for youth. One review article described the development of an outpatient adolescent 12-step program, which incorporated some elements of motivational enhancement and cognitive behavior therapy, and found that youth readily engaged in the program and adopted, implemented, and sustained what they learned. The more frequently kids attended, the greater the percentage of days abstinent from substance use. A follow-up study found that program attendees experienced fewer substance-related consequences compared to participants in a ten-session group that utilized solely motivational enhancement and CBT therapy and were equally successful in terms of reducing the frequency of substance use and sustaining abstinence over time.

Many residential facilities have now taken a more eclectic approach to treating youth, combining 12-step facilitation with other evidence-based therapies. Those therapies may include some of those featured in the 2019 article in *Current Psychiatry Reports* on effective substance use treatment for adolescents:

Multidimensional family therapy (MDFT) is a psychosocial treatment that holistically addresses the individual, family, and environmental factors that contribute to substance use and related problems. One study found that adolescents with both a substance use disorder and a co-occurring mental health condition who were treated with MDFT were more successful in maintaining improvements in both drug use and behavior than adolescents who had residential treatment. MDFT has been found to be particularly beneficial among youth with severe SUDs.

Motivational interviewing (MI) is a counseling strategy for eliciting behavior change developed by psychologists William Miller and Stephen Rollnick. A therapist using MI seeks to help strengthen their client's personal motivation "by exploring the person's own reasons for change within an atmosphere of acceptance and compassion." While its effectiveness with adolescents is still being studied, extensive studies have found good evidence that MI is effective in promoting behavior change in ambivalent patients, "particularly with regard to problematic substance use (primarily alcohol, cannabis, and tobacco)." Other studies have suggested the potential efficacy of MI when combined with other treatment modalities such as family interventions, acceptance and commitment therapy, and contingency management.

Acceptance and commitment therapy (ACT) and mindfulness-based cognitive therapy emphasize acceptance (e.g., accepting rather than avoiding or denying feelings) and mindfulness (e.g., meditation) techniques. While the effectiveness of these therapies for treating adolescents and young adults with substance use disorders is still ongoing, there is some promising early data.

Adolescent community reinforcement approach (A-CRA) is a behavioral intervention for adolescents and young adults ages twelve to twenty-five dealing with substance use issues. It is an adaptation of the Community Reinforcement Approach developed in the early 1970s by behavioral psychologist Nathan Azrin. He believed that the punitive and confrontational approaches to substance use treatment then implemented by some therapeutic communities would not be effective long term, and that what people struggling with substance use needed was strong community support for the fulfillment and joys to be found in living sober. As Dr. William Miller, creator of MI, put it, the philosophy of A-CRA "is that in order to compete with the reinforcing effects of addictive substances, it is important to help people establish a rewarding lifestyle with regular positive reinforcement that does not depend on the use of drugs." In A-CRA, clinicians focus on helping adolescents develop a rewarding, non–substance use lifestyle. Using structured protocols and methods including role play and behavioral rehearsals to help foster prosocial behaviors, and develop problem-solving, anger-management, and communication skills as well as substance use relapse–prevention skills. Participants receive homework assignments focused on practicing these skills and are encouraged to engage in positive leisure activities. The therapist also devotes some sessions to engaging caregivers, both alone and with their child.

Medication Management

For kids who have become addicted to using drugs and have difficulty stopping their use despite the challenges that they are experiencing with their overall functioning, their primary care provider or a mental health professional may recommend the use of medication. Currently, there are no FDA-approved medications to treat young people with a substance use disorder except for buprenorphine, which is used for individuals who have opioid use disorder. This drug binds to the same receptors as opioids such as heroin or prescription painkillers such as oxycodone, codeine, and fentanyl and helps prevent withdrawal symptoms, reduces cravings, and makes people feel less dependent on their drug of choice. Buprenorphine has been FDA approved for use in people as young as sixteen.

Other medications that have been studied to treat substance use disorder include n-acetylcysteine (NAC), a medication available over the counter that some evidence shows can reduce cravings and withdrawal symptoms for cannabis use disorder. Bupropion helps to mitigate urges and cravings for nicotine for people who smoke cigarettes, and naltrexone is a medication that can be helpful for treating alcohol use disorder as well as opioid use disorder. However, the majority of studies on substance use disorders and adolescents have found that medication management alone is insufficient as a form of treatment. Therapy, specifically therapy involving the family, is crucial for success.

The Value of Peer Support— for Kids and Caregivers

Especially for young people, many of whose peers may still be experimenting with drugs without apparent negative consequences, the prospect of not drinking or using drugs for the rest of their lives is hard to fathom. Many will use substances again after treatment, in the belief or hope that their experience with abstinence will allow them to use drugs now and then without the negative impacts that led them to treatment in the first place. It's important for you to know that recovery from substance use is a process and that relapses may be part of the process. If your child has a hard time staying away from the substances, it may take additional negative consequences, and more emotional pain, before they learn that they are not biologically wired to be able to use drugs "occasionally" or "recreationally."

Many people recovering from substance use disorders find peer support fundamental to staying clean and sober. This is especially true for adolescents, who are peer-oriented developmentally. Your child's treatment program may offer ongoing "alumni" support in the form of meetings, gatherings, or recreational activities. There is also a robust support community available through membership in 12-step fellowships. While teen membership is relatively small, there are meetings that draw young people in many cities as well as on or near campuses in college and university towns, and online meetings worldwide held every hour of the day and night and in many languages. All the fellowships are organized around the 12-step program originated by Alcoholics Anonymous (AA), but particular meetings are different and appeal to different people, so your child may need to try more than one to find other kids with whom they identify. AA is the oldest and largest fellowship and many AA meetings welcome people whose primary "drug of choice" is something other than alcohol. But your child may also find peer support via Narcotics Anonymous, Cocaine Anonymous, Marijuana Anonymous, or another fellowship formed specifically for people who use a particular substance or who struggle with what is called a process disorder, like compulsive gambling, shopping, or eating. For people recovering from both substance use and a mental health condition, there are also Dual Diagnosis Anonymous and Double Trouble in Recovery meetings. Some of these fellowships and organizations are small relative to AA, and offer fewer in-person meetings, but most offer online meetings.

There are faith-based recovery support programs as well. Celebrate Recovery (Christian), Millati Islami (Muslim), and the Latter Day Saints' Addiction Recovery Program (ARP) combine a 12-step approach with religious teachings. Jewish Alcoholics, Chemically Dependent Persons and Significant Others (JACS) provides information about recovery programs and meetings with a Jewish spiritual focus and hosts meetings and retreats. Refuge Recovery is a "non-theistic" spiritual program based on the Four Noble Truths and Eightfold Path of traditional Buddhist practice.

SMART Recovery is another peer-led nonprofit organization serving people struggling with addictive behaviors—including not just around drugs or alcohol but "process addictions." Whereas 12-step fellowships describe themselves as a spiritual program of recovery, SMART takes a cognitive behavioral approach. It offers what it calls a four-point program focused on building and maintaining motivation, coping with urges and cravings, managing thoughts, feelings, and behaviors, and living a balanced life. SMART Recovery does offer meetings specifically for young adults, and others for teens, both in person and online.

Finally: A young person's chronic substance use or substance use disorder affects everyone in the family, especially you as caregiver. In the family programs run by treatment facilities, or in sessions with your child's therapist, you will likely be encouraged to find support for yourself. I encourage you to take that advice to heart. NAMI regional chapters offer family support groups and some host online groups specifically for parents of children and young adults with mental health conditions. Mental Health America hosts the Parent Support Network for parents of kids up to age twenty-five dealing with any mental health concern, including substance use disorder. Many parents and caregivers find support in 12-step groups like Al-Anon, Nar-Anon, and Families Anonymous, or in SMART Recovery Family & Friends. The Partnership to End Drug Addiction holds free online support meetings several times weekly for parents and caregivers of children experimenting with, or dependent on, substances, hosted by trained parent facilitators, and overseen by clinicians. For more information about support groups in your area, you can call the SAMSHA Helpline: 1-800-662-4357.

Living with a child struggling with substance use can be scary, frustrating, and infuriating. The support of others who truly understand what you're going through will be invaluable. You can't do it alone— and you don't have to.

PART III

Lessons from Lived Experience

FOURTEEN

Speaking for Ourselves: Youth, Identity, and Mental Health

How do young people understand their own mental health? How do they understand the role of mental health in shaping the world around them, and what ideas might they have for developing a healthier culture surrounding mental health and well-being in the world around us? In my work with NAMI and as a child psychiatrist, I am consistently struck by just how articulate and thoughtful many of the young people I work with are, both about their own mental health and the mental health of others. Especially with the rise of internet culture and social media, the world has seen a wave of young people taking ownership of their experiences, sharing their stories with others, and creating communities of support and networks of advocacy amongst themselves. This new wave inspired NAMI to establish NAMI Next Gen, a ten-member young adult advisory group dedicated to advising, creating, and innovating how NAMI works with youth and young adults. As NAMI Next Gen's slogan, which originated from the peer movement in which people with lived experience from a variety of conditions including mental health conditions, "nothing about us, without us," suggests, young people are aware of the current mental health landscape, and they're asking for a seat at the table. As we discuss the youth mental health crisis, it's critical to include the voices of young people themselves.

For this book, I spoke with sixteen individuals under the age of twenty-six about their mental health journeys. I asked these young interviewees to describe their own experience of mental health symptoms and to tell me about the things that were most helpful to them in navigating life in light of those symptoms. In this chapter, my goal is to step back and let these young people speak for themselves. I'll share some of their descriptions of their symptoms and experiences, their understanding of their mental illness and its role in the larger context of their lives, and some of the coping mechanisms and strategies they employed to manage their mental health and cultivate well-being. The young people I interviewed made it very clear how important it was for them to share their stories with others, since they were motivated by the possibility that their story could make an impact on another young person's life.

Signs, Symptoms, Self-Advocacy

I asked each young person I interviewed when they first started to notice something was going on with regard to their mental health, and how they would describe what they feel when they aren't feeling good. Kids recounted how they began to notice their own emotions and mood states, and the somatic experiences they had when dealing with difficult emotions.

Jillian is a biracial Chinese, Italian, and Irish woman in her midtwenties from Massachusetts who has experienced symptoms of bipolar disorder since childhood, including depression and anxiety, mania, and psychosis. She described to us her experience of treatment-resistant depression and anxiety, something she remembers from early on in her life:

I just remember being so unhappy. No matter what I had, no matter what I was given, no matter what we did, it was like I was always going to end up depressed again. It was like it didn't matter what we did, but I just kept doing it. I was really good and compliant with my care as a kid. I took my meds. I went to therapy. I did everything right, but I had treatment-resistant symptoms of depression and anxiety, so nothing really helped.

Jillian and her mother, Marie, struggled to find an effective treatment strategy for Jillian until eventually trying electroconvulsive therapy, or ECT, which she described as the most effective form of treatment for her. She also shared how she manages her continued symptoms with a combination of medication and an attitude of hope and positivity:

I still hear voices, so I have to do things in addition to medication to try and help with the voices. Being positive, especially about yourself, and also keeping yourself in control, keeping yourself calm, keeping yourself confident, because the voices always want to take you down.

At the time of our interview, Jillian was applying to attend college at the University of Massachusetts at Dartmouth.

For Jake, a seventeen-year-old male from Missouri who has experienced symptoms of PTSD, depression, and anxiety since early childhood, indicators of negative emotions or difficulties with mental health include somatic cues or physical signals that reflect the level of his emotional distress. His advice to others struggling with similar feelings would be to work on developing strategies for releasing emotions in a healthy way:

I feel that my face gets heated, and I start popping my knuckles. My chest gets warm. But my advice to others is don't hold it in because if you hold it in, you take it out on other people. I feel fine with going for

treatment because I think I do need help. I struggle with anger issues
and some other stuff.

Jake also shared how he understands the relationship between early
trauma and his mental health:

It's hard to talk about trauma from the past. My biological mom aban-
doned me. But if I commit to treatment and talk about my past, it's not
going to boil over in the future, and I won't lash out at other people.

Jake now serves as a member of a suicide prevention program at his
school, where students are trained to help other students get connected
with mental health resources. "I like the program because I like to help
others," he told me.

J, a preteen diagnosed with bipolar disorder, described to me how
his experiences with mania contrasted with his depressive symptoms:

When I was younger, I don't think I was affected as much. It kind of got
worse about two years ago. I was pretty manic all the time—hyper and
irritable and, for me, it's being hyperirritable, just a little bit crazy. You're
freaking out. Not sleeping a lot. And recently I was pretty depressed,
but I'm starting to feel better.

I feel like depression is the opposite of being manic. It's weird how it
clashes. It's like if you split someone's personality into two. You're really
energetic, irritable, and all those things, and then you have really just
the opposite, not as energetic. When I was depressed I didn't really do
much and luckily it was over winter break, so I had a long time to get
over it. I started feeling a lot better around the end of the break, and I
was able to go back to school.

Kevin, a seventeen-year-old from Illinois, first noticed difficulties
with his mental health around seventh grade, and has since developed
coping strategies that help him manage difficult or low moods:

Definitely constant mood swings, little things setting you off, like if you're having a great day and then you see one thing online or you get a bad test back, and then that just ruins the rest of your day. If things like that continue happening or if I just start feeling consistently sad or angry or stuff like that, then I definitely know that I need to talk about it with someone or just use my own strategies to chill out. Or sometimes it just happens out of nowhere, but even then just trying to talk to someone about how I'm feeling and just have someone listen, or just taking it on with strategies, is great.

He told me that initially, he struggled to open up to anyone or reach out for support:

It's definitely a hard topic to bring up, especially when you're trying to figure it out on your own. I don't think anyone should try and figure it out on their own, now that I've gone through all that. But definitely just the pressure of trying to ask someone for help and then the thoughts that counter it like, maybe they won't know what you're feeling, maybe they'll just ignore it, maybe they'll take it more seriously than it is, that's hard to go through.

At Kevin's school, a music teacher reached out and helped him tap into external supports:

My music teacher actually noticed that I wasn't doing so great, and he eventually decided to contact my parents. We had school plays, and he was the one who coached them, so I spent more time talking with him academically than any other teacher and it felt like I could open up a little to him about my experiences. He said, this is okay, telling me, but this is to the point where we have to contact someone because it isn't healthy. He was very calm about it and that made it feel a lot more genuine than if he'd freaked out or just showed no emotion. But he was super calm about it, and he was like, "I understand how you're feeling and you're not alone," but this is a point where we have to reach out to someone.

These stories reveal that kids' ability to learn how to recognize changes in how they are thinking and feeling, and come to understand that those changes signify that they need to reach out for support, is an important part of their journey. It is inspiring that these individuals were able to articulate to others that they were struggling at such a young age, ensuring that they were able to get the treatment and support that they needed.

A common theme in my interviews with young people was their feeling that adults sometimes underestimated just how much kids understand about their own mental health and the mental health of others. Youth and young adults generally have a very strong understanding of their situation, diagnoses, and symptoms and have opinions about their treatment that caregivers should take into account. As frustrating as it might be sometimes to deal with a headstrong adolescent who is certain that not doing homework is the answer to their issues, or a stubborn six-year-old who insists that vegetables are bad for them, developing opinions on things that are different from those of caregivers is an important part of development, and kids need support from the adults around them in figuring out what it is they need and learning how to ask for it.

I asked kids about diagnoses they'd received and how they understood those diagnoses. We spoke about the role of mental health in the larger context of their lives and communities, and how it factored into their developing identities (or did not).

For Evelyn, an eighteen-year-old from Northern Virginia we met in chapter 2, it was important that her health care provider shared clinical reasoning with her for suggested forms of treatment:

When I was younger, I remember thinking: I don't want medication to change who I am. That was something that no one explained to me.

People told me that it wouldn't, but how was I supposed to know? They didn't show me any sort of research. Doctors just said, "Oh no, it won't." You need to explain to me why it won't, not just tell me it won't.

Evelyn emphasized that she believed the lack of explanation was due to providers not knowing how to communicate effectively with younger people:

I think doctors weren't prepared. The doctors I had initially were not prepared for an eleven-year-old to say, "No, I don't want to do that." Yes, I was eleven, but that is old enough to say yes and no. I would've liked people to explain to me, rather than just tell me. Don't tell me it's going to help my depression. Explain to me that this is what it might feel like, this is what it's doing in your brain. I think the biggest thing that eventually helped me get on board was my psychiatrist, who I still work with today. She explained to me why she was suggesting these things, and how she thought it would help me.

Involving young people in the decision-making when it comes to their care is critical. Even though as adults we may feel as though we're better positioned to know what our kids may need for their mental health, we can't always make that assumption. Many kids want to be involved in discussions about their mental health and to share their perspective of how it is they are experiencing their symptoms, and involving them in this process of discussing their mental health concerns and advocating for their mental health needs can provide them with the tools that will be necessary when they are adults and have to advocate for themselves independently. Participating in these conversations over time strengthens their ability to articulate their internal experiences and sharpens their self-advocacy skills.

The Meaning of a Diagnosis

Throughout the chapters of this book, we have talked about many different diagnoses young people may receive on their ever-evolving mental health journeys. The ability to contextualize these diagnoses and what they mean for you and your child can set the tone for the whole course of treatment, and also provide an opportunity to talk openly about their experiences and their hopes for what might change with treatment. Many of the young people we hear from next share that getting their diagnosis was a major relief or a puzzle piece of information that brought the full picture into focus regarding what they had been going through. However, as we learned in part I of this book, a diagnosis is merely a marker in time for a set of observable symptoms. For some, it is a huge moment in their recovery, but for others, it may be just a stop along the way. Whatever your experience with diagnosis is, we hope it is a helpful tool for you.

Jillian, whom we met earlier, described how the side effects of her medication posed challenges for her in school, and how her diagnosis made it easier to put school supports in place:

> I couldn't wake up for school because of my meds, and it only got worse, because school gets earlier as you go on. I had the greatest people put in my path at my schools. They knew I was a good kid. They knew that I was trying my best, and thankfully with the diagnosis, people tended to be like, "Okay, yep. I get it." That is what we need. That is why we need to help her adapt to a different schedule than everyone else, because she's dealing with mental illness, and specifically bipolar disorder. I feel that's when I realized, "Okay, this diagnosis might not be a bad thing."

Jillian shared with me how medication is an option that she recommends for other individuals living with mental health concerns, and how holding on to hope has been a helpful coping strategy for her:

I highly encourage medication for people who have bipolar disorder, any kind of mental illness that requires medication treatment, and no matter what the side effects are, it's so much better than the alternative. Just stick with it, and there's always something that can be done. Don't give up hope.

For Don, the Asian American agender person from Michigan whom we met earlier, a diagnosis helped them contextualize thought patterns and behaviors that they'd been experiencing throughout their childhood:

Once I was diagnosed with bipolar, it clicked for me—all these different symptoms or episodes growing up that I, at the time, thought was just a me thing, something that I would eventually get over, or maybe that this was part of my personality or character. I didn't really see the symptoms as points of concern. And with my family, communication was hard, talking about especially negative things, so I didn't bring up the subject.

Bre, a teenage girl living in Michigan, spoke to us about receiving multiple diagnoses over the course of her adolescence, and how finding the one that felt the most accurate was a process:

Before I was diagnosed with borderline personality disorder, I was mistakenly diagnosed as bipolar, because it had similar symptoms. Borderline personality, it's for me at least, rapid mood swings. One second, I'll be happy doing whatever. The next thing you know, I'll just be mad for no reason. Then twenty minutes later, I can be crying, and then five minutes later be happy again. It's definitely an emotional roller coaster, you could say.

The more research we did, the more doctors we went to, we got a more accurate diagnosis for me. I can see where borderline personality disorder and bipolar match up, but I also see where they're different.

Receiving a diagnosis for a mental health condition as a child helped place Bre on a path to receiving more tailored treatment and supports. For many kids struggling with mental health concerns, a diagnosis may not be clear at the onset of symptoms. The process of better understanding one's mental health over the course of their childhood and adolescent years is very often an evolving one.

Mental Health in the Bigger Picture

Mental health concerns don't exist in a vacuum. People experience their mental and emotional life while living in the wider world. The individuals I interviewed spoke about how they dealt with mental health concerns within the broader framework of their lives, whether that was in school, amongst friends, through advocacy, or in different community spaces. For Brandon Smith, a former NAMI Next Gen ambassador whom we heard from earlier, faith is a key pillar of his life. He spoke to us both about the importance of his faith and also how his mental health journey fits into his relationship with his faith community:

> I am part of the Christian faith and I do practice in a congregation. I think that in religious spaces, concepts of mental health issues can be very difficult to try and understand. But I'm actually so happy to see the changes in how the organization I'm a part of moved so quickly to try and meet those needs.
>
> Faith is everything to me. I realized that I was trying to go in and do all this alone and it was funny because as I thought back to all that I accomplished, I don't take full credit for that, not even in the slightest bit. And I think about all the things that I survived—either there is a divine spirit or I'm the greatest strategist that the world has ever known. And I don't believe the latter is true. So, I think the former, it feels right. I've been in situations where it's really indescribable. A lot of people will think that it's like this magical thing, but it's very, very practical. When

you ask for advice and you pray and you're like, "Look, I'm at this point, what do I do?" And then things just unfold. It is probably one of the most incredible things in my life. All the rest of this stuff that I'm doing is really just in service of my faith because that's really all that matters to me. Everything else is so unpredictable and wild and can be slated for failure in ways that you can't anticipate. But you can almost never go wrong when you're pursuing your faith and your beliefs.

Maleah Nore, a member of the Tlingit Nation from Alaska, whom we met earlier, spoke in our interview on the legacies of intergenerational trauma and systemic oppression, and specifically how understanding harm within a broader historical context can help us cultivate compassion and optimism even in the face of conflict and trauma:

I think it's always really important to keep in mind that there's a history to everything and the way that people treat each other, the way that people struggle with mental health now, the way that we experience harm, the ways in which we hurt each other even though we don't necessarily mean to, there's histories behind all of that. And some of those histories are hundreds of years old.

Those histories go back a really long time and they're also something that we live every day. And so I think really just the best way to, I guess, come to accept reality for what it is as much as you can, is just to understand the systemic nature of things. And also just to assume that everybody is doing their best, their version of the best. If you don't keep those histories and those traumas and everything in mind, there's a lot of times where you might think the whole world hates each other and that's really not the case.

We also asked young people how mental health and mental illness fit into their developing identities. Maddie Stults, the college student from North Florida we met earlier, reflected on their journey through adolescence, identifying some elements of growing up that might exacerbate feelings of stress and anxiety, and how as they grew, they incorporated their passion for mental health into their career path:

> In middle school, you're so dependent on your parents, you spend hardly any time away from them. You're more just an extension of everyone, an extension of your parents, an extension of your siblings, all that kind of stuff. And in high school, you spend more time to yourself, you spend more time in school in extracurriculars and stuff. So, you start to become an actual human being with interests and personality traits.
>
> And I remember feeling everyone around me had already developed that, while I was stressed out about it. I remember being like, okay, well who am I then? What am I interested in? What am I going to do in college? What classes do I have to take now so that I can develop those interests and stuff? It was just a lot of pressure to become a functional person.
>
> Four years later I'm medicated, going to therapy. Super helpful. I am in school for psychology, I'm a junior in college. I have an awesome support system. I have a girlfriend now. That was a big deal for me. So, I'm going to school to eventually become a clinical psychologist, do research, but also practice. It's been a full 180, because I thought of mental illnesses as such a deficit, "Oh you can't swing normal life." But so much of that journey has informed who I am now. I wouldn't be a psychology major. I wouldn't be advocating for young people's voices and stuff now. So, it definitely has been a net positive for sure.

Themes of Recovery

In our interviews, we gained important insight into how young people understand and use different modalities for managing their recovery, including medication, treatment programs, styles of therapy, and community supports. Across the country, young people are finding new ways to promote their own wellness as they navigate the world around them and form their identity. Young people we interviewed told us about a wide range of things that helped them maintain their mental health, including time outdoors, card games, video games, the support of their pets, sports, art, and more, in addition to the traditional inpatient and outpatient therapies that are often prescribed by a health care professional. What we gleaned from these conversations reinforced many of the other ideas in this chapter—that the best mental health supports are personal, engaging, and connect young people to some sense of peace and community. Two young people mentioned next validated the need for traditional care despite these, sharing their experiences of how the treatment they received got them back on track and into a healing state of mind.

Kevin, the seventeen-year-old from Illinois we met earlier shared about an inpatient experience that helped him realize he was not alone and gave him the knowledge and skills to be proactive and communicative about finding solutions:

> I definitely came out much better. I did go to an inpatient and outpatient care facility and throughout inpatient it was just like, I'm not alone. And that was just one week to make sure that I was going to be okay. And then outpatient was actually a few months straight and that really helped because I was way more educated about mental health, and I was taught way more about how to safely deal with these problems and how to not necessarily stop them but help other people understand what I was dealing with so that we could come to solutions together instead of one person trying to do it.

Kenzie, a twelve-year-old from California, told us how realizing she needed help and getting into therapy helped her deal with bullying at her school. For Kenzie, the skills she learned in a therapeutic setting helped her navigate day-to-day emotions and open up to her family about what she was going through:

Now? I feel a lot better about myself. I learned a lot. I learned how to apologize, and I was able to talk about it and my problems because I would also get mad when I would have things just bottled up inside of me. Because I would just do that. I wouldn't talk about it to anyone. I had the biggest trust issues ever. I couldn't trust anybody. Therapy taught me how to apologize. Taught me how to be a nicer person around people.

I changed a lot from therapy. I'm so much better from it. I was all the way down here and now I'm getting a little higher.

Relationships with Caregivers

While we've heard from many young people about the external supports that have helped them cope, many reach these supports through the kind hand of a caregiver steering them in the right direction. The young folks we talked to have a wide array of experiences with parent and caregiver relationships, but agreed that the most important thing was for them to feel heard, understood, and loved through all of it.

NAMI In Our Own Voice is a presentation where leaders with lived experience in mental health conditions talk openly about what it's like to have a mental health condition in their community.

Sam, a twenty-eight-year-old NAMI In Our Own Voice presenter from Colorado, who has experienced symptoms of a binge-purge eating disorder, self-harm, bipolar I, and anxiety, told us how his parents went above and beyond to understand what he was going through. He emphasized that knowing your child and not being afraid to learn more can make all the difference in their healing:

They both came together, not only as parents, but honestly as people, and tried to get to know me on a level that I really don't think a lot of parents try to understand their kids because they're afraid of that intimacy in terms of knowing too much of what their kid has gone through.

And I'm sure it was heartbreaking for them, but I really think that you have to know that if your child is giving you the option of telling you what's going on, as brutal and as heartbreaking as it is, it's an opportunity to let your child know that you are there. That is more important than your fear of asking harmful questions.

Don, the student from Michigan we heard from earlier in this chapter on the difficulty of sharing their own struggles with mental health with their mother, also told me that the pressure to succeed, in light of their mother's trauma and hardships as a new immigrant to the United States, led to feelings of shame and loneliness:

I know this brings up the concept of intergenerational trauma. My mom went through some very, very difficult times. She wanted to equip me with certain things, especially with education, so that I didn't go through what she did, having to struggle so much. That's what I mean where these feelings of being a failure, for example, or not being worth it, I shouldn't be having those feelings. They were abnormal.

During that time, the main thing that I was desperately seeking, whether it was for friends, coaches, teachers, was to be validated. It was to be told that the feelings that I was experiencing were okay, they were normal. They weren't weird, they weren't bad, they weren't wrong. I didn't even necessarily want them to go away. It was more so I just wanted it to be acknowledged that even though I could be happy, funny, goofy, perform well at school, be extroverted, even be "popular," that it was okay to also have negative feelings. I wasn't a robot. I didn't have to be happy all the time. It was okay to be sad.

I think the biggest disconnect is that my mom felt like she knew the way that I wanted to be supported, but she was not supporting me the way I wanted. And by not having that conversation, there was just this tension that was there all the time, and that's something that I really wish, thinking back, that we were able to do.

Through therapy and other treatments, Don realized that what they truly wanted was someone to navigate things together with, someone to ask and listen to what would be the most helpful, without judgment or assumption.

What I wanted was not for my mom to parent me differently, but for me to have the courage to talk about how I was feeling, so we could navigate it together. I think that's what I was really hoping for growing up, is to be able to do things together. It almost felt like I was raising myself with how I wanted to be supported, but my mom was raising me separately in the way she wanted to support me.

As generational gaps in experience become wider, it is natural that family members have differing ideas about generational trauma, mental health care, shame, and support. However, the key takeaway from Don's story is that the most valuable thing we can give to one another is to simply be there, listen, and do our best to understand what kind of help the person is seeking.

We asked many of our young people whether they had additional advice for parents and caregivers navigating mental health with their child. D'Asha, a twenty-year-old from Michigan, shared a practical tip for remaining calm in the face of things that can be upsetting and difficult to navigate, especially when emotions are running high:

If you're working with a teenager and the teenager isn't listening, it'd be best to just walk away for a little bit, give it like ten minutes for the situation to calm down. And then go back and talk about the problem, about what caused the situation, and what was the mistake or the misunderstanding. Always try to just go with the flow. Don't let your anger, stress, and anxiety get the best of you.

Nathan is a teenager living in Michigan. He was adopted from Ethiopia as a toddler and struggles with anxiety and depression. Nathan had advice for teachers who have the opportunity to be a positive influence on a child's mental health—in our interview, he pointed out that students are more aware than you think, and can internalize being dismissed or ignored. He told me helping them can be as easy as being there and acknowledging that there's something they're going through that they don't want to do alone:

> Sometimes when I talked to teachers about what I was going through, I would tell them and they would just say, "Okay," then they sent me away. And I feel like if the teacher actually talked to you about it, instead of just listening to what you say, if they were trying to at least show that they understand or care, that would be good.
>
> Tell them they're not alone. There's a lot of people in the world who feel that way. It's not just them, they're not alone and they have a lot of people that care about them, and they should try and find something that they really, really like, and then do that.

Pooja Mehta is a South Asian American mental health advocate, originally from Raleigh, North Carolina. She is a suicide-loss survivor and lives with anxiety with auditory hallucinations and depression, and currently works in mental health policy. Pooja had a similar message for the South Asian community she grew up in—on how denial and avoidance only make the problem more difficult for the whole community:

> One of the things that I say, especially whenever I'm speaking to a South Asian audience, is you can sit here and believe that this could never happen to your child, but the fact of the matter is, I was your child at one point. I gave a speech at the temple that I grew up in, and to the audience I was like, "You have seen me practice in this hall, you have seen me go to events in the community, you have seen me dance on this stage. You saw me during this time of my life. You were there for all of it. You just didn't know it."

Diana Chao, a twenty-four-year-old first-generation Buyi Chinese immigrant to California, founded Letters to Strangers, the largest global youth mental health charity, out of her experience with bipolar disorder and c-PTSD. In our interview, she described to me how even if a child's problem can be dismissed as "teenage angst," it is still an emotional experience they're having that deserves empathy and support:

> I think one thing is definitely to take kids more seriously. I think a lot of what I felt was dismissed because people just thought I was going through teenage angst, all of that, which I'm sure played a part of it. But I think if you're clearly distressed, whether or not it's teenage angst doesn't matter, it's still something that should be addressed and supported if there is a possibility to do so. I wish there was a little more education and support around that from the teachers or other adults in my life.

Diana shared her hopes that school systems will integrate more mental health curricula, the same way they have developed curricula addressing topics like drug use and physical health, and that more space will be made for children's well-being in and outside of school settings.

> I think when we go to health classes as early as fifth and sixth grade, we should be talking about mental and emotional well-being. It doesn't have to be anything super in-depth, but I remember going through the DARE program when I was in fifth grade. I'm like, if I can talk about drugs at fifth grade, I can talk about mental health. And I wish that was something that was more incorporated.
>
> I also think that having more classroom activities built around mental well-being would be helpful. So, things like, I hesitate to use the word *meditation* in this context, but a semi-meditative sort of setting when you are having, let's say on a Friday, a class discussion about

something where people can be seated maybe on the floor in a circle instead of being at their desks. And maybe you can have some music playing. It doesn't have to be anything super intense or integrated into every aspect of a curriculum, but something that creates a pattern of a safe space for a kid.

Diana noted that no adult is, or needs to be, perfect when it comes to these conversations. The ability and willingness to keep trying, apologize when you get it wrong, and remain steadfast in your support, can be worth more than you know:

I think it'd be really wonderful if more adults were forthright about their own journeys of trying to understand how to be a better supporter. I remember when I heard my mom tell me, after I explained a lot of things that had happened, "I'm so sorry, I was learning and I really did not know, and it's my fault, I'm sorry." But I think just realizing that, oh, these are not perfect people, and all that time knowing that they're in that learning process, too, would've made me feel less crazy, I think, as a kid.

Though the experiences, upbringing, identities, and dreams of the young people you've heard from in this chapter have all been different, their messages share some key similarities. Nearly all the youth I spoke to emphasize the importance of having someone to go to who makes them feel less alone, can hold hope when things seem dark, and help them navigate back to a space where they feel safe, happy, and prepared for whatever future difficulties may come.

Alice Held, the woman from Missoula we met earlier, began receiving treatment for PTSD and drug addiction as a young teenager, and is now an undergraduate research assistant completing a degree in human physiology. They shared these words of advice on remaining hopeful no matter the circumstances, and how powerful that can be for others in your life who are struggling:

There's so much that you don't have control over when you're seeing a loved one through this process of recovering. But the one thing you do have control over is you can always hold hope. You can always keep hope. And that doesn't mean it isn't super frustrating to hold hope sometimes when you really don't want to be hopeful because it feels like you're being delusional. And that's okay.

But that's why it's really important for the caregivers to have support as well, because being a part of a community is going to help energize them to continue holding that hope. Because to me, it's like, hold hope no matter what. Even when it sucks to hold hope, even when it's really painful to hold hope.

FIFTEEN

The Power of Community

I have found that iron sharpens iron, and one person's journey, and the knowledge they've gained from it, can help me improve my journey and the resources that I find for my daughter.

—**ALLEYA RAY,**
a mother of two from Arkansas

. . .

In the interviews I conducted for this book, families shared stories of what they'd been through: the difficulties they'd faced, the tips and tricks they'd learned along the way, the silver-lining moments. I heard dozens of unique stories, and each one left me awed and inspired to share the wisdom and lived experience that was shared with me. In almost every single interview, though, there was a common thread: the most important lessons families learned along the way were about the power of peers and community. By peers, I mean individuals with lived experience who can offer support and education. Families shared how they'd embarked on their child's mental health journey feeling isolated, anxious, and sometimes hopeless—and then, in learning how to share their story and lean on others, and finding places where they felt safe doing so, the path forward became clearer and more hopeful.

In my own work as a child psychiatrist and in the course of writing this book, I often see caregivers whose daily routines are entirely shaped by their child's needs. They put 110 percent of themselves into cultivating and maintaining their child's care—and ultimately, it is not sustainable. These caregivers are often exhausted and isolated and feel as though their child's well-being is entirely their responsibility. The reality is that no caregiver can or should view the process of raising a child to be happy, healthy, stable, and well-rounded as a solo sport. However we go about it, we must become comfortable with the idea of letting people in and tapping into the wealth of resources and support that an active relationship with our community can give us.

In this chapter, I'll focus primarily on sharing the knowledge and expertise of families who have lived experience of supporting a child with a mental health condition, and of people who lived with a mental health condition in childhood or adolescence. Within these pages, we've assembled a community whose stories will, we hope, provide comfort, compassion, and education to readers. My hope for this book, and NAMI's hope for this book, is that hearing this community of voices will encourage you to begin building your own community as well.

What Does Community Look Like?

Community comes in many forms. For some, it's a support group. For others, it might consist of family members or friends, or an online group of people with similar experiences or backgrounds. It can include diagnosis-specific organizations, advocacy platforms, or local chapters or meetings of larger national organizations, but can also be as simple and informal as your neighbors, extended chosen family, or members of your faith tradition.

Our community at NAMI began in 1979, when a group of mothers of adult children with schizophrenia gathered around a kitchen table in Madison, Wisconsin, to share their experiences. Now, more than four decades later, NAMI is a large community comprising hundreds of subcommunities reflecting commonalities including location, diagnosis, identity, family role, hobbies and interests, and others. To get started, you can enroll in one of the educational and advocacy programs NAMI has developed to engage with people living with mental health conditions, families, and the public. Some examples of programs specifically tailored to young people and their caregivers include:

NAMI Basics, a course for parents and other family caregivers who provide care for youth (age twenty-two or younger) who are experiencing mental health symptoms. NAMI Basics is an evidence-based practice that has demonstrated effectiveness for participants in improving self-care, empowerment, family communication, caregiver activation and engagement and also decreasing symptoms for their children. This course is led by two trained family members and also available in Spanish (Bases y Fundamentos de NAMI). Sessions are available live in person and virtually. There is also an interactive asynchronous version, NAMI Basics OnDemand that is available for parents/caregivers to take at their own pace: www.nami.org/basics.

NAMI Family-to-Family, is a course for families, significant others, and friends of people with mental health conditions. This evidence-based program has been shown to improve coping skills, problem-solving skills, and feelings of empowerment for the participants. This course is led by two trained family members, available in person and virtually and available in Spanish (De Familia a Familia de NAMI).

NAMI Peer-to-Peer, a course for adults (eighteen and older) with mental health conditions. The course is designed to encourage growth, healing, and recovery among participants. NAMI Peer-to-Peer has an evidence base that demonstrates that participants report decreased stigma regarding mental health conditions and improved recovery outcomes. This program is led by two individuals with lived experience with mental illness who have been trained, is available in person and virtually, and is also available in Spanish (De Persona a Persona de NAMI).

NAMI Ending the Silence, an evidence-based presentation designed for middle and high school students, school staff, and parents or guardians of middle or high school aged youth. Audiences learn about the signs and symptoms of mental health conditions, how to recognize the early warning signs, and the importance of acknowledging those warning signs. Research has demonstrated that students participating in presentations reported improvement in attitudes around mental health, their knowledge of the topic, reduction in negative stereotypes, and an increased willingness to seek help. The presentation is made by one young adult living well in recovery and one family member of a young adult with a mental health condition.

NAMI Next Gen, a ten-member young adult advisory group representing the voices of youth and young adults across the country. NAMI Next Gen members advise, create, and innovate by informing the work of NAMI programs, content, initiatives, and new projects to meet young people where they are.

Teen & Young Adult Helpline is a free nationwide peer-support service providing information, resource referrals, and support to teens and young adults via phone, text, or chat.

NAMI Family Support Group is a weekly or monthly peer-led support group for any adult with a loved one who has experienced symptoms of a mental health condition; you can find information about groups near you at NAMI.org.

NAMI On Campus clubs are student-led, student-run mental health clubs on high school and college campuses that work to raise mental health awareness and educate their school communities, advocate for improved mental health services and policies on campus, and provide support for peers.

• • •

There are many other support and interest groups specific to and hosted by NAMI's six hundred local affiliates, so check with your local chapter to explore the opportunities. No matter which NAMI program is the most appropriate for your situation, we welcome you to join us to find community, support, validation, and empowerment.

Many of the caregivers we spoke to in the interview process shared their experiences with NAMI affiliates all over the country. Angelina Hudson, now executive director of NAMI Greater Houston, told us that the greatest thing joining NAMI did for her was to provide perspective and empower her to deal with her family's mental health challenges:

> It's been a privilege, but I would've never, ever said it was a privilege when I first started. When people ask me, what is the one thing about NAMI? NAMI does not diagnose, NAMI does not treat, and NAMI doesn't do anything to make it all go away. It gives families the wherewithal. That time that you feel: "I can't do this. It's never going to work," NAMI says, "Yes you can." You pick up this sense of strength and endurance from the other families. NAMI helps us face what we've got to face, endure what we've got to endure. Then it gives us the idea or the notion that we can overcome. And then it happens.

Beth, a lawyer and mother from Illinois, found that NAMI brought her to a community of people with similar experiences who could listen without judgment through moments of crisis:

> It's really difficult when you're in the midst of it because you're just dealing with a crisis at that point. It's hard to get your head above water. For me, going to therapy has really helped, and building back up a community of friends and people that also have kids experiencing similar

challenges was really helpful, too, because I could go to some of my close friends and say, "We had this kind of day." And they would understand without judgment. And that's what I needed, was not to doubt myself. I needed someone that would listen without judgment and support me. So, I think it's about community, and that's why I like NAMI, and that's why I like doing social groups with NAMI, because we can go there and everybody has their challenges, but everybody comes together and can support each other and can just be there. That's been really important for me.

For the mother and family-to-family graduate from Santa Barbara County, the judgment-free community she found at NAMI provided her the space to learn to cope with difficult uncertainties when it came to her child:

When I went to my first NAMI class, it was like, "Oh, I can talk and they're not going to look at me like I'm a terrible parent. No, these people in this room, they all are going through the same struggle. And there's nothing that I can say that they're going to not be able to relate to because we've all had some sort of experience that we would never think we would have." I mean, it sounds weird to say that you're not shocked by what you hear people saying because you can relate to it. Not everything's exactly the same, but there's a common thread. And we got to the point where all of the people that were in the class had to acknowledge there are things that are out of our control, and to figure out, how do we cope with the uncertainty of our child's life being out of your control?

Alleya Ray, the mother from Arkansas we met earlier, shared a similar sentiment: Even though it's often difficult to admit there may be an issue with your child that you're not equipped to deal with alone, it's worth it to reach out and find the shared strength to keep going:

It's hard to ask for help. It's hard to tell people that you're struggling with something with your child, especially when you think your child's going to be stigmatized. But asking for that help and finding the right community of people, knowing where those resources are—that's something I would share with people who are just starting out on this journey. Have NAMI in your back pocket. I've had to call the NAMI resource line a million times. They're probably like, "Oh, it's Alleya again." But those people are there to help. They want to help. And I would say, "Give yourself grace."

I think in that moment, you discover strength that you had no clue that you possessed. And you have to dig deep and really rely on that strength and determination to find the answers that you need. Because with the mental health care system, there is no roadmap. There is nobody that I have found that is willing to hold your hand and say, "Okay, come with me. We're going to do this." Our NAMI group, absolutely. But I didn't have that back then. You feel like you're alone because there's nobody willing to help.

NAMI is lucky to share our mission and partner with many other mental health organizations that have also created spaces for community building across the country, like the JED Foundation, the American Foundation for Suicide Prevention, and Active Minds. Each of these organizations has contributed resources, insights, and information to many of the prior chapters in the book. And one of the best things about NAMI and our peer organizations is that no matter where you are, how much time and money you have, or what your day-to-day looks like, their resources are free and available to anyone.

These organizations provide a formal, accessible, and standardized way to build a mental health community and support system around both yourself and your child, but they are, of course, not the only organizations and not the only way to find community. Many of the people we spoke to in our interviews shared with us how they built their own grassroots community simply by finding and organizing with people around them who shared similar interests, struggles, or goals regarding the mental health of their child. Rachel Murray of Lansing, Michigan, shared with us her experience of forming one such group, which has grown to 450 members in just one year:

> I am a founder and co-director of Advocates for Mental Health of Michigan Youth, which is a grassroots organization that was formed by three of us parents who were struggling in different ways with the mental health system, living in crisis. We came together, and we were like, "We have to do something. This can't go on. We're all experiencing the brokenness of the system in very different ways." So, we created a Facebook group, and we just started with bringing people together. It just spread by word of mouth. Almost a year later, we have about 450 people in our group, and these are all people who have children who have complex or severe mental health issues. The system's not meeting their needs, and they're living in crisis pretty much constantly.
>
> We're all just helping each other navigate. We all have little tidbits of information about how you can get through the system and maybe get a little bit of your needs met. So, we share information, and we're also working together to advocate. We are lobbying our legislators, getting media placements, and just trying to raise awareness and push for policy change.

If you don't know where to start with forming your own group, many folks we talked to began simply by sharing their own story and advocating for change however they could.

Valerie Cantella, a mother of two from Santa Barbara, California, wrote and published a book on her experience in hopes that she could not just make sense of her experience herself, but also help others in their own journeys:

My book is called *off-script: a mom's journey through adoption, a husband's alcoholism, and special needs parenting*. I have grown up with this narrative that if you follow the script, if you love God, love your family, and help others, you'll have an easy and blessed life. I wrestled with reconciling my belief that I had been a good person who had done the right things and the reality that my life was completely in shambles.

Lori Barnes is a white woman in her midfifties from Kansas. She lost her son, Daniel, to suicide on July 8, 2021. She shared with me that immediately after losing her son, she got involved with her local Suicide Prevention Coalition and local mental health authority, and eventually formed a NAMI affiliate in her town. Lori has also done incredible individual advocacy work with her local and state representatives to try to create actionable policy changes to prevent others from experiencing the same heartache of losing a child to suicide.

Our son took his own life July 8, 2021. And I started therapy right away and I thought, "I'm going to advocate for my child and mental health." I took the NAMI Smarts for Advocacy training program online, which talked about telling your story, approaching your legislators, and having meetings. Someone at the affiliate that was giving the class was like, "What do you think about NAMI?" And I said, "I don't have it down here." And she's like, "What if we got you started down there?" And I'm like, "What do I need to do?" So Representative Riley hooked me up in another town in Caldwell County because she wanted more than one county involved, and I went over there and talked and got some people there to help. We joined with Butler County and now we are NAMI South Central Kansas.

Because mental health conditions are still very stigmatized, especially for communities of color, connection often comes from surprising places. Once people open up about their own experiences, they find others in their school, church, or even family who had been suffering in silence and who didn't know others close to them were facing the same issues. Joseline Castaños, the educator and mother of two we met in chapter 10, shared with us her experience of opening up to her family after her daughter's mental health crisis, and finding that many other members of her family had children experiencing the very same struggles:

In December, my daughter was hospitalized, and Latino families are huge about Christmas and getting together, and I thought, "Well, what am I going to tell my family about where my kid is?" I did email my family ahead of time and told them what was happening. But I explained that she was in the hospital and what could they do. I said: "You can pray for her, and I don't want you to treat her differently when you see her or ask her about it. I'm just letting you know because this is going to be something very different from now on, but we are going to continue to try to support her and we have faith, and we are going to do everything in our power to help our child." And I got responses from family and there were four other kids/youngsters going through similar things—some of them much older, who had been through this journey and were already at or approaching college age. But nobody had talked about it.

I think that a lot of us realized that you have to break that stigma and you have to talk about it. Here I was going to the doctor and the first thing they ask you is family history, and I'm like, "No, no history of mental illness in my family." Well, obviously there is a lot of history, number one. And then number two, that you're not alone and that you can support each other. So now we always share things—as we learn, or hear new information. We're a family of faith; we pray for each other as well. I'm not going to deny it: There were family members who perhaps distanced themselves or people in the church who distanced themselves and who saw us differently after that. I think it happens. But I have to believe that everyone who's still around is meant to be around.

Focused Support Groups

Support groups are an ideal entry point into building a community around you and your child as you navigate your child's mental health journey. The environment created by focused support groups, where everyone in attendance shares a common thread of experience, can ease discomfort around sharing personal details and discussing difficult topics. Support groups are also great places for asking specific questions pertaining to your child's mental health journey.

For Nina Richtman, whom we met earlier, attending an adoption support group helped her gain access to resources and recommendations:

It was really helpful to get involved with other parents or other people that were in the adoption community. The person that was leading the adoption group had eight kids that were adopted, so she'd been through all the things and was able to give me some guidance on how to find some resources. So, that's one thing that was pretty pivotal that I'd recommend to families, is go to an adoption support group or go to a family support group.

I think another reason to be really connected with other families in your area, if possible, is then you can get recommendations for things like therapists that have successfully worked with kids who have some of the same behaviors and conditions.

Nina also spoke to us about online support groups, which can be a great resource for those who live in more rural areas:

There are online communities that are really great. So, through Facebook, I joined a couple of groups, and those people are a wealth of knowledge. They're all over the country, so you don't necessarily get the local connections, but they can help you navigate all kinds of different situations, and you can read about different situations that people put on there and then you can think about how it would apply to your kids.

The real-time support Nina was able to tap into once she had established connections within her support group opened up opportunities for connection instead of isolation:

> Find some other parents that understand. For probably the first five years, I had a really good friend who was also parenting two kids adopted from foster care, and we texted real-time, and I would be like, "People are doing these crazy things." And she would be like, "You got this." And I would do the same for her. Having that person or multiple people that can be there for you, that understands, is really critical. So, get connected with other parents.
>
> The really isolating part for parents of kids that have pretty severe behaviors is that a lot of the world doesn't understand. So, the key thing is, you've got to find your people, you've got to find the people that both understand the behaviors and also choose to parent in this similar type of way.

Samantha is a queer disabled parent originally from New York City. They coparent two teens. They have lived with complex trauma and other co-morbid conditions since childhood. They hold a master's degree in social work and are also an artist. Samantha shared with us several experiences around the importance of community, especially LGBTQ+ youth centers that gave them support and a place to go when they were in crisis as a young person:

> I left my community, went to a state school in New York, and basically just broke down. I couldn't go to classes. I was sleeping all the time. I wound up having to leave the school and I didn't get therapy, but I also was "coming out" at that period of time, and I was superbly lucky. And

I will say that over and over again, that it was the 1990s and I was in New York City where there were gay and lesbian organizations that were open for LGBTQ+ youth. And if it wasn't for those centers, I don't know that I'd be here, because all of them, one, they all still exist. And two, they were in existence because there was such a severe issue with homelessness and suicidal ideation and suicide attempts and deaths from suicide among LGBTQ+ youth. These organizations pretty much set themselves up to make sure that we stayed alive into adulthood.

When Samantha couldn't access in-person communities later in life when they needed support for their children, they described the validating experience of finding and connecting with an online community who had similar views and goals:

The way that I have found help for myself has literally been scouring the internet for any place that has a support that's virtual. Why? Because I live in a very insular place and it's hard for me to connect to other people otherwise. That has been very helpful. On Facebook I'm on a particular Facebook page called Latinx Parents Practicing Nonviolence, or something about nonviolence . . . It's basically a group of people who want to talk about being culturally aware and sharing our cultural values but not sharing the cultural value of hitting children or punishing children for things that are age appropriate and so forth and so on. And in those conversations, people do talk about mental health, and I think that the most important thing, I would say, is as much as you think that you're the only person dealing with it, you're not.

If you just mention it, even to a teacher, talk to somebody about your concerns, you are going to start getting those connections on how to help. How I learned how to get help from the State of New Jersey was because I was in social work school and through my internship I had to get all these resources and one of them was resources for parents. I Googled resources for parents in New Jersey and there it was. I'm very good with the internet and yet I never knew to look it up like that. I think one of the things that's happening right now is that mental health is being discussed much more within the media. However, we still need more POC to be talking about it. We still need more people with more intersections to really talk about how they're approaching getting mental health services.

Finding Support in Schools

There is another community that should not be left out of the conversation here. The educational system is made up of individuals who spend large amounts of time with children—caring for them, sharing knowledge, supporting them, and encouraging them to grow. The educational community is one of the first communities our children will experience away from primary caregivers. Teachers, classmates, coaches, administrators—in schools, children are learning more than just the formal curriculum. They're learning to build relationships with peers and teachers, create and respect boundaries, and communicate their wants and needs. The educational system is a critical pillar of support in the development of our young people. In school, children start to develop as individuals embedded in the social fabric of the world around them.

Of all the incredible individuals we interviewed for this book, our educators stood out as exceptionally dedicated to the mental health and well-being of the children they worked with. Teachers and administrators spoke to us about the ways in which they build community for the children in their classrooms, from small day-to-day interactions to more serious conversations about mental health and well-being. Educators are a part of our community in a critical way—and learning to see the educational system as a place where the type of community necessary for healthy development can flourish opens up so many avenues of support for our children.

Jodi Bullinger of Ann Arbor, Michigan, whom we met earlier, started as a psychology teacher and has since moved into an administrative role at the high school where she has taught for years. She summarized it well: "At the end of the day, our goal is to provide the young people who come through the school system with the skills to be able to live the life that they want and be contributors to the world around them in a positive and meaningful way."

Classroom Communities

It takes a village—that is one of the underlying themes of all of our interviews for this book. Recognizing the potential for the educational system to set our children up not only for academic success, but for personal well-being, educators shared with us a myriad of ways they support the children who come through their schools and classrooms. Many teachers discussed explicitly the need for significant programming in schools directed at the youth mental health crisis and described specific curriculums they've developed for addressing mental health and well-being in the classroom.

Alby Zander, a health educator and coach from Illinois, has been teaching health classes for the entirety of his thirty years in the educational system. He described how his students start by learning the basics of mental health, which provides a foundation for learning about other components of physical health and how to build sustainable well-being:

> Our first unit is mental health because we have found that everything else makes much more sense once kids have the mental health knowledge. I know from asking our students that they usually think of health classes as physical health, and exercise, and "eat your vegetables," and all that, so I think it's really interesting for them to really get into the mental and emotional aspects of health, because they can all relate to that. So that's kind of our starting point: the brain, the most important part of your body. And then we get into things like general wellness, which impacts your brain more than anything. So, sleep, social media, all these

things that impact your brain are things that make you more susceptible to mental illness at your age. This is why the numbers are what they are. It's not necessarily anything you're doing wrong, it's just that when your brain is growing at such a rapid rate, you become more susceptible to those things. And therefore because of your susceptibility, it's even more important to get enough sleep, more important to exercise, more important to self-care in these other ways.

We were the first school in our area to have our local NAMI chapter come in, and they were very impressed by how much we talked about it, and how open we were with mental and emotional health. That's something that I'm very proud of, that we've always approached mental health with the understanding that a brain disorder, it's a physical disorder. I've been using this illustration forever: If you have someone that has cancer, a loved one, you do everything you can to help them get the best treatment. How come it's different with mental and emotional disorders? And so, ending the silence, decreasing the stigma, all that stuff, it's really nice to see that we are raising more awareness of it.

Alby also talked about how, when the students knew the administrators and social workers at their school, it increased the number of kids who came forward seeking help for mental health—and additionally, how when parents advocate for increased social services in schools, their voices carry significant weight:

Many years ago, we reached out to student services and said, "I think more kids would seek help if they could put a face to student services." And so, they started coming into classrooms and just introducing themselves, and saying, "Hey, here's who we are, we're the social workers, here's why students come to us." And that has significantly impacted the number of students that feel safe, just self-referring.

What's happened even in the last few years is that the community has been very vocal about, hey, we got to do something about this. It's hard to ignore. And so that has kind of changed things, and I've told parents forever that if you seek change, you're the most likely to be listened to, because you're direct stakeholders.

Nora Flanagan, the Chicago-based teacher and mother we met in chapter 2, described how in coming back from the pandemic, the physical environment in which kids had been learning for the time they spent away from school had changed significantly. She told us how she sat down with her own son and asked him about what would make the transition back into the classroom environment easier, and then implemented some of those ideas in her own tenth and twelfth grade classrooms:

> We've got blankets, Legos. There's a bin of stress toys and Play-Doh over there. I've got standing desks because sometimes you can't sit still for entire one-hundred-minute classes; that's a long time. I've got bean bags and disc chairs. There's a quiet corner, where you can come and sit, and I have a lava lamp. There are some instructions about self-care and how to do calm-down breathing. This space has its own box of stress toys and fidgeters that don't leave this part of the room. I've got some soft fur plushies and squeezies. If a student needs to just come be back here, it's "no questions asked, take your time, and come back to us when you're ready."
>
> There was this vibe among some, not all, teachers and parents to the effect of, "Well, you just need to settle down. I know it is hard, but we've all been through some difficult stuff. Just sit down and sit still and do your work." Nobody wanted to accept that it wasn't that the kids didn't want to; they physically couldn't. They went to school in their rooms for a year. There's a top-down compulsion from grown-ups to tell kids what they need to do to succeed instead of asking them what they need in order to succeed.

Astrid Ross, a mother of five living in Georgia, has been an educator for the past twenty-four years and is currently the lead administrator of

City of Knowledge Islamic School, which serves children from preschool to eighth grade. She spoke to us about the concept of social-emotional Learning (SEL), which is an approach to learning that emphasizes the importance of fostering social and emotional skills within an educational environment. When I asked Astrid what this looked like in the classroom, she described a school day full of meaningful, intentional interactions between teachers and students that cultivated an environment of community, safety, and support:

In the mornings, we'll have at least three to four teachers out in the car lane. And we will greet the child, we will walk them in, we're assessing the child. We know them by name. We're talking a bit. "How was your night? What do you have for lunch today? Tell Mommy bye, we'll see you at three o'clock." So that's our smooth transition. That's SEL for us. That's the first thing they get.

Then, we have a breakfast club. Because most of my middle schoolers, anyone from third grade up, do not eat in the morning. They do not eat, they refuse, they fight their parents in the morning. "I don't feel like eating." But they love to eat and socialize. So, we offered breakfast clubs. So don't fight your mom in the morning, just get up, get enough sleep, get cleaned up, come to school, eat breakfast with your friends. They get to get their little conversations out before the instruction begins. That is extremely successful. That's SEL.

So, it's attending to this whole child and understanding that their needs have to be met from those necessities first. Education is not an instinctive necessity. They have to eat, they have to sleep, they have to feel safe, they have to feel connected to the people who are their caregivers, and then learning can start.

Many teachers mentioned the concept of social-emotional learning during the interview process—and many of them commented on how, even though the term was coined only recently, social-emotional learning principles have been present in educational settings for a long time.

Bethann, a woman in her late fifties who teaches high school and college-level health education in South Carolina, shared with me how these principles have always been in action in her classroom:

> Social-emotional learning has always been taught in health education. It's a buzzword now. But for those of us who are health educators, mental, emotional, and social health, really that little package, has always been an extremely important part of teaching young people about how to live and breathe and move. It's one thing to say, "We got to eat well, and we've got to drink enough water and get enough sleep." But having a job you love, being with people you love, being supported, all those things are on those lists as the key things that actually give you longevity, that really make you healthy.

Bethann also described some of the positive changes she's noticed since the Covid-19 pandemic when it comes to the mental health of her students:

> What I see lately, particularly because of Covid, is this big focus on helping kids. And I like it. I like the fact that somebody having that rough time, or that anxiety, or that depression, or just difficulty coping well in whatever situation, is being recognized and being taken seriously. I don't believe that we put as much credence in the necessity to take care of these young people's emotional situation prior to now.

Justin D. is a forty-year-old educator and strength and conditioning coach in North Carolina. He is also an NAMI Ending the Silence lead presenter. Justin told me a story from an earlier point in his career. In 2016, he'd been hired to teach at a public school in rural Oregon. He moved from Florida to start the job, and when he arrived, he was informed he'd be manning the adult education program—essentially helping thirty students who either hadn't graduated on time or weren't expecting to succeed in getting their diploma. Justin was given freedom over the curriculum, and assigned a trailer slightly away from the main school building to teach in:

> When I got in that trailer, I thought, "I'm in this crusty trailer, everyone else is in a real building. My students have to walk down a path to this thing. It feels more like being incarcerated than it does being at school." I decided, "You know what? We're going to make this the best place on earth. You will be dying to get out here and you'll never want to go back. I will have to kick you out the door. You know when you're real comfortable at home and mama's got to kick you out when you're eighteen? You're not going to want to leave."

Over the months spent with his group of students, Justin noticed that a community was forming and that they were helping keep each other accountable:

> I remember I walked up onto the main campus one time, and I thought, "Our room is better than anything going on up here." It was cleaner because we cleaned it ourselves. So, it was cleaner, it was safer, it was more focused, it was quieter. A controlled environment where we could play around a little bit and then you could be like, "Okay, okay. Let's dial it back down and focus back up." And everybody kind of policed themselves. We would make tea. If somebody spilled water, somebody else was like, "Aren't you going to get that?" and they'd give them a paper towel. And I just nodded like, "Mm-hmm." One guy peed on the toilet seat and a girl got very upset and she handed him a Lysol wipe and said, "Go back in there and take care of business. We are not in a barn." They policed themselves. It was a community, at the end.

I asked Justin what he thought it was about that particular environment that lent itself to the feeling of community, and how he got students to "buy in" to the curriculum he designed:

I did it all too. For example, our physical health curriculum, I lifted weights with them. I walked the track with them. They saw what I was eating, and they knew that I was trying my best. I'm not the thinnest person in the world. They knew I was trying my best to eat better and to stop eating junk all the time. Because I didn't come in there eating the same way. I was drinking Diet Pepsi like there was no tomorrow and eating crappy food, too, and would come in eating a grilled chicken or baked or fried chicken sandwiches and fries and stuff. And I was like, "No, I'm not going to do it either. I'm going to eat pretzels and carrots and hummus and we're going to switch this up even so you're going to see me do it." The buy-in I think just came because I did it with them.

In the end, trust is a by-product. Trust is an end result. It's an outcome. It's not a core value because you can't just, "Well, I'm going to be trusted." No, you're not. You have to earn it. I think eventually they realized I was there for their betterment, not out to get them. We had a lot in common.

In the end, improving youth mental health in schools is about so much more than just implementing education about mental health and wellness and increasing access to services. It's also about investing time, thought, and resources into strengthening preventive care measures, which include relationships between students and teachers, students and their peers, and also, parents and educators.

Barriers to Student Well-Being

While I heard many stories of successes teachers had with their students, both in directly improving mental health initiatives and in fortifying community supports as preventive care, I also heard about the many challenges teachers faced within the educational system. These barriers, primarily related to resources, contribute significantly to the teacher shortage facing American schools today.

Our teachers are on the front lines of a youth mental health crisis. And they are being asked to support students' mental health needs with limited financial and clinical resources. There are some school districts that receive funding to support the delivery of mental health services to students while students are in the school building. School-based mental health clinicians can provide individual therapy to students in a private and confidential setting, sidestepping the challenge of requiring caregivers to transport their kids to appointments that may be scheduled at inconvenient times and locations. Investing resources into school-based mental health supports can serve as a relief for our teachers. They don't have to feel solely responsible for a child's emotional well-being since they know that a mental health provider with clinical expertise is also monitoring the student. It can also be helpful for teachers to have access to these school-based clinicians, so they can share with the therapist any particular challenges that the student may be experiencing and inquire about ways in which they could better support that student in the classroom.

Besides resources for mental health supports, we need to ensure schools have resources to support students' exploration of different sports and activities that can provide an invaluable outlet for our kids to express themselves and channel some of their emotional strife.

Nora Flanagan, the Chicago-based teacher we met earlier, discussed how a lack of funding for after-school activities is a significant barrier to student well-being:

School funding has to stop being a "Hunger Games." We've been fighting austerity for a generation. I'm in one of the districts with a strong union that fights for funding and fights for staffing, but we don't have everything we need. I work at a selective enrollment school where students test to get in. It's a deeply flawed system, but one of those deep flaws is that students from more affluent backgrounds are advantaged because they can take test prep programs and get a leg up. We do draw from all over the city. We are one of the most diverse high schools in a historically very segregated city. We're winning on some angles, but we are fortunate to have a student body that comes from relative affluence compared to some other schools, so we have a fundraising organization attached to our school that means we're doing better than a lot of those other places.

That's not fair, because the kids at schools with a much lower average family income are having the same struggles, and their teachers might not be getting paid to sponsor a school activity. The funding model has to prioritize students and not elected officials who want to forever promise that taxes won't go up a dime. When schools had to go remote, we heard, we got yelled at about students' mental health. But once we came back into the buildings for in-person instruction, we stopped talking about student mental health.

I'm telling you, the kids were in rough shape last year. They're still in rough shape. There's a lot of struggles. If I were going to wave a magic wand and get us what we needed, it would be to not have to fight for every penny when we have all this evidence of what we need and what helps. That's not just mental health, that's violence prevention. Having stuff for kids to do after school is violence prevention. I'm in a city that likes to talk a lot about youth violence but then not fund solutions for it. A lot of this comes down to money, which isn't romantic or sexy, but a lot of this comes down to paying for what we know we need.

Jodi Bullinger, whom we also heard from earlier, spoke in our interview about how educators often feel ill-equipped to deal with student mental health:

I think we have a lot of educators in the field right now that feel very under-resourced to be able to provide therapeutic supports and interventions. And I look at our long-standing model of school leadership and response to students that are exhibiting certain kinds of behaviors, and think there's a need for people who are school leaders and building supports that are trauma-informed and that are informed in mental health, quite frankly.

The future of children's mental health is tied up in the future of the educational system. It is critical that we do not neglect the educational system when thinking about how to address the youth mental health crisis.

Looking Forward

Throughout the pages of this book, you've heard from parents, grandparents, teachers, chosen family, health care providers, children, and young adults. Each individual who contributed their story to this book did so with you in mind—whether you are a concerned parent, a teacher, a young adult, or just generally interested in the mental health and well-being of young people. Each interviewee recognized the power of sharing their own story to help others. While I hope you've found some helpful and practical tools, strategies, and ideas that you can implement in your own life, I hope the message you ultimately take from this book is that you are not alone.

The importance of community cannot be understated. Community is where we find solace, joy, resilience, and growth. Everyone deserves a network of support that can ease some of the burden of navigating life's ups and downs, especially when it comes to living with a mental health condition. We hope that the stories we've shared from real families and kids inspire and encourage you to find or create a community of people around you and your child who will be there to share in the successes and hardships of whatever mental health journey you are on.

People within your community—whether that be your family, friends, neighbors, teachers, health care team, or another support system—are essential allies in caring for a young person with a mental health condition. As many of us know, parenting is already one of the most challenging (and rewarding) endeavors a person can embark on. Especially in our individualistic American culture, it can be easy to feel as though successful parenting means figuring things out on your own, and never needing to ask for help or support in raising your child. But each caregiver I interviewed shared one common thread of belief: It takes a village to raise a child. And not only to raise a child through times of difficulty or distress, but to share in the celebration of seeing that child grow and flourish, to witness their successes, and to partake in the joy that comes from watching that child become a unique individual. While it is critical to have community around you when your child is struggling, remember that that community is also incredibly valuable once the crisis passes. Consistent, caring relationships in any corner of a child's life can be a powerful protective factor and enhance the joy they feel in simply being alive.

The perspectives, supports, and comforts of a caring community are essential not only to your child's well-being, but also to your own. When we give ourselves the grace of knowing we cannot and should not shoulder the responsibility of caring for a child on our own, we can take a breath, look around, and take stock of the resources around us. The variety of perspectives and skill sets within a community helps us to develop distress tolerance and withstand difficult times. Given all the challenges of raising a child and existing in a complex and changing world, we at NAMI believe no one can or should do it alone.

At NAMI and beyond, there are people who understand what it is like and who can help you to weather the storm. There are classes to learn from, validating stories to hear from others, and helping hands reaching out to offer resources, ideas, or just a friendly face and willingness to listen.

Maleah Nore, the twenty-five-year-old Tlingit woman from Alaska who uses her lived experience with depression and PTSD to advocate for the needs and rights of Native people, left us with these words of wisdom on caregiving within community, realizing one's limitations, and ultimately, just being there for your child.

I think it is really hard to accept that it takes a village because there are a lot of high expectations and stigma around parenting and a fear of being a burden to the people around you through your situation and perhaps your child.

And I think it's important to remember that perfection is 100 percent not the goal. It really is not at all, and okay parenting is the best parenting that there is. And as long as you're present with your child, even when you mess up or even when you don't know what to do or even when you say, "I honestly do not know. I don't know, sweetie pie. This sucks. This is hard," that can be enough.

Being willing to lean on the people around you and not feeling bad about it is really important because traditionally that's the way it was. That's the way it should be. And all of these changes brought about by colonization and just by the breakdown of family structure and community structure, you shouldn't have to bear that weight on your shoulders.

And so, leaning on your aunties and your cousins and your grandparents and your friends and all of the people who are there to be present for you and for your kids, that is an act of decolonization. That is an act of moving you and your community forward. It's setting an example that you want other people to follow and it's something that you should feel proud of instead of shamed about or stigmatized about or worried about.

I hope that the stories and the words of validation and encouragement shared by the children, young adults, caregivers, teachers, and other people who I interviewed for this book have assured you that you do not have to take this journey to support your child's mental health by yourself. They, and many other members of the NAMI community who understand what it's like to live with or love someone with a mental health condition, are here if you need more information, support, or just someone to listen. We welcome you and your family. You are not alone.

ACKNOWLEDGMENTS

This book would not have been possible without Dr. Ken Duckworth. His dedication and determination to make *You Are Not Alone,* NAMI's first book, a reality created this opportunity to highlight the unique challenges that caregivers of children and adolescents face. I thank Dr. Duckworth for introducing me to the world of NAMI when I was a third-year resident at Massachusetts General Hospital/McLean Hospital. I was captivated when he gave a lecture to my residency class, speaking with such passion about the importance of community psychiatry and the power of amplifying the voices of those with lived experience. I am forever grateful that when I approached him after his lecture and said yes to his offer to grab a cup of coffee at a local bakery in Roslindale, Massachusetts, that one meeting has blossomed into an amazing friendship that has completely transformed my life. I often find myself in awe of his generosity as well as his unwavering confidence in me. Thank you, Ken, this is all possible because of you.

The amazing book team at NAMI, made up of Alexa Zielinski and Jordan Miller, who dedicated nearly two years of their lives to this project, were absolute lifesavers. Since day one of this project, Alexa poured her heart and soul into making this book a reality. She was an amazing support during the early days of this project, when I was struggling to figure out how to write this book. Our calls would be full of laughter, tears, and intense discussions in which she would challenge me with her amazing insights. She always believed in me, especially at times when I did not believe in myself. Alexa is an exceptional writer and a creative genius, and I am so happy that this project brought her into my life.

Jordan Miller's presence infused a sense of energy and optimism during a period when I honestly felt completing this book wouldn't be possible. She remained unflappable throughout this process and approached all tasks with speed and efficiency. Her calmness and steadfast confidence in this project made it impossible for me to give up. She is such an incredible human being with a heart of gold, and I cannot thank her enough for everything that she has done for this book.

Lisa Kaufman, my amazing writing partner, is an absolute angel. Lisa has the patience of a saint and a writing talent that is truly a gift from God. She was exceptionally skillful at transforming my thoughts and ideas into powerful words that shaped the spirit of the book. Our calls discussing how best to approach this huge undertaking of writing about such a broad topic truly helped to shape the book's direction. I cherish the calls that we had, which evolved from talking about the book into discussing the inherent challenges of being a working mother, and I am so appreciative of the time that we spent together on this project.

Will Lippincott, an exceptional book agent from Aevitas Creative Management, helped shine light on the path toward making this book a reality. I thank him for his guidance throughout this process from day one. He is truly a professional and an absolute gem. I'm so fortunate that he always believed in this project, even during my moments of panic. He always remained such a fierce advocate for this project, and I thank him for doing so.

Sarah Ried from Zando is the absolute best editor any first-time author could possibly ask for. I thank her for appreciating my vision for this book and for being an amazing coach supporting me throughout this process. I thank her for not only caring about this project and ensuring that an audience will be able to access this critical information but also for believing in me. I am so grateful for her persistently communicating her ongoing support for me, and I can't thank her enough for her ongoing validation of the wide range of emotions that I experienced throughout this journey. Also, thank you to Molly Stern, CEO and founder of Zando, for saying yes to this book.

The exceptional staff at NAMI National served as an amazing foundation of support under the leadership of our CEO, Dan Gillison Jr. Dan always believed in this project and the importance of getting this critical information about youth mental health and the tremendous supports offered through NAMI to a broader audience. He is the reason why NAMI now has books, and I thank him for making it possible for people to have this resource. Teri Brister is best described as my fairy godmother. I thank her for ensuring that I had all the resources, time, and support that I needed to get this project done. She always understood everything that it would take to execute this tremendous undertaking, and I thank her for always advocating on my behalf and protecting me from saying yes during times when I really needed to say no. Despite being exceptionally busy, Teri took the time to read countless drafts of this book to ensure that the spirit of NAMI was maintained throughout. Jessica Edwards, NAMI's chief development officer, was an incredible cheerleader for this project, sharing encouraging words and positivity all along the way. Thank you to NAMI leadership and staff, including Hannah Wesolowski, Barb Solish, Jen Rothman, Dominique Freeman, Dawn Brown (Cross-Cultural Innovation), Richele Keas, Lindsey Brown, and Roseanna Ramirez.

I am so blessed to have an amazing village of support at Boston Medical Center (BMC) and Boston University Chobanian & Avedisian School of Medicine that is dedicated to the field of psychiatry and inspires me every day in my clinical and professional work. Dr. David Henderson, who was there throughout this journey, bearing witness to the ongoing challenges of writing the book while maintaining my career in academic medicine, thank you for always supporting me. Dr. Laura Prager is the reason why I am the child psychiatrist that I am today, and I cannot thank her enough for not only being an incredible mentor and teacher but for also being such an amazing friend. Thank you for reading early drafts, as your comments helped to elevate this book. A special shout-out to all my dear friends at BMC, including Drs. Natalija Bogdanovic, Lovern Moseley, and Cara Fuchs. Dr. Alex

Chang, former mentee turned colleague and friend, provided helpful insights for the book and was instrumental in making sure that medical students at Boston University had a meaningful educational experience in our psychiatry module and clerkship while I was working on this project. Dr. Hannah Brown, an extraordinary educator, clinician, and friend, provided me with constant joy and laughter even during the most challenging times. Dr. Michelle Durham, mentor turned dear friend, inspired me to say yes to this project, acknowledging the tremendous undertaking of writing a book while navigating the ongoing balancing act of serving in multiple roles, including motherhood.

Thank you to all my childhood and college friends who have helped shape the person that I am today: Katrina McCoy, Leah Field, Ramona Gravesande, Atty. Danielle Webb, Teresa Eng, Atty. Lisa Andre, Irina Shteyn, and Dr. Emily Zarookian. Thank you to Dr. Nicole Benson, who epitomizes what it means to be the ultimate working mother and has always remained an incredible friend.

Dr. Ann Epstein, a skillful child psychiatrist, therapist, and most importantly an unbelievable person, thank you for being you.

The driving force for writing this book really stems from my interactions with my patients and their caregivers. I have been seeing many of my current patients since I was a resident at Massachusetts General Hospital/McLean Hospital, and I am so honored that they have continued to grant me the privilege of being their psychiatrist. I wanted to ensure that the caregivers would never have to worry alone about their child, and I wanted my patients to know that they should have adults in their lives empowered with the necessary tools and resources to care for them. To all the countless caregivers, teachers, clinicians, and others who have approached me about what they should do for their child struggling with a mental health concern, thank you for empowering me with the sense of urgency to complete this book so that it can get into the hands of those who need it most.

And to my family, you have all served as the foundation for allowing me to grow and develop in a way that has allowed me to achieve this dream of becoming a psychiatrist and to have this incredible career. To my mother, who has always loved me and has been in support of everything that I do, thank you for everything that you have done for me, and I will always love you. To Jasmine, my little sister who has witnessed my entire educational journey and career trajectory, and has been continuously rooting for me all along the way, I love you so much. My father, who passed away in 2007, remains an enduring presence who continues to look after me and guide me through life's ups and downs.

To the rest of my family, your steadfast love and support has not gone unnoticed: Grandma Addie, Grandpa Vernal, Auntie Dawn, Aunt Loretta, Auntie Opal, Davina, Amanda, Gulaid, Julie, Bobbi-Jewel, Sekou, Paul, Nadine, Roger, Mel, Mya, and Wilhemina. Thank you to Teresa McDonald for being an absolute godsend, looking after my girls while I was busy writing.

To my beautiful daughters, Sophia and Olivia, my entire world revolves around the two of you. When I first started writing this book, Olivia was two and a half, and Sophia was sixteen months old. Over the course of writing this book, I have witnessed so many milestones in your short lives, including transitions to preschool, potty training, and the developing love and bond between the two of you. I cannot believe that I was able to complete this book during a time in your lives that was full of so much excitement, anxiety, and joy. Thank you for allowing me to be a mommy and to also be a writer.

And to my husband, Nate, who has been a part of this journey long before I even started medical school, you have been there for every major milestone in my educational and professional life and have been instrumental in all decisions that I have made along the way. Thank you for all the times that you had to juggle childcare, with two toddler girls constantly clamoring for your attention, while simultaneously conducting important Zoom calls from our dining room. I love you and thank you.

Finally, I want to thank all the contributors to this book. You shared your expertise, wisdom, and lived experience with me over memorable

Zoom calls that served as the backbone and spirit for this book. Thank you for sharing your stories with me and for sharing them with the world. None of this would have been possible without each of you. Every single one of you made this book a reality, and I am incredibly grateful for your generosity and vulnerability. Thank you.

Alleya Ray
Amy
Amy Edgar
Angelina Hudson
Ann Lettes
Anonymous
    Contributor
    from Santa
    Barbara County
Astrid Ross
Beth
Bethann
Brandon Smith
Bre
Cheryl Hayes
D'Asha
Diana Chao
Dominique
Don
Doreen Marshall
Dr. Blaise Aguirre
Dr. Bruce Perry
Dr. Chase TM
    Anderson
Dr. Claudia Gold
Dr. Emily Kline
Dr. Kelsey
    Evans-Amalu

Dr. Lori
    Desautels
Dr. Mona
    Delahooke
Dr. Mona Potter
Dr. Oscar
    Bukstein
Dr. Ross Greene
Dr. Sheldon
    Jacobs
Evelyn
Holly Miles
J
Jake
Jen Hart
Jen Rothman
Jennifer
Jeremiah
Jeremy Daigle
Jessica Rienstra
Jillian
Jocelyn Vega
Jodi Bullinger
Johanna
Jose Julio Murrilo
Joseline Castaños
Justin D.
Karen Simon

Kelley Elliot
Kenzie
Kevin
Kirsten Colston
Laura Horne
Lori Barnes
Maddie Stults
Maleah Nore
Marc DeGregorio
Marie
Mike Lambert
Nathan
Nina Richtman
Nora Flanagan
Olivette Orme
Pooja Mehta
Rachel Murray
Rebecca Benghiat
Renee Albertson
Sam Piscitelli
Samantha
    Martinez
Sarah Horne
Sierra Grandy
Todd Benson
Valerie Cantella
Yeska Aguilar
Ziona

RESOURCES

Books and Other Media

- *A Peek Inside: Illustrated Journeys in Life with Mental Illness* by Micah Pearson

- *ADHD 2.0: New Science and Essential Strategies for Thriving with Distraction—from Childhood Through Adulthood* by Edward M. Hallowell, MD, and John J. Ratey, MD

- *Anxiety Relief for Teens: Essential CBT Skills and Mindfulness Practices to Overcome Anxiety and Stress* by Regine Galanti, PhD

- *Beyond Behaviors: Using Brain Science and Compassion to Understand and Solve Children's Behavioral Challenges* by Mona Delahooke, PhD

- *Borderline Personality Disorder in Adolescents: A Complete Guide to Understanding and Coping When Your Adolescent Has BPD* by Blaise Aguirre, MD

- *Bowling Alone: The Collapse and Survival of American Community* by Robert D. Putnam

- *Brain-Body Parenting: How to Stop Managing Behavior and Start Raising Joyful, Resilient Kids* by Mona Delahooke, PhD

- *Building a Life Worth Living: A Memoir* by Marsha M. Linehan

- *Cognitive Behavior Therapy: Basics and Beyond* by Judith S. Beck

- *Connections Over Compliance: Rewiring Our Perceptions of Discipline* by Lori L. Desautels, PhD

- *Coping with BPD: DBT and CBT Skills to Soothe the Symptoms of Borderline Personality Disorder* by Blaise Aguirre, MD, and Gillian Galen, PsyD

- *Crazy: A Father's Search Through America's Mental Health Madness* by Pete Earley

- *Do They Have Bad Days in Heaven?: Surviving the Suicide Loss of a Sibling* by Michelle Linn-Gust

- *Done with the Crying: Help and Healing for Mothers of Estranged Adult Children* by Sheri McGregor, MA

- *Family Guide to Mental Illness and the Law: A Practical Handbook* by Linda Tashbook

- *Gizmo's Pawesome Guide to Mental Health Guide*, a free PDF available through United Way of Connecticut website.

- *Hiding in Plain Sight: Youth Mental Illness* documentary by Erik Ewers and Christopher Loren Ewers, produced by Ken Burns

- *I Am Not Sick I Don't Need Help!* by Xavier Amador

- *Intentional Neuroplasticity: Moving Our Nervous Systems and Educational System Toward Post-Traumatic Growth* by Lori L. Desautels, PhD

- *Youth-for-Youth Mental Health Guidebook* by Letters to Strangers

- *Lost and Found: Helping Behaviorally Challenging Students (and, While You're at It, All the Others)* by Ross W. Greene, PhD

- *Lost at School: Why Our Kids with Behavioral Challenges and How We Can Help Them* by Ross W. Greene, PhD

- *More Than a Body: Your Body Is an Instrument, Not an Ornament* by Lindsay Kite, PhD, and Lexie Kite, PhD

- Motivational Interviewing for Loved Ones (MILO) by Dr. Emily Kline

- *Motivational Interviewing: Helping People Change* by William R. Miller and Stephen Rollnick

- *Meet Little Monster* by NAMI, a free online resource available through NAMI.org

- *New Hope for Children and Teens with Bipolar Disorder: Your Friendly, Authoritative Guide to the Latest in Traditional and Complementary Solutions* by Boris Birmaher, MD

- *off-script: a mom's journey through adoption, a husband's alcoholism, and special needs parenting* by Valerie Cantella

- *Parenting a Bipolar Child: What to Do and Why* by Nancy Austin, PsyD, and Gianni Faedda, MD

- *Perfect Chaos: A Daughter's Journey to Survive Bipolar, a Mother's Struggle to Save Her* by Linea Johnson and Cinda Johnson

- *Raising a Moody Child: How to Cope with Depression and Bipolar Disorder* by Mary A. Fristad, PhD, and Jill S. Goldberg Arnold, PhD

- *Raising Human Beings: Creating a Collaborative Partnership with Your Child* by Ross W. Greene, PhD

- *Social and Emotional Development in Early Intervention: A Skills Guide for Working with Children* by Mona Delahooke, PhD

- *Surviving a Suicide Loss: Resource and Healing Guide* by the American Foundation for Suicide Prevention

- *The Behavior Code: A Practical Guide to Understanding and Teaching the Most Challenging*

Students by Jessica Minahan and Nancy Rappaport, MD

- *The Bipolar Child: The Definitive and Reassuring Guide to Childhood's Most Misunderstood Disorder* by Demetri Papolos, MD, and Janice Papolos
- *The Boy Who Was Raised as a Dog* by Bruce D. Perry, MD, PhD
- *The Deepest Well: Healing the Long-Term Effects of Childhood Trauma and Adversity* by Nadine Burke Harris, MD
- *The Explosive Child* by Ross W. Greene, PhD
- *The Grieving Child* by Helen Fitzgerald
- *The School of Hard Talks* by Emily Kline, PhD
- *Thinking Differently: An Inspiring Guide for Parents of Children with Learning Disabilities* by David Flink
- *Turtles All the Way Down* by John Green
- *What Happened to You?* by Bruce D. Perry, MD, PhD, and Oprah Winfrey
- *You Need Help: A Step-by-Step Plan to Convince a Loved One to Get Counseling* by Mark S. Komrad, MD, and Rosalynn Carter

Organizations

- Academy of Special Needs Planners, a group of professionals such as attorneys, financial planners, and trust officers who support those planning for family and friends with special needs
- Active Minds, an organization that uses education, awareness, and advocacy programs to change the conversation around youth mental health.
- Alateen, a group helping young people affected by someone else's drinking
- American Academy for Child and Adolescent Psychiatrists, professional group
- American Association for Marriage and Family Therapy, professional group
- APA SMI Adviser, an online database of resources for individuals and families
- Balanced Mind Parent Network, an online support community for parents
- Center for Youth Wellness, improving health of youth impacted by adverse childhood experiences (ACES)
- Center on the Developing Child, organization driving science-based innovation for children facing adversity.
- Child Mind Institute, organization transforming lives of children with mental health conditions and learning disorders
- Clay Center for Young Healthy Minds, Massachusetts General

Hospital program providing free online resources on supporting young people

- Clubhouse International, local community-based services for people living with mental illness

- Coordinated Specialty Care/ NAVIGATE (1st Episode Psychosis), program providing early treatment to individuals who have experienced their first episode of psychosis

- Crisis Intervention Training International, community partnership organization promoting CIT training and response systems

- Dougy Center for Grieving Children and Families, support, resources and connection before and after a death

- Drug Story Theater, young adults in recovery share their stories onstage to encourage kids to avoid drugs and alcohol

- Families for Depression Awareness, organization providing resources to help families recognize and cope with depression to prevent suicides

- Fresh Hope for Mental Health, network of Christian mental health peer support groups for individuals and families

- Hearing Voices Network, small national charity raising awareness and encouraging more positive responses to people who hear voices or have related experiences

- Indian Health Service, Department of Health and Human Services providing services to American Indians and Alaska Natives

- Letters to Strangers, global youth for youth organization destigmatizing mental illness through letter writing

- Me2/Orchestra, classical music organization created for individuals with mental illnesses and those who support them

- Motivational Interviewing Network of Trainers (MINT), resource for those seeking information on motivational interviewing

- National Alliance on Caregiving, organization dedicated to improving quality of life for friends and family caregivers and those in their care

- National Center for PTSD, center researching and educating on PTSD and traumatic stress

- National Child Traumatic Stress Network, organization working to raise the standard of care and improve access to services for traumatized children, their families, and communities

- National Eating Disorder Association, organization supporting individuals and families affected by eating disorders through prevention and access to quality care

- National Empowerment Center, organization promoting recovery, empowerment, hope, and healing to people with lived experience with mental health issues and trauma

- National Guardianship Association, organization providing education and resources to protect the interests of guardians and people in their care

- Project HEAL, organization advocating for equitable access to eating disorder treatment and resources

- SAVE.org Suicide Survivor Support Group, network of groups working to prevent suicide and support survivors

- Shatterproof, national nonprofit dedicated to transforming addiction treatment, end stigma, and support communities

- Sources of Strength, organization preventing adverse outcomes by increasing well-being, help-seeking, resiliency, healthy coping, and belonging

- Stand Up for Mental Health, organization teaching stand-up comedy to people with mental health issues as a form of therapy

- Students with Psychosis, global nonprofit fostering community and collaboration to empower students and advocates

- The American Academy of Child and Adolescent Psychiatry, professional medical organization promoting mentally healthy children, adolescents, and families

- The JED Foundation, nonprofit protecting emotional health and preventing suicide for teens and young adults

- The Trevor Project, suicide prevention organization providing 24/7 crisis support services, research, and advocacy for LGBTQ+ young people

- This Is My Brave, organization using the performing arts to end stigma surrounding mental illness and addiction

- Trans Lifeline, peer support and crisis hotline serving transgender people

INDEX

ABOUT THE AUTHOR

CHRISTINE M. CRAWFORD, MD is a Harvard-trained adult, child, and adolescent psychiatrist who currently serves as at the associate medical director for the National Alliance on Mental Illness (NAMI). She is an assistant professor of psychiatry and the vice chair of education at the Boston University Chobanian & Avedisian School of Medicine. Additionally, she's the medical director for the Boston Public Health Commission's School Based Clinician Program, in which she provides guidance on how best to support the socioemotional well-being of children within the Boston public school system. She is also a trusted source of child mental health expertise for major media outlets, including the *New York Times*, the *Washington Post*, NPR, the *Boston Globe*, and *Medscape*, and makes on-camera appearances for NBC, ABC, CBS, and Fox. She lives with her family just outside of Boston.